UN Security Council

Drawing largely from primary sources, it opens with a look at the conditions, expectations, and politics that shaped its creation in the early 1940s. The soaring public rhetoric of the day is contrasted to the hard-headed realism that conditioned the drafting in Dumbarton Oaks and San Francisco of the Charter's provisions concerning the composition and practices of the Council. It notes that the pointed debates over these matters at the founding conference are echoed in the current struggle over Council reform and expansion.

The heart of the book traces how the four key tools at the Council's disposal – peace operations, military enforcement, sanctions, and empowering partners – have evolved through practice and experience. It finds that the Council has proven to be remarkably adaptable to changing circumstances, no doubt a key to its longevity. The final section addresses how the Council is seeking to confront three current challenges – humanitarian atrocities, terrorism and weapons of mass destruction, and demands for reform – that will largely define its future.

Remarkably little has been written about the Council, though it has become one of the most dynamic, ambitious and controversial institutions in contemporary world politics. Filling this gap, *UN Security Council* is essential reading for those with interests in international peace and security and international politics and relations.

Edward C. Luck is Director of the Center on International Organization and Professor of Practice in International and Public Affairs at Columbia University. A past president and CEO of the United Nations Association of the USA and one of the architects of the UN reform efforts from 1995 to 1997, he has published widely on UN affairs, US foreign policy, and a range of security and political issues. Among his publications are *Mixed Messages: American Politics and International Organization, 1919–1999* (1999); *Reforming the United Nations: Lessons from a History in Progress* (2003); and, with Michael Doyle, *International Law and Organization: Closing the Compliance Gap* (2004).

Routledge Global Institutions

Edited by Thomas G. Weiss
The CUNY Graduate Center, New York, USA
and Rorden Wilkinson
University of Manchester, UK

About the series

The Global Institutions series is designed to provide readers with comprehensive, accessible, and informative guides to the history, structure, and activities of key international organizations. Every volume stands on its own as a thorough and insightful treatment of a particular topic, but the series as a whole contributes to a coherent and complementary portrait of the phenomenon of global institutions at the dawn of the millennium.

Books are written by recognized experts, conform to a similar structure, and cover a range of themes and debates common to the series. These areas of shared concern include the general purpose and rationale for organizations, developments over time, membership, structure, decision-making procedures, and key functions. Moreover, current debates are placed in historical perspective alongside informed analysis and critique. Each book also contains an annotated bibliography and guide to electronic information as well as any annexes appropriate to the subject matter at hand.

The volumes currently under contract include:

The United Nations and Human Rights
by Julie A. Mertus (American University)

The UN Secretary-General and Secretariat
by Leon Gordenker (Princeton University)

United Nations Global Conferences
by Michael G. Schechter (Michigan State University)

The UN General Assembly
by M. J. Peterson (University of Massachusetts, Amherst)

Internal Displacement
Conceptualization and its consequences
by Thomas G. Weiss (The CUNY Graduate Center) and David A. Korn

Global Environmental Institutions
by Elizabeth R. DeSombre (Wellesley College)

The World Intellectual Property Organization
Resurgence and the development agenda
by Chris May (University of the West of England)

UN Security Council
Practice and promise
by Edward C. Luck (Columbia University)

The North Atlantic Treaty Organization
The enduring alliance
by Julian Lindley-French (European Union Centre for Security Studies)

World Economic Forum
A multi-stakeholder approach to global governance
by Geoffrey Pigman (University of Kent)

Group of 7/8
by Hugo Dobson (University of Sheffield)

The International Monetary Fund
The politics of conditional lending
by James Vreeland (Yale University)

The World Bank
From reconstruction to development to equity
by Katherine Marshall (World Bank)

The African Union
Past and future governance challenges
by Samuel M. Makinda (Murdoch University) and Wafula Okumu (McMaster University)

Organisation for Economic Co-operation and Development
by Richard Woodward (University of Hull)

Non-governmental Organizations in Global Politics
by Peter Willetts (City University, London)

Multilateralism in the South
An analysis
by Jacqueline Anne Braveboy-Wagner (City College of New York)

The European Union
by Clive Archer (Manchester Metropolitan University)

The International Labour Organization
by Steve Hughes (University of Newcastle)

The International Committee of the Red Cross
A unique humanitarian actor
by David Forsythe (University of Nebraska) and Barbara Ann J. Rieffer (Bethany College)

The Commonwealth(s) and Global Governance
by Timothy Shaw (University of London)

A Crisis of Global Institutions? International Security and New Multilateralism
by Edward Newman (United Nations University)

UN Conference on Trade and Development
by Ian Taylor (University of St Andrews)

The Organization for Security and Co-operation in Europe
by David J. Galbreath (University of Aberdeen)

UNHCR
The politics and practice of refugee protection into the twenty first century
by Gil Loescher (University of Oxford), James Milner (University of Oxford), and Alexander Betts (University of Oxford)

The World Health Organization
by Kelley Lee (London School of Hygiene and Tropical Medicine)

The World Trade Organization
by Bernard Hoekman (World Bank) and Petros Mavroidis (Columbia University)

The International Organization for Standardization and the Global Economy
Setting standards
by Craig Murphy (Wellesley College) and JoAnne Yates (Massachusetts Institute of Technology)

For further information regarding the series, please contact:

Craig Fowlie, Publisher, Politics & International Studies
Taylor & Francis
2 Park Square, Milton Park, Abingdon
Oxford OX14 4RN, UK

+44 (0)207 017 6665 Tel
+44 (0)207 017 6702 Fax

Craig.Fowlie@tandf.co.uk
www.routledge.com

UN Security Council

Practice and promise

Edward C. Luck

Routledge
Taylor & Francis Group

LONDON AND NEW YORK

First published 2006
by Routledge
2 Park Square, Milton Park, Abingdon, Oxon OX14 4RN

Simultaneously published in the USA and Canada
by Routledge
270 Madison Avenue, New York, NY 10016

Routledge is an imprint of the Taylor & Francis Group, an informa business

©2006 Edward C. Luck

Typeset in Garamond by
Taylor & Francis Books

Printed and bound in Great Britain by
Antony Rowe Ltd, Chippenham, Wiltshire

British Library Cataloguing in Publication Data
A catalogue record for this book is available from the British Library

Library of Congress Cataloging in Publication Data
A catalog record for this book has been requested

ISBN10: 0–415–35530–3   ISBN13: 978–0–415–35530–8 (hbk)
ISBN10: 0–415–35531–1   ISBN13: 978–0–415–35531–5 (pbk)
ISBN10: 0–203–96933–2   ISBN13: 978–0–203–96933–5 (ebk)

In Memory of Professor David J. Luck

Contents

Illustrations

Foreword

The current volume is the seventh in a new and dynamic series on "global institutions." The series strives (and, based on the initial volumes we believe, succeeds) to provide readers with definitive guides to the most visible aspects of what we know as "global governance." Remarkable as it may seem, there exist relatively few books that offer in-depth treatments of prominent global bodies and processes, much less an entire series of concise and complementary volumes. Those that do exist are either out of date, inaccessible to the non-specialist, or seek to develop an in-depth understanding of narrow aspects of an institution or process rather than offer an overall account of its functioning. Similarly, existing books have often been written in highly technical language or have been crafted "in-house" and are notoriously self-serving and narrow.

The advent of electronic media has helped by making information, documents, and resolutions of international organizations more readily available, but it has also complicated matters. The growing reliance on the internet and other electronic methods of finding information about key international organizations and processes has served, ironically, to limit the educational materials to which most readers have ready access – namely, books. Public relations brochures, raw data, and loosely refereed websites do not make for intelligent analysis. Many official publications and a vast amount of electronically available information are suspect because of their ideological or self-promoting slant. Paradoxically, a growing range of purportedly independent websites offering analyses of the activities of particular organizations has emerged, but one inadvertent consequence has been to frustrate access to basic, critical, and well researched texts. The market for such has actually been reduced by the ready availability of electronic materials of varying quality.

For those of us who teach, research, and practice in the area, this access to information has been at best frustrating. We were delighted, then, when Routledge saw the value of a series that bucks this trend and provides key reference points to the most significant global institutions. They are betting that serious students and professionals will want serious analyses. We have assembled a first-rate line-up of authors to address that market. Our intention, then, is to provide one-stop shopping for all readers – students (both undergraduate and postgraduate), interested negotiators, diplomats, practitioners from non-governmental and inter-governmental organizations, and interested parties alike – seeking information about most prominent institutional aspects of global governance.

The UN Security Council

Among the galaxy of specialized agencies, independent bodies, dedicated programs and funds within the UN system, none carries greater weight in reality or in the literature of international organization than the Security Council. The UN's defunct predecessor, the League of Nations, was without enforcement capabilities; and virtually all observers saw this as the number one reason for its demise. Central in the planning exercise for the next generation of world organization that began during World War II was the realization that military "teeth" would be necessary once the Allied military alliance that was called the "United Nations" morphed into an organization with the same name.

As the principal organ with "primary responsibility for the maintenance of international peace and security," the Security Council was in our minds from the outset as an absolutely essential volume in this series. When we brainstormed about the person to write it, Edward C. Luck was in a category of one. We were delighted that we were able to pull him away from his administrative duties as the director of the Center on International Organization and his teaching as a professor of practice at Columbia University's School for International and Public Affairs.

In many ways a lifetime of work in and around UN headquarters – as a scholar and policy analyst, as a consultant for the world organization and an advocate for informed multilateral decisions in the United States – are amortized in this very accessible but authoritative volume. With the same depth of historical, legal, and political acumen that is invariably present in his articles, monographs and book chapters, but especially in his classic, *Mixed Messages*,[1] Luck pulls no punches. His probing examination of the Security Council will surely have something politically incorrect to please and irritate every reader. "One day it is heralded, the next disdained or, worse, dismissed," Luck writes. "Each action it takes is celebrated by some and despaired by others."

As an institution, the Council fascinates. It has demonstrated a degree of institutional longevity, resilience, and dynamism shown by few other intergovernmental organizations. While its numbers were increased from eleven to fifteen in 1965, the Security Council functions pretty much as the same club of great powers as it was at the outset. Luck ends his analysis with a critical scrutiny of the 2005 World Summit at which over 150 presidents, prime ministers, and princes sought to coax the world organization into the twenty-first century. Although the Secretary-General's so-called High-level Panel on Threats, Challenges and Change, and Kofi Annan himself, put forward what they thought were compelling arguments to transform the Council's membership and procedures,[2] no change was politically possible. After everyone agreed that the Security Council and its five permanent members with vetoes represented the world of 1945 rather than six decades later, every solution raised as many problems as it solved.

Rhetorical fireworks over the last decade have, however, contributed to a permissive environment that facilitated pragmatic modifications in working methods. As Luck argues, these have injected more openness, accountability, and diverse inputs into Council deliberations and should be expanded.[3] They have not, of course, made a dent in national-interest decision-making, but what would? Will the inability to move ahead with dramatic alterations in the UN's most important institution compromise UN credibility and legitimacy? Not more than in the past.

As Luck tells us, "Few institutions are as well known or as little understood as the UN Security Council. It is, in that regard, one of those classic enigmas hiding in plain sight." This engaging book remedies this dearth in understanding. It is invaluable not only for those interested in international peace and security but also for those seeking to better understand the political realities and limitations of global governance in contemporary international society. We are pleased to recommend this readable volume to all. As always, comments and suggestions from readers are welcome.

Thomas G. Weiss, The CUNY Graduate Center, New York, USA
Rorden Wilkinson, University of Manchester, UK
April 2006

Preface

This is a short book on a long subject. Once seen as a bold experiment whose potential had been thwarted by Cold War tensions, the Security Council has acquired a history almost as long as its agenda. More than a decade and a half since the unlamented demise of the Cold War, the Council has now been tested by the freer but less predictable politics of an evolving international system. How it is responding to the new expectations and challenges is a matter of some controversy. Many, dissatisfied with its performance or desiring a seat at its table, are calling for sweeping changes in its composition and working methods. The very intensity of the rhetoric on both sides of this debate, however, testifies to the prominence the Council has come to assume in contemporary international politics and security affairs.

This book, then, is motivated by a paradox: few institutions have generated so much commentary yet so little systematic analysis. Countless volumes have been devoted to the crises the Council seeks to address and the tools it wields. Few of these have been shy about offering opinions about whether the Council did or did not contribute to resolving the particular conflict, threat, or humanitarian calamity at hand. There is no shortage of snapshots of the Council at work. Most of the numerous texts and collections of essays on the United Nations contain a chapter on the Council or, more likely, on one or more of the peacekeeping, sanctions, or humanitarian measures it authorizes. But there have been remarkably few books devoted to the Security Council as an institution. An early effort, *Fifteen Men on a Powder Keg: A History of the UN Security Council* by Andrew Boyd (London: Methuen, 1971) is lively but badly dated. The Council today bears only a surface resemblance to its form and image of thirty, even twenty, years ago.

A much more ambitious and valuable attempt to narrow this literature gap was David M. Malone's 2004 collection, *The UN Security Council: From the Cold War to the 21st Century* (Boulder, CO: Lynne Rienner). Then the energetic President of the widely respected International Peace Academy, Malone assembled a team of no less than fifty authors, many of them practitioners, to give insiders' accounts of how the Council has sought to cope with a variety of themes and crises. There is an immense amount of valuable material in these thirty-nine essays, and the 746-page tome is bound to have an unusually long shelf life. Only a couple of the chapters, however, seek to grapple with the Council's identity – its pedigree, history, value, and future – as an institution.

This slimmer and single-authored volume seeks to complement the Malone book, even as it draws on the material compiled in its predecessor at a number of points. In relatively short order, this book tells the Council's story from its inception to its current challenges. For practitioners as well as scholars and students, it offers one-stop shopping, a single source for a wide range of information about what the Council was supposed to be, how it operates, and what it has become. Its central theme is the historical evolution of the Council, as an institution that has proven repeatedly to be adaptable to a range of conditions, demands, and opportunities. Rather than offering a snapshot, its begins to paint a panorama.

Part I provides a context for thinking about the Council and for assessing how it is doing. Chapter 1 offers a series of broad criteria for gauging the Council's performance. Noting the lack of comparable bodies, the chapter suggests the utility of comparing the Council to itself by assessing how it is doing over time, decade by decade, issue by issue. The second chapter relates the founding conception and the ways this Council was to be an improvement over the League of Nations' Council. It points out that many of today's debates about the Council echo equally heated ones from 1945. Chapter 3 takes a hard look at the Council-related provisions of the Charter, at the struggles at Dumbarton Oaks and San Francisco that shaped them, and at how they have been interpreted over time.

Part II offers four chapters on the primary tools in the Council's arsenal of persuasion and coercion: peace operations; military enforcement; economic sanctions, arms embargoes, and diplomatic instruments; and enlisting and empowering partners. It looks at how each of these tools has developed and been employed over the course of six decades of practice and, in some cases, of learning.

Finally, Part III addresses, in greater detail, three of the biggest challenges facing the Council: the humanitarian imperative; terrorism and weapons of mass destruction; and its own reform, adaptation, and evolution. Each chapter reaches a similar conclusion. The Council is proving itself to be a dynamic and responsive body, if not a markedly successful one. It is learning new tricks, new ways of going about its business, even as the nature of that business seems to be ever expanding and ever more demanding. Whether its glass is half full or half empty, one thing is clear: the proverbial glass itself is getting bigger. How to reform such a moving target is proving to be an especially intriguing and difficult task. In speculating about the Council's future, the final chapter underlines that the only way to get a sense of where it is going is to begin with some understanding of where it started, what route it has taken, and how far it has come. Given that the demand for its services keeps growing and diversifying, there is reason to be modestly bullish about its future. The Council, in short, is proving to be as vibrant as it is flawed – a truly human institution.

In preparing this book, the author has acquired deep debts to a few rather than shallow debts to many. As so often in the past, Marilyn Messer is responsible not only for turning illegible scribbles on yellow legal pads into presentable manuscript pages, but also for conducting endless hours of invaluable primary research, for preparing the illustrations and appendices, and, at appropriate points, for inquiring tactfully of the author if he really meant to say such and such. By keeping the author's calendar and the wider work of Columbia's Center on International Organization in reasonable order, she has managed to keep sufficient blocks of time open – here and there at least – to complete the manuscript within the limits of the editors' and publisher's patience. In that regard, the author appreciates the forbearance of the series editors, Thomas G. Weiss and Rorden Wilkinson, as much as their encouragement. The manuscript benefited, as well, from Professor Weiss' carefully targeted and eminently sensible suggestions. As always, my most profound debt is to my wife Dana and daughter Jessica for their endless encouragement and support.

Abbreviations

CTAG	G-8 Counter-Terrorism Action Group
CTED	United Nations Counter-Terrrorism Committee Executive Directorate
ECOSOC	Economic and Social Council
FATF	Financial Action Task Force
GDP	Gross Domestic Product
HLP	High-level Panel on Threats, Challenges and Change
IAEA	International Atomic Energy Agency
ICAO	International Civil Aviation Organization
ICJ	International Court of Justice
ICTR	International Criminal Tribunal for Rwanda
ICTY	International Criminal Tribunal for the former Yugoslavia
MSC	Military Staff Committee
NATO	North Atlantic Treaty Organization
NGOs	Non-governmental Organizations
NPT	Treaty on the Non-Proliferation of Nuclear Weapons
OAU	Organization of African Unity
OCHA	UN Office for Coordination of Humanitarian Affairs
OHCHR	United Nations Office of the High Commissioner for Human Rights
OIOS	United Nations Office of Internal Oversight Services
ONUC	United Nations Operation in the Congo
PSI	Proliferation Security Initiative
RUF	Revolutionary United Front
TPB	United Nations Terrorism Prevention Branch
UNAMIR	UN Assistance Mission for Rwanda
UNEF	United Nations Emergency Force
UNHCR	United Nations High Commissioner for Refugees
UNITA	National Union for the Total Independence of Angola

UNMOGIP	United Nations Military Observer Group in India and Pakistan
UNMOVIC	United Nations Monitoring, Verification and Inspection Commission
UNFICYP	United Nations Peace-keeping Force in Cyprus
UNOSOM	United Nations Operation in Somalia
UNPROFOR	United Nations Protection Force in the former Yugoslavia
UNSCOM	United Nations Special Commission on Iraq
UNTAG	United Nations Transition Assistance Group (Namibia)
UNTSO	United Nations Truce Supervision Organization
WMD	Weapons of Mass Destruction
WTO	World Trade Organization

Part I
Context

1 Grading the great experiment

The Security Council is a special place. Over several centuries of institutional evolution, it is the closest approximation to global governance in the peace and security realm yet achieved. Its enforcement authority is unique in the history of inter-governmental cooperation. The UN's 192 sovereign member states have agreed, under its Charter, to accept the decisions of the Council's fifteen members as binding, despite ceaseless complaints about its undemocratic and unrepresentative character. Having survived more than six decades of hot and cold wars, its durability has proven unprecedented. As the centerpiece of the UN system, it is the depository of ageless dreams and recurring disappointments about the prospects for a more peaceful and cooperative global order.

Yet even the Council's most ardent admirers have to admit that its track record in maintaining international peace and security – its mandate under the Charter – has been spotty at best. Surely nothing close to the dependable system of collective security sought by the UN's far-sighted founders has been achieved. Clearly the Council has been more willing and able to grapple with some kinds of conflicts and with some regions than others. And the degree of consensus among its more influential members has ebbed and flowed, with the divisive debate in 2002–3 over the use of force in Iraq among its more public low points. So the Council appears to be caught in a historical limbo. Far more ambitious and accomplished than its predecessors, the Council's performance nevertheless offers compelling testimony to the limits of global governance in an era of sovereign nation states.

All of this argues against sweeping endorsements or indictments of the Council's place in the current and evolving world order. It also helps explain why the Council has proven to be such a lightning rod for commentary of all persuasions, as well as symbolic of so much that is right and wrong with the international system. Both sides in the debate over Iraq, for example, were quick to assert that they had the Council's core purposes in mind, though they held starkly divergent images of what the Council's role, place, and priorities ought to be. To those who believe that the Council's first task is to decide when force can legitimately and legally be employed, it acted properly in denying the coalition seeking to oust Saddam Hussein's regime its blessing. But for those who stress the Council's responsibility for organizing collective action to enforce institutional law and norms, the episode capped a dozen years of equivocation and division in the face of Iraqi non-compliance.

This slim volume does not seek to decide such weighty debates or to pass judgment on the Council. Rather it aims to provide the reader with a sufficiently wide range of information, analysis, and historical background to understand and assess the Council's place in past and contemporary efforts to bolster international peace and security. For those intent on weighing the merits of the Council's work, it would be useful to begin by identifying some possible criteria for gauging the Council's performance and potential. What standards are appropriate for weighing the value of a body that is historically unique both in its ambitions and in its legal and political authority?

At the basest level, it could be asked whether states are interested in participating in the Council's deliberations and in influencing its decisions. The annual competition to be elected a non-permanent member, the lines of member states seeking to speak at open sessions, and the fierce, and seemingly endless, debate over ways to recast and broaden its composition suggest an affirmative response. Not only do states send their top diplomatic talent to represent them in Council deliberations, but, over the past dozen years, the Council has convened a number of times at the foreign minister or summit level, the latter most recently in September 2005 on aspects of terrorism.

Do states care, as well, about the content of the Council's resolutions and presidential statements? In other words, do national political leaders look to the Council for more than photo-ops and political grandstanding on a global stage? Again, the protracted negotiations over the wording of sensitive resolutions – whether on Iran, Iraq, Palestine, the Balkans, or the mandate for a new peacekeeping force – suggest that this content matters for reasons of law, politics, and policy. The very act of bringing a matter to the Council, such as efforts by Iran and North Korea to acquire nuclear weapons, or Syrian involvement in Lebanon, is considered by the parties involved to be a serious and consequential step. Once a contentious case is before the Council, the major powers are rarely shy about bringing pressure to bear in the capitals of undecided non-permanent members. Words often matter. Despite all of the ups and (mostly) downs of the Middle East peace process, for example, the wording of resolution 242 of 1967 – and differing interpretations of it – still is cited by the parties as a critical plank in any formula for a durable peace in the troubled region.

On the other hand, even if the Council is central to the life of international diplomacy, what evidence is there that its words and actions matter to ordinary people, to the work of non-governmental organizations (NGOs), and to the media? Realists, after all, have long dismissed the work of the Council as marginal, at best, to the course of power-based politics in a largely anarchical world.[1] Indeed, for much of its life, constrained by the tensions of the Cold War, the Council had relatively few opportunities to make a difference. So publics and journalists looked elsewhere for the seminal events of the day. Many news outlets closed or severely trimmed their UN bureaus. Now some of the action is returning to Turtle Bay. The Council's growing activism since the end of the Cold War has spurred renewed interest among the public, press, and pundits, if not always their approval.

The political fallout from the Council's bitter and ultimately indecisive debate over the use of force in Iraq included declining public confidence in the UN, according to various opinion surveys, in a broad range of developed and developing countries.[2] While not encouraging for the world body, the results confirmed that publics were neither disinterested nor uninformed about the Council's struggles to find common ground on how to deal with the crisis. What was most striking was the degree to which people throughout much of the world had come to accept the premise that the Council's authorization was either mandatory or highly preferable prior to the use of force. Even for a Bush administration once dismissive of the UN's relevance, the goal of getting the Council on board, both before and after the use of force in Iraq, appeared to be a high priority. Hardheaded realists should take note, for something is changing in terms of international norms and public perceptions regarding the rules of warfare, the use of force, and sources of legitimacy. The Council's boosters, on the other hand, should beware that public expectations concerning the Council's performance may well be rising with its increasing activism.

While this quick review argues that the Council does matter at the level of political relevance, steeper tests would ask whether it has succeeded (1) in eliciting substantial and sustainable commitments from member states to support its decisions; (2) in carrying out its operational activities and missions competently and efficiently; and, ultimately, (3) in making a real difference to the maintenance of international peace and security. Should the Council be deemed to have surmounted all of these hurdles, a final question of comparative advantage would remain. Has the Council been the best placed vehicle for pursuing some set of core international security goals?; if so, which ones?; and which should be left to others or be addressed in partnership with other groups and institutions?

There are any number of ways to measure member state commitment to carrying out Security Council resolutions. One would be whether they have altered their policies in substantial ways to conform with Council edicts on important matters. Have they faithfully and fully implemented, for instance, sanctions regimes approved by the Council, whether related to diplomatic, political, economic, social, or arms control activities? Another set of measures would consider the material, political, and human assistance states have provided for Council-mandated missions, whether of a humanitarian, peace-keeping, or enforcement nature. While most peacekeeping operations are funded through assessed contributions, humanitarian, nation-building, and enforcement actions generally need voluntary contributions, human as well as financial. Since member states retain their sovereignty under the UN Charter, compliance, cooperation, and participation are not automatic (even if expected under Article 25). They require action within national capitals, and the response rate obviously varies greatly by country and issue. Whether the commitment glass should be considered to be half full – filling or ebbing – would no doubt depend on where and when one looks. The glass, moreover, is itself expanding as the Council takes on new issues and asks more of the member states (see Part III, on challenges, below). The pull of Security Council decisions, especially binding ones under Chapter VII of the Charter, on national capitals has surely been more than negligible given the vast quantity of money, soldiers, and effort – now including reporting – that has been devoted to Council-sponsored activities and operations over the years. But, as the chapters that follow attest, the unevenness and selectivity of member state responses to Council appeals have been equally impressive.

Has the Council gone about its ambitious work in an efficient and productive fashion? The UN's management reforms of the last decade have put considerable emphasis on instituting modern management techniques, such as results-based budgeting, a more flexible human resources system, an inspector general's office, lessons-learned and best practices units, and cross-sectoral integration of planning and operations. Much has been achieved, yet the oil-for-food scandal underlines how very far there still is to go. The Council itself has undertaken a series of reforms of its working methods in the name of greater transparency and accountability, even as deeper reforms in decision-making and composition have been resisted.

How can the competency and efficiency of efforts to advance peace and security be measured, given the moving targets, the raft of unknowns and hypotheticals, the indefinite timeframes, the vagaries of politics, and the preference for prevention over cure? How does one account for tragedies avoided? Is it a sensible expenditure of resources, for example, to maintain a peacekeeping force in Cyprus for over forty years, or of political capital to devote so much of the Council's time and attention to the more intransigent aspects of the Middle East crisis? Should the Council devote more resources to those crises most ripe for solution or to those with the most troubling implications? Are there times when conflict can produce constructive change and the Council should step aside and let history follow its own course? How does one introduce factors of efficiency and productivity into the deliberations of such an intrinsically political body? Where one stands on such questions depends largely, of course, on where one sits. And yet how can such considerations not be taken into account when political, financial, and military resources are in limited supply?

Surely the first rule for the Council, as for the medical profession, should be to do no harm. Sometimes, as in Srebrenica and Rwanda, its unprincipled neglect had tragic consequences. The Council is unhelpful, at best, when it raises false expectations with rhetorical flourishes or paper-thin deployments, or adds layers of polarizing global politics to local ones. In East Timor, Central America, West Africa, Southern Africa, and Southeast Asia, on the other hand, most would agree that it has made a positive, and often pivotal, difference. In reviewing the issues raised in the following chapters, one would do well to keep asking where, when, and why the Council has – or has not – been able to achieve positive results. In particular, to what extent might lessons learned from past experience help or hinder the UN's understanding of how to address the emerging challenges of human security, failing states, terrorism, and the proliferation of weapons of mass destruction? Likewise, what do such lessons tell us about which reform steps might boost or hinder the Council's capacity to make a difference in the future?

Finally, it should be asked, relative to each of the policy tasks addressed in this volume, whether the Security Council is the best placed and equipped organ for dealing with the problem at hand. Under Chapter VIII of the Charter, it is envisioned that the parties to a conflict themselves should endeavor to resolve their differences peacefully, that the involvement of regional arrangements would be a second recourse, and that referral to the Council would be undertaken when a resolution of a crisis could not be managed at these lower levels. While the employment of enforcement measures could only be authorized by the Council, it was contemplated that regional cooperation would ease much of the burden on the Council for maintaining international peace and security. The founders, in this regard, seemed to be early proponents of the principle of subsidiarity, in which policy issues are to be resolved at the lowest responsible level. Successive secretaries-general, moreover, have asserted that the UN is not capable of organizing or overseeing military enforcement measures, which must be left to coalitions of the willing. In operational terms, the doctrines of subsidiarity and of coalitions of the willing may be eminently sensible, but they fit awkwardly with the assertion elsewhere in the Charter that the ultimate legal authority for the use of force resides in the Council.

Before turning to the founders' hopes, dreams, and expectations, much less to an assessment of the Council's performance to date, two further caveats should be borne in mind. One is that there are problems without solutions, or at least without any feasible or cost-effective answers in a reasonable time-frame. Member states habitually bring just such problems to the Council. As noted above, the Charter stipulates that the Council is not expected to handle every crisis, only those that no-one else can resolve. The second is that the world changes, and with it the prospects for successful Council action. It is not coincidental that the Council moved in slow motion for four decades of Cold War and has been hyperactive since its end. As Figure 1.1 illustrates, the rate at which it managed to pass resolutions and, importantly, Chapter VII enforcement resolutions, accelerated exponentially following the Cold War, even as the number of vetoes cast precipitously declined.

Clearly, the Council is not above the vagaries of international politics. Indeed, it is all about politics: local, national, regional, and global. The story of the Council, in other words, is a narrative on the evolution of global geopolitics. But the Council is more than just a barometer, it is also an actor that seeks to change the course of human events, even if incrementally and imperceptibly.

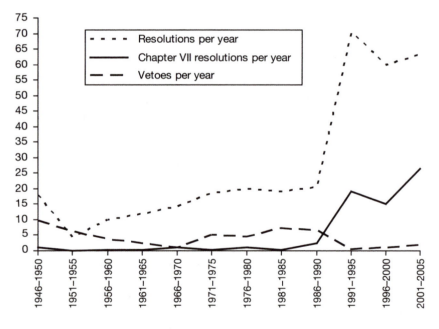

Figure 1.1 Average number of Security Council resolutions, Chapter VII resolutions, and vetoes per year for each five-year period 1946–2005

Sources: www.un.org/documents/scres.htm.; Sydney D. Bailey and Sam Daws, Procedure of the Security Council (Oxford: Clarendon Press, 1998).

2 The founding vision

Old council, new council

Of one thing, the proponents of the infant United Nations were absolutely certain: the new world body would be a very different animal than its predecessor, the League of Nations. It would have to be if it was to deliver on the opening pledge of its Charter "to save succeeding generations from the scourge of war, which twice in our lifetimes has brought untold sorrow to mankind." The League had, Soviet Foreign Minister Vyacheslav M. Molotov reminded the opening plenary of the UN's founding conference in San Francisco,

> betrayed the hopes of those who believed in it. It is obvious that no one wishes to restore a League of Nations which had no rights or power, which did not interfere with any aggressors preparing for war against peace-loving nations and which sometimes even lulled the nations' vigilance with regard to impending aggression.[1]

Yet in many respects the shape and structure of the new organization bore an uncanny resemblance to those of the old one. As the League's foremost chronicler, F. P. Walters, phrased it:

> As the new [UN] organizations took shape, each absorbed in one form or another, the functions, the plans, the records, and in many cases the staff, of the corresponding organ of the League. In the wider vision of a time of rebirth, and with the additional confidence, initiative, and resources supplied by the adhesion of the United States, most of the new agencies were able to start their career on a scale which those of the League could never attain. But continuity remained unbroken.[2]

At a time of fresh starts and institutional succession, however, the UN's founders had little incentive to point out these similarities, particularly to members of the US Senate. One of the few scholars to remark on how much the new emperor's clothes looked like the last one's, Leland M. Goodrich, reported that

> quite clearly there was a hesitancy in many quarters to call attention to the essential continuity of the old League and new United Nations for fear of arousing latent hostilities or creating doubts which might seriously jeopardize the birth and early success of the new organization.[3]

So why were expectations for the new body so much higher than for the old, when, as Grayson Kirk acknowledged in 1946, the League had "died more from political anemia than from organic failure"?[4] What capacities set it apart from its predecessor? The most telling answers were provided by the delegates to the final meeting of the League's Assembly in April of that year. Other than overseeing the transfer of its functions, activities, and assets to its successor, the main business conducted in the grand Palais des Nations in Geneva that spring was some revealing soul searching about what had gone wrong with their beloved League and what could go right under the new architecture.[5] Four themes stood out, all related to the special features of the new Security Council. One, the new Council included all of the major powers and, in particular, would serve to embed American power and dynamism in the new structure. Two, the most powerful states were given special rights and responsibilities concerning the maintenance of international peace and security. Three, the new Council was to be of limited size, without what the Dutch delegate labeled the "exaggerated equality between great and small Powers" that characterized the consensus rule in the League's Council. The latter reached its greatest girth – double its initial eight members – in 1934, on the eve of the World War it was supposed to prevent.[6] And four, the new Council had the authority to enforce its decisions, while its members had the capacity – and the experience – to crush aggressors through the collective use of force if necessary. The Council, in short, was to be the centerpiece of the boldest attempt yet to institutionalize collective security.

The Big Three, Four, Five

The far-reaching conception of the UN, and of its core, the Security Council, grew out of the devastation of the second global war in two generations. That contest was still being waged at the time of the San Francisco founding conference. The very term United Nations, on which the US insisted, was the title used by the anti-Axis alliance.[7] Indeed, the postwar extension of the alliance, and particularly of the collaboration among its key members, was to be the central task of the new Council. US President Franklin Delano Roosevelt was an especially keen champion of the notion that these Four Policemen could and should enforce the peace. His Christmas Eve speech in December 1943 captured this vision:

> Britain, Russia, China and the United States and their allies represent more than three-quarters of the total population of the earth. As long as these four nations with great military power stick together in determination to keep the peace there will be no possibility of an aggressor nation arising to start another world war.[8]

Cautioning that "we must be prepared to keep the peace by force," he declared that the people of the world "are fighting for the attainment of peace – not just a truce, not just an armistice – but peace that is as strongly enforced and as durable as mortal man can make it." In an interview with the *Saturday Evening Post* earlier that year, the President stressed that the postwar organization must be built on a clear foundation of power politics, not welfare politics or wishful thinking. Given the prospect of American military dominance in the postwar world, he opposed any sort of autonomous or distinct United Nations military capacity or the delegation of sovereignty from member states to the world body.[9]

America's two major partners in winning the war and designing the peace, the Soviet Union and United Kingdom, came to similar conclusions. They, too, had strong strategic reasons for preferring a small Security Council built around the cooperation of the chief wartime allies. Moscow and London, even more than Washington, insisted that the new organization not be able to act on security issues without the unanimity of the great powers. They were keenly aware that the alliance had been forged by necessity, as a reaction to Axis ambitions, rather than by any confluence of ideology or societal values. True, cultural ties between England and its former North American colonies ran deep. But the dismantling of British and other European colonial empires was among Washington's postwar aims, while London was well aware that it would need to scramble to maintain its strategic position in the face of growing American and Soviet power. For the once-revolutionary USSR, neither capitalist America nor imperialist Britain made for prime ideological soulmates. But war against a common enemy had brought them together, and the UN, particularly the Security Council, provided a potential means for perpetuating the wartime collaboration should other potential aggressors appear or should differences arise among the wartime allies.

While the allies recognized the advantage of bringing additional countries under the UN umbrella, they hardly envisioned a universal organization.[10] Moscow, in particular, was wary of being outnumbered in the new forum. Nor was the UN produced by multilateral diplomacy. Instead, most of the intensive planning for the postwar system was conducted in one country: the United States, whose territory and infrastructure were least touched by the war's devastation.[11] Anglo-American consultations and then the series of wartime conferences between Roosevelt, Churchill and Stalin brought a high degree of convergence on the basic structures and purposes of the prospective world body. More detailed proposals were worked out at a two-part series of "conversations" at Dumbarton Oaks, an elegant private estate in the Georgetown section of Washington DC, from August to October 1944. Because Moscow refused to meet with a Chinese delegation representing the Chiang Kia-Shek regime, the Dumbarton Oaks meetings had to proceed in two tripartite phases, the first including the Soviet Union and the second, and briefer, China. This awkward process served both to reinforce the centrality of the Anglo-American partnership to the novel enterprise and to foreshadow what a trying task it was going to be to hold the major powers together in the new Council. The resulting "Proposals for the Establishment of a General International Organization" formed the basis for broader discussions at the UN's founding conference in San Francisco the following spring, which was sponsored by the four powers represented at Dumbarton Oaks. It was only over the course of the founding conference that France began to participate in the inner deliberations among the leading powers. In San Francisco, the Big Four became the Big Five.

Invitations to San Francisco, moreover, were to be limited to those states that had declared war on one of the Axis countries. Rather than espousing the goal of universality, the resulting Charter left membership "open to all other peace-loving states which accept the obligations contained in the present Charter and, in the judgment of the Organization, are able and willing to carry out these obligations" (Article 4). This judgment was to be expressed through a two-thirds vote of the General Assembly upon recommendation of the Security Council. The latter provision gave each of the Big Five the opportunity to veto membership applications. Unlike the League's Covenant, moreover, the Charter includes three references to possible actions against "any state which during the Second World War has been an enemy of any signatory of the present Charter." Though painfully archaic, these provisions have not been removed during the three rounds of Charter amendment to date, though in the Outcome Document from the September 2005 World Summit the heads of state and government resolved "to delete references to 'enemy states' in Article 53, 77, and 107 of the Charter."[12]

The non-negotiable veto

The Dumbarton Oaks proposals provided a detailed blueprint of the new organization's purposes, principles, procedures, and structure.[13] Most of this language found its way into the UN Charter, including several highly controversial provisions related to the Security Council.[14] Despite pointed debate at San Francisco, the big powers held firm given the centrality of the Council to their larger vision. There were gaps in the Dumbarton Oaks plans, of course, none more consequential than what the voting procedures in the Security Council would be.[15] The Big Four agreed on the need for unanimity among them for the authorization of collective enforcement action, so as to insure that the organization would not be turned against any one of them. But there were distinct views about how far this veto should extend. Should it cover matters of peaceful settlement of disputes, the admission of new members, the appointment of the Secretary-General, the amendment of the Charter and/or the inclusion of matters on the Council's agenda? Stalin favored the most sweeping and absolute application, Churchill initially leaned toward a relatively broad interpretation, while an often divided American delegation tended to favor some restrictions on the use of the veto. The best that the Dumbarton Oaks proposals could do was to candidly admit that "the question of voting procedure in the Security Council is still under consideration."[16]

Rather than leave such a central and potentially divisive item to the more multilateral, inclusive and hence less predictable deliberations in San Francisco, the Big Three scrambled to resolve their differences at their next wartime summit, at the Black Sea resort of Yalta in February 1945. There, however, the veto question became entwined with a complex set of trade-offs relating to Stalin's demand that all sixteen Soviet republics be given seats in the General Assembly (he was eventually granted three seats), to the invitation list for San Francisco, and to such weighty geopolitical issues as the future of Germany, Poland, and much of Eastern Europe after the war and the conditions for Soviet entry into the war in the Pacific.[17] On the veto, at least, the American formula prevailed at Yalta.[18] Each of the eleven Council members would have one vote; decisions on procedural matters would require seven affirmative votes; on all other matters decisions would be made "by an affirmative vote of seven members including the concurring vote of the permanent members." Parties to a dispute were to abstain from voting in cases of pacific settlement (though the veto would still apply).[19]

To no one's surprise, none of the proposed Charter provisions spurred greater acrimony in San Francisco than those related to the veto.[20] There was little dissent over whether the great powers should have a veto over the authorization of enforcement measures that might well involve the use of their armed forces. But the notion that great power unanimity should be required for peaceful settlement efforts provoked debate even within the US delegation. Many countries, led by Australia, expressed deep reservations.[21] Neither Dumbarton Oaks nor Yalta, moreover, had produced a clear understanding of what matters should be considered procedural. The Soviet delegation, for example, surprised its partners at San Francisco by announcing that it had interpreted Yalta as requiring great power unanimity even for introducing a topic onto the Council's agenda.[22] Though a united opposition and appeals all the way to Stalin in Moscow's Kremlin led to a reversal of the Soviet position, the incident underlined how thin and fragile was the political foundation for the new enterprise.

The dilemma for most delegations in San Francisco could not have been starker. On the one hand, they objected to the veto both because it was inequitable and because it could prevent Council action when most needed. On the other hand, they realized that the viability and effectiveness of the UN – like the League before it – would depend heavily on the continued collaboration of the great powers. As the New Zealand delegate put it, "although it might be necessary to accept the Yalta voting formula as a part of the present international situation, there was no need to extol it."[23] Their dilemma was heightened by the fear, shared by presidents Roosevelt and Truman as well, that not only might Stalin walk away from the San Francisco negotiations, but that the US Senate could well refuse to give its consent to the ratification of the Charter, just as it had to the League Covenant.

During the debate over the veto, Tom Connally (D-Texas), an active member of the US delegation and Chairman of the Senate Foreign Relations Committee, decided to graphically underline the point. As he describes the incident, he warned those insisting on further constraints on the veto:

> "You may go home from San Francisco – if you wish," I cautioned the delegates, "and report that you have defeated the veto. Yes," I went on, "you can say you defeated the veto. . . . But you can also say, 'We *tore up the Charter!*'" At that point I sweepingly ripped the Charter draft in my hands to shreds and flung the scraps with disgust on the table.[24]

Point made, the Yalta formula for Council voting was eventually accepted by the delegates, veto and all. While Moscow did not get its way on requiring unanimity for the Council even to discuss a matter, the veto was to apply to peaceful settlement, new members, appointment of the Secretary-General, and Charter amendment, as well as to all other non-procedural matters.

By placing some high hurdles on the path to Charter amendment, moreover, the Dumbarton Oaks proposals reflected the reluctance of the Big Four to see any quick or easy tampering with the provisions they had so laboriously worked out. Amendment would require a vote of two thirds of the members of the General Assembly and ratification by two thirds of the members of the United Nations, including all five permanent members of the Security Council (Article 108). Any of the five would have the option, in other words, of vetoing any attempts to constrain or limit their veto power. The numerous delegations unhappy with the veto provision did manage, however, a modest quid pro quo. Concerned that the inequities built into the Council voting provisions not be set in stone for perpetuity, they managed to insert a provision for a General Conference, to be held no later than the tenth annual session of the General Assembly, to review the provisions of the Charter (Article 109). By that point, of course, world politics had entered the depths of the Cold War and there was little inclination to reopen a document whose provisions reflected a much more optimistic and forward-looking time.

3 Defining the Council through charter and practice

Chapter V (Articles 23–32)

The Security Council is not an independent actor. It is one of the six principal organs of the United Nations (Article 7). As Article 24(2) spells out, it is to "act in accordance with the Purposes and Principles" of that body. According to Article 1(1), the first purpose of the UN is:

> To maintain international peace and security, and to that end: to take effective collective measures for the prevention and removal of threats to the peace and for the suppression of acts of aggression or other breaches of the peace, and to bring about by peaceful means, and in conformity with the principles of justice and international law, adjustment or settlement of international disputes or situations which might lead to a breach of the peace.

To those ends, "members confer in the Security Council primary responsibility for the maintenance of international peace and security, and agree that in carrying out its duties under this responsibility the Security Council acts on their behalf" (Article 24(1)). This simple provision sets the Security Council apart from the League's Council, which did not have such specific and differentiated responsibilities. Council decisions, moreover, unlike those of the General Assembly, are to be binding. As Article 25 puts it, "members of the United Nations agree to accept and carry out the decisions of the Security Council in accordance with the present Charter."

The Council is to function continuously (Article 28(1)), can meet away from headquarters (Article 28(3)), and can "establish such organs as it deems necessary" (Article 29). With the end of the Cold War and the subsequent expansion of Council activities, the number and scope of subsidiary bodies began to grow, just as they have for the General Assembly and the Economic and Social Council. The UN has taken to the principle of subsidiarity like a duck to water. By mid-2006, the Security Council had acquired 25 such bodies, including six working groups in addition to the ongoing monitoring and supervisory organs charged with carrying out much of the Council's operational responsibilities. Among these subsidiary bodies were nine devoted to overseeing various country-specific regimes, such as sanctions, imposed by the Council, the two criminal tribunals for the former Yugoslavia and Rwanda established by the Council, three committees devoted to countering terrorism and the proliferation of weapons of mass destruction, and two related to claims and financial matters involving Iraq. The six working groups focused on generic questions related to sanctions, peacekeeping, conflict prevention and resolution in Africa, children and armed conflict, counter-terrorism and Council procedures. Box 3.1 provides the mid-2006 list of subsidiary bodies.

Because few of these groups are chaired by permanent members, they provide non-permanent members with opportunities to lead important aspects of the Council's work, and, because the subsidiary bodies generally operate by consensus, to have a virtual veto over their decisions. Like the proverbial iceberg, much of the Council's work, therefore, occurs beneath the surface and away from the public eye. Since much of the action now takes place either in informal consultations or in these subsidiary bodies, the popular image of the Council meeting around the famous horseshoe table in the formal Security Council Chamber to do its business is becoming increasingly anachronistic. Should the Council be enlarged again, this tendency would likely become even more pronounced.

While the Council can establish its own rules of procedure (Article 30), it continues to find it convenient to operate under provisional ones adopted in 1982.[1] These can be found in Appendix 1. Among those rules is the selection of its president, a post that is rotated monthly and alphabetically among its members. In recent years, it has not been uncommon for the Council to meet at the foreign minister level to address major crises or thematic issues. Occasionally it has met at the summit level, as it did to mark the post-Cold War revival of the Council in January 1992 and for the UN summits in 2000 and 2005. Any member state can participate in Council deliberations without a vote should the Council decide that the member's interests "are specially affected" (Article 31). Likewise, a member or even a non-member that is "party to a dispute under consideration" by the Council also may be invited to participate without vote (Article 32).

In practice, the Council meets either in formal meetings that are public and largely devoted to speechmaking or in private meetings and informal consultations where most of its deliberative work is accomplished out of the public eye. These days, the line of non-Council members seeking to speak at formal meetings of the Council can, at times, resemble a queue for a popular first-run movie. The increasing activism of the Council with the end of the Cold War can be seen in the impressive growth in the numbers of its formal

Box 3.1: Subsidiary bodies of the Security Council (25)

Standing committees (2)

The Committee of Experts on Rules of Procedure
The Committee on the Admission of New Members

Ad Hoc committees (2)

The Committee on Council Meetings away from Headquarters
The Governing Council of the United Nations Compensation Commission

Sanctions and similar matters (11)

Security Council Committee on Somalia
  Established by Resolution 751 of 24 April 1992
Security Council Committee on Rwanda
  Established by Resolution 918 of 17 May 1994
Security Council Committee on Sierra Leone
  Established by Resolution 1132 of 8 October 1997
Security Council Committee Concerning Al-Qaida and the Taliban
  Established by Resolution 1267 of 15 October 1999
Security Council Committee on Counter-terrorism
  Established by Resolution 1373 of 28 September 2001
Security Council Committee on Iraq
  Established by Resolution 1518 of 24 November 2003
Security Council Committee on Liberia
  Established by Resolution 1521 of 22 December 2003
Security Council Committee on the Democratic Republic of the Congo
  Established by Resolution 1533 of 12 March 2004
Security Council Committee on Weapons of Mass Destruction and Terrorism
  Established by Resolution 1540 of 28 April 2004
Security Council Committee on Côte d'Ivoire
  Established by Resolution 1572 of 15 November 2004
Security Council Committee on the Sudan
  Established by Resolution 1591 of 29 March 2005

Tribunals (2)

International Criminal Tribunal for the Former Yugoslavia
  Established by Resolution 808 of 22 February 1993
International Criminal Tribunal for Rwanda
  Established by Resolution 955 of 8 November 1994

Working groups (6)

General issues of sanctions
  Established by Note by the President of the Security Council S/
    2000/319 of 17 April 2000
UN Peacekeeping Operations
  Established by President Statement S/PRST//2001/3 of 31 January 2001
Conflict Prevention and Resolution in Africa
  Established by Note by the President of the Security Council S/
    2002/207 of 1 March 2002
Terrorism
  Established by Resolution 1566 of 7 October 2004
Children and Armed Conflict
  Established by Resolution 1612 of 26 July 2005
Documentation and Other Procedural Matters

Other matters (2)

United Nations Monitoring, Verification and Inspection Commission
  (UNMOVIC)
Established by Resolution 1284 of 17 December 1999
Peacebuilding Commission
Established by Resolution 1645 of 20 December 2005

Source: Security Council website,
http://www.un.org/Docs/sc/unsc_structure.html. List as of July 2006

meetings and informal consultations. These totaled 117 in 1988, grew to 321 by 1992, and reached 532 in 2002.[2] Twice-a-day sessions have become the norm for the Council, which usually has several items on its agenda for each session.[3] Though traditionally informal consultations had generally outnumbered formal meetings, in recent years that ratio has been reversed with the chorus of demands by other member states for greater transparency and wider participation in its work.

Initially, as proposed at Dumbarton Oaks, the Council had eleven members, five permanent and six non-permanent (or elected) ones, with seven affirmative votes required for a decision. But, with the success of the UN-brokered decolonization movement, pressures grew to expand the Council to make room for the newly independent countries. By 1963, the membership of the organization had swelled from 51 to 114, with more than half from underrepresented Africa and Asia. In December of that year, the General Assembly voted overwhelmingly to add four more non-permanent members to the Council, with the majority required for a decision going from seven of eleven to nine of fifteen. Though only one of the five permanent members, China (Taiwan), voted for the expansion, by mid-1965 all five had ratified the amendment.[4] In the four decades since, the topic of further Council expansion has been incessantly debated as the organization's membership has risen to 192, but, as Chapter 10 below details, a widely agreeable formula has proven elusive.

Non-permanent members serve two-year terms and are not eligible for "immediate re-election" (Article 23(2)), so each year there is an influx of five new members into the Council. As an "important question," election to the Council requires a two-thirds vote of the General Assembly, though the veto does not apply (Article 18). According to Article 23(1) "due regard" is to be paid "in the first instance to the contribution of Members of the United Nations to the maintenance of international peace and security and to the other purposes of the Organization, and also to equitable geographical distribution." In practice, these criteria often appear to be reversed, with regional groups as likely to put forward candidates on the basis of rotation or intra-regional politics as for their global contributions.

Debates over the composition of the Council, as well as over the veto power of the five permanent members (P-5), reflect the inherent tension between the founding goal of assuring the leadership and collaboration of the states most capable of enforcing the Council's will and the norms of universality and representativeness espoused by a growing and increasingly diverse membership. Those calling for radical reform of the Council often ask, if "the Organization is based on the principle of the sovereign equality of all its Members," as Article 2(1) asserts, then why should such inequities among the rights and privileges of members of the Council persist? Part of the answer lies in the founders' employment of sovereign equality as a legal term, not one describing rules for inter-governmental decision-making. Indeed, again adopting one of the Dumbarton Oaks proposals, the delegates in San Francisco agreed that the term indicated:

- that states are juridically equal;
- that they enjoy the rights inherent in their full sovereignty;
- that the personality of the state is respected, as well as its territorial integrity and political independence; and
- that the state should, under international order, comply faithfully with its international duties and obligations.[5]

Tellingly, the term is cited neither in Chapter V describing the Council nor in Chapter IV describing the General Assembly, even with the latter's one-nation, one-vote rules.

Chapter VI (Articles 33–8)

According to a New Zealand delegate to San Francisco, the language on pacific settlement of disputes had "the doubtful distinction of being regarded as one of the most poorly drafted sections" of the Dumbarton Oaks proposals. Even after much debate and some reworking at San Francisco, what had become Chapter VI of the Charter was described by the Canadians as containing "continuing obscurities."[6] Article 33(1), as well as Article 52(2), makes it abundantly clear that the first responsibility of parties to any dispute is to seek peaceful settlement themselves or through a regional agency or arrangement. Reference to the heavily burdened Council is not to be the first option, though the Council may "call upon the parties to settle their dispute by such means" (Article 33(2)). Should the parties fail to resolve their differences by means of the mechanisms under Article 33, then Article 37 instructs them to refer their dispute to the Council.

Though it has become commonplace for commentators to opine that the founders sought to restrict the Council's competence to cases of inter-state conflict, the provisions of Chapter VI suggest otherwise. Under Article 34, the Council "may investigate any dispute, or any situation which might lead to international friction or give rise to a dispute" to determine whether there exists a potential threat to international peace and security. Article 35 stipulates that any member state may bring "any dispute, or any situation of the nature referred to in Article 34, to the attention of the Security Council or of the General Assembly," while non-member states may do so if they accept in advance "the obligations of pacific settlement" contained in the Charter. "At any stage" of such a dispute, according to Article 36(1), the Council may "recommend appropriate procedures or methods of adjustment." However, "as a general rule," Article 36(3) reminds the Council members, legal disputes should be referred to the International Court of Justice (one of the UN's six principal organs).[7]

The thrust of Chapter VI is that the Council should begin to investigate situations that have conflict potential at an early stage, well before they erupt into inter-state conflict. It is encouraged to make recommendations for peaceful settlement at any point that it deems helpful, though Chapter VI, unlike Chapter VII, contains no enforcement measures. These provisions respond to the Article 1(1) declaration that the UN's first purpose encompasses "collective measures for the prevention and removal of threats to the peace," as well as for addressing "situations which might lead to a breach of the peace." True, Article 2(7) cautions that "nothing contained in the present Charter shall authorize the United Nations to intervene in matters which are essentially within the domestic jurisdiction of any state or should require the Members to submit such matters to settlement under the present Charter."

But it goes on to underline that "this principle should not prejudice the application of enforcement measures under Chapter VII."

The delegates from New Zealand and Canada had a point. The drafters, no doubt for good political reasons, made it less than crystal clear when the Council might determine that conditions within a state might hold the seeds to international conflict. But the Council's latitude for conducting investigations in such cases is cast broadly under Chapter VI and, should it decide that enforcement action is necessary under Chapter VII, then the non-intervention caveats under 2(7) would not apply. Though giving a respectful nod to the core principle of sovereignty in 2(7), the founders evidently put greater weight on the need for the Council to have sufficient leeway to address problems within states if necessary to fulfill its paramount responsibility of maintaining international peace and security.

Chapter VII (Articles 39–51)

If the Security Council was to be the manifestation of the new seriousness of purpose that animated the allied powers, it was Chapter VII and its enforcement provisions that were to give teeth to its potential. Decisions of the Council taken under Chapter VII were to be enforceable, not just legally binding. While the Covenant had expressed aspirations toward collective security, especially in its vaguely worded Article 10 commitments, the elaboration of enforcement machinery in Chapter VII was unprecedented in its scope, detail and ambitions.[8] The existence of these provisions, of course, is no guarantee that the members of the Council will agree on the wisdom of invoking them in any given situation – much less that their implementation will prove effective. The collective will to employ Chapter VII measures has, of course, varied with the political seasons. Over the first forty-four years of the Council's work, roughly corresponding to the Cold War years, on average one Chapter VII resolution was passed every two years (22 in 44 years). Since 1990, in contrast, the Council has invoked Chapter VII on an average of about eighteen resolutions per year (or more often in an average month than in two years during the first four decades).[9]

Chapter VII opens with an unassuming, but quite powerful, assertion. According to Article 39, it is the Security Council that "shall determine the existence of any threat to the peace, breach of the peace, or act of aggression and should make recommendations, or decide what measures shall be taken . . . to maintain or restore international peace and security." Under Article 99, "the Secretary-General may bring to the attention of the Security Council any matter which in his opinion may threaten the maintenance of international peace and security." But only the Council has the authority to make that determination. Likewise, the General Assembly may discuss any security question brought before it (Article 11(2)), but if the Council is addressing the matter, then the Assembly "shall not make any recommendations with regard to that dispute or situation unless the Security Council so requests" (Article 12(1)). Chapter VII makes no reference either to the International Court of Justice or to any guidelines or standards by which the Council should make its determinations about the existence of a threat or about the need to take collective action to deal with it. These are to be political decisions, produced through the votes of sovereign states, not necessarily by reference to a higher authority or set of standards, beyond the general admonition in 24(2), noted above, that the Council should "act in accordance with the Purposes and Principles" spelled out in the Charter.

While commentators are no doubt correct to conclude that the founders were chiefly concerned about the need to join forces to oppose and defeat aggressor states, it is worth recalling that Article 39 is cast much more broadly. It poses a spectrum of concerns, ranging from "the existence of any threat to the peace" to "breach of the peace" to "act of aggression." As with the provisions of Chapter VI discussed above, Article 39 encompasses the notion of early intervention, whether of a diplomatic, political, economic, or military character. This notion is reinforced by Article 40's authorization for the Council to "call upon the parties concerned to comply with such provisional measures as it deems necessary or desirable" in an effort "to prevent an aggravation of the situation." At the same time, delegates from a range of countries stressed in San Francisco that the Council needed to be able "to act quickly and effectively" as the Norwegian President of Commission III, on the Council, put it. "On the authority and ability of the Security Council to act with all possible dispatch and forcefulness may very well depend, at some future date," he warned, "the security, the peace, and the very existence of the freedom- and justice-loving nations of the world."[10] Neither the inclusion of the provisional measures clause nor the sequence of Articles laying out the tools available to the Council were meant to suggest that the Council was expected to invoke them in that order.[11]

The Council, in short, is given wide latitude to pick the cases, the timing, and the tools for its interventions. There is no language in Chapter VII urging the members of the Council to be consistent, fair, or equitable in their judgments about when and how to get involved. The Charter, after all, was largely drafted by those permanent members of the Council whose political, economic, and security capacities were most likely to be called upon to implement Chapter VII mandates (see Chapter 2 above). They wanted maximum flexibility in the application of its provisions, even as they sought to make the Council's decisions binding on the rest of the membership.[12] At the same time, the more far-sighted figures also recognized – and the smaller delegations repeatedly reminded them – that the system would not be viable if the

Council gained a reputation for double standards, narrow agendas, and half-hearted implementation. A feckless Council, as they had already learned with the League, would do them little good when they turned to it in distress. Credibility and legitimacy would have to be earned.

The tools to get the job done are laid out in Articles 41, 42, 43 and 47. According to 41,

> The Security Council may decide what measures not involving the use of armed force are to be employed to give effect to its decisions, and it may call upon the Members of the United Nations to apply such measures. These may include complete or partial interruption of economic relations and of rail, sea, air, postal, telegraphic, radio, and other means of communication, and the severance of diplomatic relations.

The terms of Article 41 are much broader and more flexible than those of its counterpart in the League Covenant (Article 16). The League's boosters had put much greater stake in the power and persuasiveness of economic statecraft. The failure of key members to embargo strategically important oil shipments to Italy as part of the League's economic sanctions – imposed in response to Mussolini's invasion of Abyssinia (now Ethiopia) in 1935 – however, had left this tool in rather poor repute. Nevertheless, the UN's architects appreciated that there might be times and places where such steps could be helpful, if only to offer an alternative or a political stepping stone to the use of military force.

Unlike the Covenant, Article 41 posits the possibility of "partial" measures and does not restrict the application of sanctions to nation states. Indeed, as addressed in Chapter 6 below, the Council has on several occasions imposed sanctions against non-state actors in recent years. Though the economy was not as globalized in 1945 as it is today, the Charter recognizes that sanctions taken against one state may have an unintended negative impact on its neighbors and trading partners as well. According to Article 50, those third-party states, whether members of the UN or not, that "are confronted with special economic problems arising from the carrying out of those measures shall have the right to consult the Security Council with regard to a resolution of those problems." Less clear, of course, is what the Council might decide to do to remedy such cases, other than to ask the member states to do their best to be helpful.

Though it has become commonplace to assert that the Charter relegates the use of force to a last resort, it would be hard to prove it either by the comments in San Francisco about sequencing noted above or by the wording of Article 42:

> Should the Council consider that measures provided for in Article 41 would be inadequate or have proved to be inadequate, it may take such

action by air, sea, or land forces as may be necessary to maintain or restore international peace and security. Such action may include demonstrations, blockade, and other operations by air, sea, or land forces of Members of the United Nations.

The phrase "would be inadequate" – added at Canada's suggestion at the San Francisco conference – underlined the founders' keen appreciation that members of the Council may well face situations in which time is of the essence and there is good reason to believe that non-military measures would not get the job done.[13] In such cases, the responsible course may be to resort early to the collective threat, demonstration, or use of force instead. Article 42, in that regard, provides a suitably broad and flexible constitutional framework. While action under Article 42 is generally assumed to have a coercive character, the Council and successive secretaries-general have developed a remarkably varied repertoire of ways in which the creative application of force can, at times, assist the organization's diplomatic efforts and political purposes. The continuum ranges from classical peacekeeping, with the consent of the parties, to preventive deployment, such as in Macedonia, in which only one side gives its consent, to authorizing the collective use of force to repulse inter-state aggression, as in Kuwait in 1990–1.[14]

Doctrine and legal authority aside, the new organization faced the same quandary that the old one had: where were the forces to come from to enforce Council decisions taken under Chapter VII? The old Council could only "recommend to the several Governments concerned what effective military, naval or air force the Members of the League could severally contribute to the armed forces to be used to protect the covenants of the League" (Article 16(2)). In practice, the collective responsibility that was to undergird collective security lacked the critical element of automaticity in a world of fully sovereign member states. Even its most ardent advocate, President Woodrow Wilson, had declared that the League could not require the dispatch of US forces abroad, nor would they be placed under an international command.[15]

The drafters of the UN Charter tried to circumvent this core dilemma by establishing a stand-by system under which individual member states would decide which of their forces would be earmarked for international contingencies and could be called into action by the Council. Under Article 43(1), all member states were "to make available to the Security Council, on its call and in accordance with a special agreement or agreements, armed forces, assistance, and facilities, including rights of passage, necessary for the purpose of maintaining international peace and security." However, while these stand-by agreements were to be "negotiated as soon as possible" with the Council (Article 43(2)), no member state stepped forward to undertake such a commitment. Article 43 was allowed to languish. Only a pale reflection could be discerned in the stand-by arrangements system developed in the 1990s for identifying possible national contingents that states might volunteer for use in certain situations under a Chapter VI peacekeeping mandate, rather than for Chapter VII enforcement action.[16]

The question of who should command such hypothetical forces proved equally troubling and similarly elusive. Again, the Charter's architects started down a bold road. They called for

> a Military Staff Committee to advise and assist the Security Council on all questions relating to the Security Council's military requirements for the maintenance of international peace and security, the employment and command of forces placed at its disposal, the regulation of armaments, and possible disarmament.
>
> (Article 47(1))

Embodying the notion of the Four (Five) Policemen, the Committee was to "consist of the Chiefs of Staff of the permanent members of the Security Council or their representatives." Others could be invited to be "associated with it" and "regional sub-committees" could be established as needed (Articles 47(2) and (4)). The Committee, further, was to "be responsible under the Security Council for the strategic direction of any armed forces placed at the disposal of the Security Council" (Article 47(3)). Whatever was meant by "strategic direction," it clearly fell short of the actual command of any UN forces.[17]

Neither at Dumbarton Oaks nor at San Francisco was it possible to gain agreement on any specific command formula, so it was left that "questions relating to the command of such forces shall be worked out subsequently" (Article 47(3)). Sixty years later, "subsequently" has still not arrived and the member states are no closer to solving the international command riddle.[18] The differences and uncertainties over command issues served, of course, to fuel member state doubts about the wisdom of negotiating with the Council Article 43 agreements to provide national forces with any automaticity to the world body.

In retrospect, it is sobering to realize that one of the most important provisions of the Charter – Article 51, at the conclusion of Chapter VII – was a last-minute insertion into the text.[19] It was, and remains, one of the more controversial elements as well. It consists of two wordy, even awkward, sentences:

> Nothing in the present Charter shall impair the inherent right of individual or collective self-defence if an armed attack occurs against a

Member of the United Nations, until the Security Council has taken measures necessary to maintain international peace and security. Measures taken by Members in the exercise of this right of self-defence shall be immediately reported to the Security Council and shall not in any way affect the authority and responsibility of the Security Council under the present Charter to take at any time such action as it deems necessary in order to maintain or restore international peace and security.

While the Dumbarton Oaks proposals had not contained an explicit affirmation of the inherent right of self-defense, it was widely assumed that this was not necessary since that right was so well established under international law and nothing in the proposals sought to undermine a country's right to defend itself against aggression. At San Francisco, however, the more inclusive multilateral format introduced new voices and concerns. The Latin American delegations were acutely worried that resting the authority to invoke enforcement measures solely with the Security Council, especially with the veto provision, could destroy the credibility of the inter-American security system. Sympathetic to their position, Senator Vandenberg cautioned his fellow US delegates that, without a self-defense provision, the Charter would be vulnerable to the same sort of attacks in the US Senate as the League Covenant had been for undermining the Monroe Doctrine.[20] From a second flank, the Soviet delegates were becoming increasingly restive about whether the Charter could make it more difficult for Moscow and others to respond to some future threat from a rearmed Germany. (For them, the enemies clauses noted in Chapter 2 above provided part of the answer.)

Initially drafted by the US delegation, Article 51 underwent several substantial revisions before it received general acceptance among the assembled states. It seeks both to offer a clear reaffirmation of the right of self-defense and to balance this with the Council's ultimate legal authority for the maintenance of international peace and security. If the Council cannot take the "measures necessary to maintain international peace and security," for example because of the employment of a veto, member states, singly or collective, may defend themselves if "an armed attack" has occurred. Over the years, of course, member states have sought to justify a wider range of actions on the basis of Article 51. Importantly, as many at San Francisco expected, 51 was used to provide a legal framework for the development of regional defense pacts in many parts of the world at the outset of the Cold War. And, yes, its addition to the text proved very helpful in getting the US Senate's consent to the ratification of the Charter without damaging reservations or interpretations.

Part II

Tools

4 Peace operations

The UN Charter painted an expansive canvas of ways in which the world body could contribute to the maintenance of international peace and security. As Chapter 3 explained, the provisions relating to peaceful settlement in Chapter VI offer a particularly rich array of political and diplomatic tools. In part, this reflected the League's experience. As Leland Goodrich noted in the UN's early days,

> The powers of the United Nations organs for the pacific settlement of disputes are substantially the same as those of the principal organs of the League. Under the Charter, as under the Covenant, the functions of the political organs in this connection are limited to discussion, inquiry, mediation and conciliation.[1]

Building on this foundation, however, time and experience would suggest even more options and refinements to the members of the Security Council and to successive secretaries-general. The flowering of the UN's creativity in the realm of peaceful settlement, like the League's before it, could be attributed in part to the political conditions that soon stymied the development of the Council's bold enforcement powers and mechanisms (see Chapters 5 and 6 below). As Chapter VII wilted under Cold War constraints, Chapter VI began to prove its utility.

In its first few years, the Council faced a series of regional conflicts with broader security implications, yet none of these fit the mold of classic state-to-state aggression. Nor, for political reasons, were they candidates for the imposition of Chapter VII enforcement measures.[2] First to come before the Council was the matter of the withdrawal of Soviet forces from northern Iran, followed by the question of whether the continuation of the Franco regime in Spain constituted a threat to international peace and security; tensions in Northern Greece; the Corfu Channel dispute between the United Kingdom and Albania; and colonial hostilities between the Netherlands and Indonesia.

Traditional diplomatic tools, such as mediation, conciliation, good offices, and fact-finding, were invoked by the Council, often in tandem with the efforts of the Secretary-General and his envoys.

In the Council's pivotal third year, 1948, it was confronted by two bitter conflicts, in Palestine and in South Asia, that required both urgent political action and innovative approaches to conflict resolution. The latter included the first two UN peacekeeping missions. On 21 April, in Resolution 47 (1948), the Council called on India and Pakistan to end their hostilities over Jammu and Kashmir and to hold a plebiscite there. It also expanded the fact-finding commission it had established in January, instructing it both to provide good offices to the parties and to create an observer group. The latter became UNMOGIP (the United Nations Military Observer Group in India and Pakistan). Two days later, in Resolution 48 (1948), the Council established a Truce Commission for Palestine, including a group of international military observers (UNTSO, the UN Truce Supervision Organization). These initial two peacekeeping ventures, employing modest contingents of international military observers, are still deployed today, attesting both to their durability and to their inability to produce a resolution of the underlying conflicts.

Barely five months later, the Security Council was relegated to expressing its shock at the assassination of the UN's mediator in Palestine, Count Folke Bernadotte, which it blamed on "a criminal group of terrorists" (Resolution 57 (1948)). This tragedy was followed, over the first four months of 1949, by Ralph Bunche's diplomatic feat of negotiating armistice accords between the infant state of Israel and its four Arab neighbors.[3] For this signal accomplishment, Bunche received the UN's first Nobel Peace Prize. In little more than a year, the Council had launched its first peacekeeping venture, made its initial condemnation of terrorism, and experienced the contrasting highs and lows that are so often associated with efforts to bring peace to those who have other agendas. These early episodes also defined the practice of fluid and intense cooperation among the Council, the Secretary-General, and a range of other actors that has characterized UN peace operations ever since. While the Council's role is at times more central than at others, it never acts alone. Quite often, in fact, regional groups or great powers take the lead in mediation efforts and the UN plays, at best, a marginal role in the peace process.[4]

Today, despite some significant refinements and innovations along the way, the UN's repertoire of peace operations bears a close resemblance to the patterns established in its early years.[5] The value of many of the UN's traditional methods in producing "quiet successes" that are "politically invisible" was confirmed by a high-level panel, headed by Lakhdar Brahimi, the former Foreign Minister of Algeria, and convened by Secretary-General Kofi Annan in 2000 to review the world body's peace and security activities.[6] The panel divided UN operations into three categories: (1) conflict prevention and peacemaking; (2) peacekeeping; and (3) peace-building; as follows:

- Peacemaking addresses conflicts in progress, attempting to bring them to a halt, using the tools of diplomacy and mediation. Peacemakers may be envoys of Governments, groups of States, regional organizations or the United Nations, or they may be unofficial and non-governmental groups, as was the case, for example, in the negotiations leading up to a peace accord for Mozambique. Peacemaking may even be the work of a prominent personality, working independently.

- Peacekeeping is a 50-year-old enterprise that has evolved rapidly in the past decade from a traditional, primarily military model of observing ceasefires and force separations after inter-State wars, to incorporate a complex model of many elements, military and civilian, working together to build peace in the dangerous aftermath of civil wars.

- Peace-building is a term of more recent origin that . . . defines activities undertaken on the far side of conflict to reassemble the foundations of peace and provide the tools for building on those foundations something that is more than just the absence of war. Thus, peace-building includes but is not limited to reintegrating former combatants into civilian society, strengthening the rule of law (for example, through training and restructuring of local police, and judicial and penal reform); improving respect for human rights through the monitoring, education and investigation of past and existing abuses; providing technical assistance for democratic development (including electoral assistance and support for free media); and promoting conflict resolution and reconciliation techniques.[7]

Most of these measures are firmly grounded on the provisions of Chapter VI on pacific settlement of disputes. None rely heavily on coercion. But, as the Charter's architects understood, the persuasive powers of Chapter VI methods could at times be dramatically enhanced by the realization that resort to credible Chapter VII options might be around the corner. As Secretary-General Kofi Annan put, "if diplomacy is to succeed, it must be backed both by force and by fairness."[8]

Conflict prevention and peacemaking

Among the UN's multiple purposes, the Charter places none higher than preventing conflict (Article 1(1)). As former Secretary-General Boutros Boutros-Ghali points out, "the most desirable and efficient employment of diplomacy is to ease tensions before they result in conflict – or, if conflict breaks out, to act swiftly to contain it and resolve its underlying causes."[9] As the old saying goes, an ounce of prevention is worth a pound of cure. Containing local conflicts and preventing small ones from escalating into larger ones took on special urgency during the Cold War years, when the dangers and the potential costs of the East/West polarization of local disputes were so acute. With the end of the Cold War, however, long-simmering rivalries and dissatisfactions were allowed to boil over in many parts of the world in the early 1990s. The UN, in turn, was faced with an over-abundance of choices: more places where it might make a difference, but also more doubts about the commitment of major powers to becoming involved given the ebbing threat of escalation.[10]

Once again, as in the founding goal of avoiding a third world war, to many the answer to the UN's strategic dilemma appeared to be prevention. But would the doctrine and techniques employed during the Cold War by the Council and the Secretary-General need to be adjusted to meet the changing circumstances? In 1997, the influential Carnegie Commission on Preventing Deadly Conflict claimed to provide part of the answer.[11] There were two varieties of prevention, it posited, operational and structural. The former encompassed traditional peacemaking and peacekeeping, while the latter addressed root causes. Adopting this sweeping taxonomy, Secretary-General Kofi Annan claimed that "in every diplomatic mission and development project that we pursue, the United Nations is doing the work of prevention." In addition to such traditional elements as early warning, preventive diplomacy, and preventive deployments, he added early humanitarian action, preventive disarmament, development, peace-building, human rights, democratization, and good governance to the roster of preventive measures.[12] "Healthy and balanced development," he told the World Bank, "is the best form of conflict prevention."[13] Since most of these tasks went well beyond the Security Council's competence, he urged that body to coordinate its efforts with those of the Bretton Woods institutions, the UN Development Programme, the Economic and Social Council (ECOSOC), and the International Court of Justice (ICJ), as well as with NGOs and the private sector.[14]

The Security Council, rather than fretting about this widening circle of actors, embraced the more expansive notion of prevention. In a pair of thematic statements by its monthly President, in November 1999 and July 2000, the Council endorsed a comprehensive definition of prevention and acknowledged the need for enhanced cooperation with regional bodies and with ECOSOC.[15] The recognition of the importance of structural factors has undoubtedly given the members of the Council a keener appreciation of the advantages of enlisting the UN system as a whole, as well as other relevant actors, in its peace operations, particularly in complex cases of intra-state or transnational conflict. Agency heads, regional experts, and even field-based NGOs have been invited more frequently in recent years to address the

Council, whether in formal sessions, in Council retreats, or in unofficial gatherings of the Council under the Arria formula (see Chapter 7 below). It is less clear, however, whether the adoption of such a broad and elastic concept has had much operational significance. If virtually everything the UN does constitutes preventive action, then what power and traction can the concept have in policy terms?[16] The member states have certainly not rushed to provide the world body with the financial, institutional, or human resources to implement any major new initiatives in the prevention realm.

Questions of prevention doctrine aside, how has the UN – chiefly the Council and the Secretary-General – been doing in meeting its peacemaking objectives? The answer depends on what standards are applied: not a simple matter when there are no comparable organizations. The League's supporters were extolling its unparalleled success at resolving local disputes even as the Axis armies were on the move in the early to mid-1930s.[17] Apparently the League was good at small things and not so good at large ones. The UN's first task, then, was to prevent aggression against the allied powers and to forestall a third world war in the twentieth century. That very big goal achieved, though only partly by the UN, the debate has revolved around its track record at resolving lower levels of conflict.[18] Here, the proliferation of non-UN mediators, fact-finders, legitimizers, and guarantors in recent years makes a definitive answer problematic.[19] Whoever deserves the credit, there is reason to believe that all of the attention by multiple actors to conflict resolution is making a difference. According to the Secretary-General's High-level Panel on Threats, Challenges and Change, "in the last 15 years, more civil wars were ended through negotiation than in the previous two centuries in large part because the United Nations provided leadership, opportunities for negotiation, strategic coordination, and the resources needed for implementation."[20]

The UN's mediation record, however, has been decidedly mixed. The High-level Panel, acknowledging that there is plenty of room for improvement, points out that "mediation produced settlement in only about 25 per cent of the civil wars" and that the two big failures to implement the accords on Angola and Rwanda cost several million lives.[21] Fen Hampson, on the other hand, points to some significant accomplishments in the 1980s and 1990s: the Iran-Iraq war, El Salvador, Cambodia, Mozambique, Guatemala, and Tajikistan. In his view, the ingredients for success in these cases included the ripeness of the case (are the parties looking for a way out of a costly conflict that has lost its meaning?); the breadth and depth of Council support; the ability to back mediation efforts with a credible capacity for rewards or punishments; having the right personnel involved; and having had previous success in the region.[22] On the other hand, as Hampson and others have observed over the years, some regional disputes have proven just too tough and intractable, not only for the UN, but for others as well. Palestine,

Kashmir, Korea and Cyprus stand out in the stubbornness category. Some of the multiple conflicts in the former Yugoslavia may eventually reach that sorry status, despite enormous, intrusive, and continuing international involvement by Europe, the US and the UN. Conditions do change on the ground, of course, and hopeless situations, as once was the case in Angola, Mozambique, South Africa, and East Timor, can over time become ripe for international mediation and intervention.

Peacekeeping

Even at the UN, necessity often acts as the mother of invention. In the fall of 1956, war again erupted in the Middle East, this time with global security implications. Following fedayeen raids on Israel from the Sinai and the nationalization of the Suez Canal, Israeli forces invaded the Sinai, supported by British and French air strikes on Egyptian airbases. As London and Paris prepared their own ground assault and Moscow threatened a massive military response, Lester Pearson, the Canadian Prime Minister, proposed in the General Assembly the creation of something quite new: "a truly international peace and police force . . . large enough to keep these borders at peace while a political settlement is being worked out."[23] The General Assembly moved expeditiously to approve the Canadian proposal "for the setting up, with the consent of the nations concerned, of an emergency international United Nations Force to secure and supervise the cessation of hostilities" (Resolution 998 (ES-1) of 4 November 1956).[24] It gave Secretary-General Dag Hammarskjöld all of forty-eight hours to develop a plan for this peacekeeping force, something far more ambitious than the two previous observer missions in Palestine and Kashmir.

The experiment worked. One, it proved that peacekeeping could act as a valuable adjunct to peacemaking efforts. Two, it established the cardinal principles that would guide UN peacekeeping missions for more than three decades: consent, impartiality, and use of force only in self-defense. By putting some physical and political space between combatants, the blue-helmeted peacekeepers could both buy time for diplomacy to work and give the parties an external excuse for explaining to domestic constituencies why they were backing away from heated rhetoric or provocative actions. If the Council could not or would not coerce or induce the parties into stepping down, it could at least provide a face-saving and highly visible rationale for their doing so. Peacekeeping and pacific settlement worked best when they worked together, each reinforcing the other. Peacekeeping might help to stabilize a situation by keeping combatants apart and discouraging dangerous incidents, but it was no substitute for patient and determined diplomacy aimed at resolving the underlying disputes. In Cyprus, for example, where the deployment of

UNFICYP, the United Nations Peace-keeping Force in Cyprus, has managed to keep the Greek and Turkish communities apart for over three decades, diplomatic efforts at bringing them back together have repeatedly fallen short.[25] The sense of security induced by the peacekeepers' presence, in fact, may have added to the lethargy that has characterized the parties' approach to resolving their underlying differences.

Not only has peacekeeping proven to be a better medicine for some ailments than for others, it also has raised some perplexing doctrinal puzzles. With its heavy reliance on military officers, units, and deployments, peace-keeping has been something of a hybrid, embracing elements of both Chapters VI and VII, while occupying some ill-defined legal space frequently labeled Chapter VI1/2.[26] It had no place, and no mention, in the Charter. Though generally with a non-coercive mandate, peacekeepers have been asked by the Council to tame unruly elements, to protect certain populations or facilities, to uphold a modicum of human rights and legal standards, to assure the delivery of humanitarian assistance, and to perform other services that spoilers have sought to disrupt. They cannot always be soldiers without enemies. Indeed, more than 2,200 peacekeepers have been killed in the line of duty, more than one half of them since 1993.[27]

In the eyes of parties to a conflict, the blue helmets' military potential may derive less from the arms they carry than from the deterrent they represent. At times, the deployment of lightly armed peacekeepers has acted as a stepping stone to more forceful action under Chapter VII when their mandate was force-fully challenged. In the Congo in the early 1960s and Somalia in the early 1990s, peacekeeping missions initially deployed under a Chapter VI mandate were later given more robust roles under Chapter VII.[28] UNPROFOR, the misnamed and ill fated United Nations Protection Force in the former Yugoslavia, on the other hand, had its mandate repeatedly recast in confusing and occasionally inconsistent ways.[29] Tasks were added under Chapter VII, including insuring the delivery of humanitarian assistance, the maintenance of no-fly zones, and – tragically – the protection of so-called safe havens, though the basic mandate remained under Chapter VI. The resulting muddle, reflecting persistent divisions and ambivalence among key Council members, only encouraged the parties to challenge the peacekeepers on the ground.

Two other developments severely taxed UN peacekeeping doctrine and capacity in the 1990s: (1) the growing demand for UN interventions; and (2) the evolving nature of the kinds of conflicts for which peacekeeping services were sought. The result was a rapid growth in the size and complexity of the peacekeeping burden. In 1991, the UN peacekeeping budget was about $490 million and the number of deployed blue helmets about 15,300. Just two years later, those figures had grown to $3.059 billion and 78,500, increases of more than sixfold in spending and fivefold in troop strength.[30] (See Figure 4.1

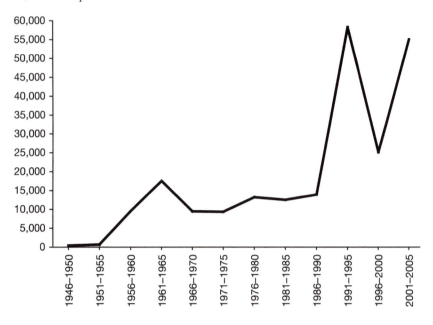

Figure 4.1 Average annual number of peacekeepers deployed for each five-year period 1946–2005

Sources: http://www.globalpolicy.org/security/peacekpg/data/pcekprs1.htm (data through 1994 by William Durch, Stimson Center; data from 1995 forward, http://www.un.org/Depts/dpko/dpko/contributors/)

for deployment trends.) Later in the decade, as UN forces ran into the kinds of problems and frustrations noted above and NATO took over peacekeeping assignments in the Balkans, the mix of UN troop contributing countries shifted dramatically. In 1993, the four largest troop contributors were France, the United Kingdom, Canada, and the Netherlands. A decade later all of the top troop contributors were from the developing world. (See Table 4.1 for the leading troop contributors in 2003, 2004 and 2005.) The major military powers kept voting in the Council for new missions, but they expected others to carry them out.[31]

The qualitative story in terms of the types of missions was more critical, because a number of the new situations did not fit the classic mold. Either consent was begrudging or uncertain, or the parties unreliable or even ill defined. The Council had dealt with civil and transnational conflicts before, most prominently in the Congo, but a much larger share of the new missions was in places where local governmental authority was weak, under challenge,

Table 4.1 Top ten contributors of troops and police personnel to UN operations based on monthly averages over a three-year period (2003–2005)

Rank	Country	Total	Monthly	2005	2004	2003
1	Pakistan	264,236	7,340	114,235	94,344	55,657
2	Bangladesh	233,393	6,483	103,007	87,344	43,042
3	India	146,539	4,071	75,708	36,902	33,929
4	Nigeria	111,886	3,108	36,068	41,485	34,333
5	Ghana	98,577	2,738	36,799	36,350	25,428
6	Nepal	84,537	2,348	41,551	28,501	14,485
7	Jordan	79,648	2,212	36,180	24,507	18,961
8	Uruguay	76,476	2,124	29,644	25,743	21,089
9	Ethiopia	72,439	2,012	41,041	30,315	1,083
10	Kenya	62,244	1,729	17,914	22,834	21,496

Source: Note of the Secretary-General, 1 February 2006, pursuant to Resolution A/60/180, circulated to the member states by the President of the General Assembly, 2 February 2006.

or, as in Somalia, non-existent. Under such conditions, according to Michael W. Doyle *et al.*, "the future of UN peacekeeping, it seems, lies between the extremes of forcible intervention and absolute respect for sovereignty."[32] As the Brahimi panel noted, "in the context of modern peace operations dealing with intra-State/transnational conflicts, consent may be manipulated in many ways by the local parties."[33] The panel concluded that rules of engagement should be more robust and "impartiality for such operations must therefore mean adherence to the principles of the Charter and to the objectives of a mandate," rather than to "neutrality or equal treatment of all parties in all cases for all time, which can amount to a policy of appeasement."[34] Even as geopolitics has permitted the Council to make much more frequent reference to Chapter VII, experience and local conditions are blurring the lines between VI and VII and between peacekeeping and peace enforcement.

Peace-building

The founders of the UN recognized that security was not solely a military matter. Only the first of the four purposes stipulated in Article 1 makes reference to the military dimensions of security. The third underlines the need "to achieve international co-operation in solving international problems of an economic, social, cultural, or humanitarian character, and in promoting and encouraging respect for human rights and for fundamental freedoms." Likewise, many of them shared the then-prevalent conviction that the flawed peace arrangements following World War I – both among and within states – made the next world war all but inevitable. The UN, then, was not just to address the broader aspects of postwar peace-building, its very creation was, to a great extent, the manifestation of just such an urge. The allies recognized that they would have to win the peace as well as the war, if the UN was not to be just another inter-war institution.

Although the term peace-building was not widely used until the 1990s, the Congo operation thirty years before certainly immersed the Security Council deeply into that country's internal affairs, even helping to determine the shape of its future governance. At the same time, the liabilities of that operation exposed the risks inherent in undertaking robust peacekeeping missions without coupling them with careful planning for postwar peace-building. Though at a much higher cost than had been anticipated, the operation did achieve its immediate objectives, including forestalling a much larger regional crisis.[35] But little was done to address the deep social, economic and governance deficits that have haunted the Congo, its people, and its neighborhood ever since. Forty years after the ONUC operation ended in mid-1964, the Congo is again one of the most frustrating and intractable challenges on the Council's security and humanitarian agenda.

The peace-building operations in Namibia, El Salvador, Cambodia, and Mozambique, undertaken between 1989 and 1995, demonstrated the Council's growing penchant for getting deeply involved in the process of reconstructing existing states or giving birth to newly independent ones following periods of severe strife.[36] The relative success of these early efforts encouraged similar ventures in the Balkans, Haiti and East Timor that have proven more troublesome and intractable, as well as the more promising ones in Liberia, Angola, and Sierra Leone.[37] Asserting that "social peace is as important as strategic or political peace," Boutros-Ghali observed in 1992 that

> once these [peace-building and peacekeeping missions] have achieved their objectives, only sustained, cooperative work to deal with underlying economic, social, cultural and humanitarian problems can place an achieved peace on a durable foundation. Preventive diplomacy is to avoid a crisis; post-conflict peace-building is to prevent a reoccurrence.[38]

Eight years later, the Brahimi report underlined the symbiotic relationship between those who keep the peace and those who build it: "while the peacebuilders may not be able to function without the peacekeepers' support, the peacekeepers have no exit without the peacebuilders' work."[39]

Post-conflict peace-building, like structural prevention, has two character-istics that make it seductively attractive to the Council and to the UN secretariat alike. One is that, by forestalling the resumption of conflict, it promises to avoid the dilemmas, costs, and risks inherent in the re-employ-ment of economic and/or military coercion under Chapter VII. Recent history has confirmed the downside risks and costs of failed peace-building. Stephen Stedman points out, in this regard, that the two worst humanitarian disasters of the 1990s, in Angola in 1993 and Rwanda in 1994, followed failures to properly and fully implement peace agreements.[40] On a more modest scale, the festering poverty and instability in Haiti testify to the consequences when the repeated peace-building efforts of the UN and regional actors fail to estab-lish sustainable and credible local institutions.

The second attraction is that post-conflict peace-building promises to involve the capacities of many parts of the far-flung UN system, while playing to the UN's presumed comparative advantage in implementing the soft side of security. Indeed, a pair of studies by the Rand Corporation, comparing cases of peace-building by the United States and by the United Nations, concluded that the latter were both more cost effective and more likely to succeed. As the second study put it,

> assuming adequate consensus among Security Council members on the purpose for any intervention, the United Nations provides the most suit-able institutional framework for most nation-building missions, one with a comparatively low cost structure, a comparatively high success rate, and the greatest degree of international legitimacy.[41]

The UN, it noted, is well suited for "low-profile, small-footprint" operations and "has an ability to compensate, to some degree at least, for its 'hard' power deficit with 'soft' power attributes of international legitimacy and local impartiality."[42] This symbiosis between the UN's comparative advantages and those enjoyed by militarily potent member states helps to account for the rebound in the number of UN peacekeeping and peace-building operations following the declining use of these tools in the latter half of the 1990s. As Box 4.1 indicates, there were fifteen ongoing UN peace operations as of early 2006, about half (seven) in Africa.

The fact that peace-building operations require a meshing of efforts by a wide range of actors from inside and outside of the UN system, however, raises important questions of decision-making coherence and operational coordination and integration. At those stages of a peace operation that entail the use of military forces, clearly the Security Council has to exercise close

Box 4.1: United Nations peacekeeping operations

Peacekeeping operations since 1948: 60.

Current peacekeeping operations: 15.

United Nations Disengagement Observer Force (UNDOF/Golan
    Heights): since June 1974

United Nations Interim Administration Mission in Kosovo (UNMIK):
    since June 1999

United Nations Interim Force in Lebanon (UNIFIL): since March 1978

United Nations Military Observer Group in India and Pakistan
    (UNMOGIP): since January 1949

United Nations Mission for the Referendum in Western Sahara
    (MINURSO): since April 1991

United Nations Mission in Ethiopia and Eritrea (UNMEE): since July
    2000

United Nations Mission in Liberia (UNMIL): since September 2003

United Nations Mission in the Sudan (UNMIS): since March 2005

United Nations Observer Mission in Georgia (UNOMIG): since August
    1993

United Nations Operation in Burundi (ONUB): since June 2004

United Nations Operation in Côte d'Ivoire (UNOCI): since April 2004

United Nations Organization Mission in the Democratic Republic of the
    Congo (MONUC): since November 1999

United Nations Peacekeeping Force in Cyprus (UNFICYP): since March
    1964

United Nations Stabilization Mission in Haiti (MINUSTAH): since June
    2004

United Nations Truce Supervision Organization (UNTSO/Middle East):
    since May 1948

Past Peacekeeping Operations

Africa (16)

United Nations Aouzou Strip Observer Group (UNASOG/Chad-Libya):
    May – June 1994

United Nations in Sierra Leone (UNOMSIL): July 1998 – October
    1999

United Nations Observer Mission in Uganda-Rwanda (UNAMIR):
October 1993 – March 1996

United Nations Mission in Liberia (UNOMIL): September 1993 –
September 1997

United Nations Mission in Sierra Leone (UNAMSIL): October 1999 –
December 2005

United Nations Mission in the Central African Republic (MINURCA):
April 1998 – February 2000

United Nations Observer Mission in Angola (MONUA): June 1997 –
February 1999

United Nations Operation in Mozambique (ONUMOZ): December
1992 – December 1994

United Nations Operation in Somalia I (UNOSOM I): April 1992 –
March 1993

United Nations Operation in Somalia II (UNOSOM II): March 1993 –
March 1995

United Nations Operation in the Congo (ONUC): July 1960 – June
1964

United Nations Transition Assistance Group (UNTAG/Namibia): April
1989 – March 1990

United Nations Verification Mission I (UNAVEM I): December 1988 –
May 1991

United Nations Verification Mission II (UNAVEM II): May 1991 –
February 1995

United Nations Verification Mission III (UNAVEM III): February
1995 – June 1997

Americas (8)

United Nations Civilian Police Mission in Haiti (MIPONUH):
December 1997 – March 2000

United Nations Mission in Haiti (UNMIH): September 1993 – June
1996

United Nations Mission of the Representative of the Secretary-General
in the Dominican Republic (DOMREP): May 1965 – October 1966

United Nations Observer Group in Central America (ONUCA):
November 1989 – January 1992

United Nations Observer Mission in El Salvador (ONUSAL): July
1991 – April 1995

United Nations Support Mission in Haiti (UNSMIH): July 1996 – July 1997

United Nations Transition Mission in Haiti (UNTMIH): August – November 1997

United Nations Verification Mission in Guatemala (MINUGUA): January – May 1997

Asia and the Pacific (8)

United Nations Advance Mission in Cambodia (UNAMIC): October 1991 – March 1992

United Nations Good Offices in Afghanistan and Pakistan (UNGOMAP): May 1988 – March 1990

United Nations India-Pakistan Observation Mission (UNIPOM): September 1965 – March 1966

United Nations Mission of Observers in Tajikistan (UNMOT): December 1994 – May 2000

United Nations Mission of Support in East Timor (UNMISET): May 2002 – May 2005

United Nations Security Force in West New Guinea (UNSF): October 1962 – April 1963

United Nations Transitional Administration in East Timor (UNTAET): October 1999 – May 2002

United Nations Transitional Authority in Cambodia (UNTAC): February 1992 – September 1993

Europe (7)

United Nations Civilian Police Support Group (UNPSG/Croatia): January – October 1998

United Nations Confidence Restoration Operation (UNCRO/Croatia): March 1995 – January 1996

United Nations Mission in Bosnia and Herzegovina (UNMIBH): December 1995 – December 2002

United Nations Mission of Observers in Prevlaka (UNMOP): February 1996 – December 2002

United Nations Preventive Deployment Force (UNPREDEP/Former Yugoslav Republic of Macedona): March 1995 – February 1999

United Nations Protection Force (UNPROFOR/Former Yugoslavia): February 1992 – March 1995

United Nations Transitional Authority in Eastern Slavonia, Baranja and
Western Sirmium (UNTAES/Croatia): January 1996 – January
1998

Middle East (6)

First United Nations Emergency Force (UNEF I/Middle East):
November 1956 – June 1967
Second United Nations Emergency Force (UNEF II/Middle East):
October 1973 –July 1979
United Nations Iran-Iraq Military Observer Group (UNIIOG): August
1988 – February 1991
United Nations Iraq-Kuwait Observation Mission (UNIKOM): April
1991 – October 2005
United Nations Observer Group in Lebanon (UNOGIL): June –
December 1958
United Nations Yemen Observation Mission (UNYOM): July 1963 –
September 1964

oversight. But is it best positioned to oversee those aspects of a post-conflict
reconstruction that involve economic and social development, judicial reform,
restoring respect for human rights, and strengthening civil and governmental
institutions? Yet, through fifteen years of growing UN involvement in such
multi-faceted operations, no other inter-governmental body has been in a
position to assume these responsibilities. To fill this gap, Secretary-General
Kofi Annan, based on one of the primary recommendations of his High-level
Panel, in March 2005 urged the establishment of an inter-governmental
Peacebuilding Commission backed by a Peacebuilding Support Office in the
secretariat.[43] After months of debate about the relative relationships of the
Security Council and ECOSOC to the new enterprise, the September 2005
Summit endorsed the establishment of the Commission.[44] The concurrent
resolutions of the Security Council and General Assembly creating the
Peacebuilding Commission as an inter-governmental advisory body described
its main purposes as the following:

(a) to bring together all relevant actors to marshal resources and to advise on
and propose integrated strategies for post-conflict peace-building and
recovery;

(b) to focus attention on the reconstruction and institution-building efforts necessary for recovery from conflict and to support the development of integrated strategies in order to lay the foundation for sustainable development;

(c) to provide recommendations and information to improve the coordination of all relevant actors within and outside the United Nations, to develop best practices, to help to insure predictable financing for early recovery activities and to extend the period of attention given by the international community to post-conflict recovery.[45]

In addition to a thirty-one-member Organizational Committee, the Commission will work primarily through a series of country-specific committees that will include representatives of the country under consideration, some of its neighbors, regional organizations, regional banks, and international financial institutions.

Whether there is an institutional fix to this problem – and whether the somewhat unwieldy Commission will be the right one – remains to be seen. Either way, the good news is that the Security Council, and the UN as a whole, continues to refine its approach to peace operations. Perhaps we are not condemned to live in "a world of endless conflict," as William Shawcross' book title so vividly suggested. On the one hand, there is no danger that the Security Council is going to succeed in putting itself out of business. Interstate war and internal or transnational strife are not about to disappear from the course of history, nor are they going to be entirely displaced on the international agenda by the growing threat of terrorism and the conflict it inspires. But, on the other hand, there are unmistakable signs of progress.

Several studies have concluded that the numbers and ferocity both of interstate and intra-state/transnational warfare have declined markedly since a peak towards the end of the Cold War.[46] "According to our calculations," notes Monty G. Marshall, "the general magnitude of global warfare has decreased by over 50 percent since peaking in the mid-1980s, falling by the end of 2002 to its lowest level since the early 1960s."[47] In recent years, the ranks of international refugees have fallen dramatically as well.[48] Consistent with these trends, the global outlay of human and material resources for defense purposes has also declined since Cold War days. According to figures compiled by the International Institute for Strategic Studies (IISS), the numbers serving in national armed forces fell by 27 percent from 1985 to 2002, while the portion of gross domestic product (GDP) devoted to defense was cut in more than half, from 6.2 to 2.6 percent.[49]

While such trends are not linear and should not be assumed for the future, they are encouraging. Marshall and his collaborator, Ted Robert Gurr, see some extension of these trends for the immediate future, at least, since "the first years of the new millennium have produced a virtual cascade of peace talks and settlements in civil wars and negotiations in international conflicts".[50] Many of these initiatives, as noted earlier, have been sponsored by other inter-governmental or non-governmental institutions or by governments, so the Council's growing activism should be seen as only part of the explanation for these encouraging developments. Nevertheless, there is now some reason to believe that the Council's repertoire of peacemaking, peace-keeping and peace-building is beginning to make a positive difference, at the very least by propagating the notion that the extinguishing of even localized conflicts should be a matter of both global and regional concern.

5   Military enforcement

Whatever their political and cultural differences, the disparate delegates who gathered at Dumbarton Oaks and San Francisco to plan the postwar world had three things in common. One, they were determined not to repeat the mistakes of the past, principally by insuring that the new world body would have real teeth. Two, they understood how critical the maintenance of the wartime alliance would be to the achievement of this shared vision. And three, like most planners, their hindsight was far superior to their foresight.

As Chapters 2 and 3 above chronicle, no portion of the Charter received as much concerted attention from the big powers as the enforcement provisions of Chapter VII. The military ones, in particular, were widely regarded as the centerpiece of the new international machinery and as the innovations that would most differentiate the muscular UN from the feeble League. Just a few years after San Francisco, however, it had become painfully clear that none of the military enforcement mechanisms were going to be realized in anything close to their initial conception. No member state had rushed to negotiate an Article 43 agreement to place any of its forces on stand-by for potential use by the Council. Once the Military Staff Committee (MSC) had deadlocked in 1948 over the question of what kinds of forces the Council would need, it was not assigned anything of real consequence to do.[1] And there were scant prospects of having international command arrangements worked out for the non-existent force.

Two strategic developments of historic proportions insured that the implementation of these enforcement provisions would be relegated indefinitely to a back burner. The most consequential, but for some canny observers not the most unexpected, development was the emergence of the Cold War in the late 1940s. While the wartime alliance among the Western powers had deep cultural, economic, and political roots, the marriage with the Soviet Union was at best one of convenience, forged largely by the dictum that my enemy's enemy is my friend. With the defeat of the Axis powers, the ideological and strategic differences that had repeatedly surfaced, and then been finessed, during the wartime conferences, including those on postwar institutions, came to the fore. The unity of the five permanent members was soon shattered, as the Soviet Union, regularly outnumbered in the Council and the Assembly, habitually resorted to its veto power to block Council action.[2] The enemy, it seemed, was within.[3]

The second, generally unforeseen, development was the atomic bomb. The UN Charter was negotiated and signed before the first detonation of the new weapon of mass destruction. Worries about sudden sneak attacks from across oceans – something that would only become feasible with the development of intercontinental delivery systems some years later – began to trouble publics and military planners alike. Under such conditions, there would be no time for Security Council deliberations, even if the veto power had not already sidelined the Council for Cold War contingencies. In such a scenario, at what point would it be determined that an "armed attack" under Article 51's parlance had occurred and who would be in a position to make that determination? Under such extreme circumstances, would pre-emption be justified when there appeared to be convincing evidence that the other side was preparing a first strike? Had technology made the Charter strictures on the use of force obsolete?

Given the magnitude of these unfavorable developments, it is remarkable not only that the UN managed to survive the Cold War, but that sixty years after San Francisco the debate over how to organize international military force remains lively, engaging, and relevant. The vision has long outlasted the machinery, and those states seeking to employ Chapter VII methods found creative ways to improvise and to reinterpret the Charter even during the darkest days of the Cold War. The North Korean invasion of South Korea in June 1950 was a case in point. The Council responded with its second, third, and fourth resolutions under Chapter VII. The first (83 of 27 June) labeled the attack a breach of the peace and recommended that member states "furnish such assistance to the Republic of Korea as may be necessary to repel the armed attack and to restore international peace and security in the area." The second, and critical one (84 of 7 July), welcomed the offers of assistance that had been forthcoming, called for a Unified Command under a commander designated by the United States, and authorized use of the UN flag in the enforcement action. The third (85 of 31 July) called on the Unified Command to help organize a humanitarian relief effort to assist beleaguered civilians.

Although no negative votes were cast, none of the three resolutions could have passed either if the Soviet delegation had not been boycotting Council sessions at that point or if Beijing, rather than Taipei, had occupied the Chinese seat (the latter being the reason for the Soviet protest). The very perversities of the Cold War, oddly enough, permitted the Council to initiate military enforcement measures for the first time. When the Soviets returned to the Council, of course, the latter ceased to be a productive venue for overseeing the UN-sponsored, but US-led, war effort on the Korean Peninsula. Seeking a way to bypass a Council that had been repeatedly frustrated by the threat or use of Soviet vetoes, the US engineered the passage of the legislatively creative but constitutionally dubious "uniting for peace" resolution in the General Assembly.[4] Though spurred by the Korean experience, the resolution was cast in a generic mode. The key operative paragraph

> Resolves that if the Security Council, because of lack of unanimity of the permanent members, fails to exercise its primary responsibility for the maintenance of international peace and security in any case where there appears to be a threat to the peace, breach of the peace, or act of aggression, the General Assembly shall consider the matter immediately with a view to making appropriate recommendations to Members for collective measures, including in the case of a breach of the peace or act of aggression the use of armed force when necessary, to maintain or restore international peace and security. If not in session at the time, the General Assembly may meet in emergency special session within twenty-four hours of the request therefore. Such emergency special session shall be called if requested by the Security Council on the vote of any seven members, or by a majority of the Members of the United Nations.

Though Article 11(2) of the Charter provides for the Assembly making recommendations on security matters, this prerogative is qualified by 12(1)'s clear admonition that the Assembly is not to do so "while the Security Council is exercising in respect to any dispute or situation the functions assigned to it in the present Charter." The British Foreign Office had cautioned Washington about pursuing this route, in part, for the practical reason that the innovation might be employed to circumvent British or American vetoes in the future.[5] The West, after all, might not be able to depend on automatic majorities in the Assembly forever.

The "uniting for peace" resolution also established a Peace Observation Commission for fact-finding purposes and a Collective Measures Committee to consider ways to strengthen the world body's peace and security capacities. Echoing Article 43, it further urged member states to earmark standby forces, though in this case for meeting calls from either the Assembly or the Council. In the end, however, it has been the provision for emergency special sessions of the Assembly that has been most frequently invoked, sometimes by the Council itself.[6] Even under "uniting for peace," of course, the Assembly cannot take enforcement action. So the power of the resolution, to this day, has been to provide the large majority of states that are not represented in the

Council with a way of expressing their views both for public consumption and for nudging the members of the Council to resolve their differences and to act more boldly and decisively in particular cases.

More than a decade would pass before the Council would again invoke Chapter VII. And then, as Chapter 4 noted, the Council backed in to giving the beleaguered ONUC operation in the Congo an enforcement mandate (Resolution 161 (1961)). It did so reluctantly – with Soviet and French abstentions – and only after ONUC's initial Chapter VI mandate had proven inadequate. The costs and controversies generated by that mission underscored what should have been obvious: declaring Chapter VII is one thing, implementing it quite another. Duly chastened, the Council would not take military measures under Chapter VII again until the end of the Cold War.

It took a case of blatant inter-state aggression of the sort envisioned by the organization's founders – Iraq's invasion and occupation of Kuwait – to trigger the fullest use of the Charter's enforcement provisions in history. Yet when Iraq had invaded another neighbor, Iran, a decade before, the Council had only responded with a relatively timid Chapter VI resolution that called for a cessation of hostilities, but not for Iraqi forces to return home.[7] What had changed?: most importantly, the victim. Less than a year before being assaulted by Iraq, the new revolutionary regime in Iran had condoned the occupation of the US embassy in Tehran and the subsequent holding of American hostages. Not only had the International Court of Justice – one of the UN's principal organs – ordered the release of the hostages, the Council had threatened Iran with unspecified Chapter VII measures if it failed to comply.[8] Iran and Iraq, moreover, had a lot in common: unattractive and undemocratic regimes, substantial human resources and military establishments, and a long and sometimes violent rivalry. Kuwait, on the other hand, was relatively small and vulnerable, like most other UN member states (though distinguished by its great oil wealth). When Baghdad declared Kuwaiti sovereignty to be artificial and promised to absorb it into a greater Iraq, even determinedly non-aligned states found the violation of international norms to be unambiguously unacceptable. There was another big change in the intervening years, of course: the Cold War had all but faded and the Council members had, for once, begun to work as a team. Helping the Secretary-General mediate the end of the bloody war between Iran and Iraq, in fact, had been the clearest manifestation of the new spirit in the aging body.

With strong encouragement from Washington, the Council moved through its enforcement toolkit with unaccustomed alacrity, at each stage warning Baghdad of tougher steps to come if it did not withdraw its forces from Kuwaiti territory. Growing deployments of US and allied military assets in the area gave an unusual degree of credibility to the Council's demands. On 2 August, the Council, acting under Chapter VII, demanded the immediate and unconditional withdrawal of Iraqi forces (Resolution 660 (1990)). Four days later, it imposed a comprehensive trade and arms embargo, exempting any food, medicine, and humanitarian goods (Resolution 661 (1990)). Two more Chapter VII resolutions on Iraqi treatment of Kuwaiti and third-state nationals followed.[9] On 29 November, these escalating steps culminated in the passage of Resolution 678, which authorized, under Chapter VII, those member states cooperating with Kuwait to employ "all necessary means" to uphold and implement 660 and the subsequent resolutions unless Baghdad had done so by 15 January 1991.[10]

Saddam Hussein, of course, decided to flout the Council's demands and US-led coalition forces proceeded to expel Iraqi forces from Kuwait with impressive dispatch in Operation Desert Storm. To many hopeful observers, this successful combination of American military capacity and Security Council legal authority represented a long-delayed realization of the founding vision of a world order that married power and legitimacy. In the United States, the apparent evidence of a more united and militarily assertive Security Council led to a resurgence of public support for the world body.[11] This was beginning to look like the sort of UN promised at San Francisco.

Seeking to build on this political momentum, the following January the Council met for the first time at a summit level and called on the new Secretary-General, Boutros Boutros-Ghali, to prepare what became his classic *An Agenda for Peace*. In it, he voiced two ill fated proposals concerning the use of force under Chapter VII. First, regarding Article 43, he asserted that "the long-standing obstacles to the conclusion of such special agreements should no longer prevail." As he noted, "the ready availability of armed forces on call could serve, in itself, as a means of deterring breaches of the peace since a potential aggressor would know that the Council had at its disposal a means of response."[12] Second, as a provisional measure under Article 40, he called for the creation of a new kind of force – better armed than traditional peace-keepers but smaller in number than Article 43 forces – to restore and maintain ceasefires.[13] These "peace enforcement units" were to be composed of volunteers from the forces of member states. While their use would need to be authorized by the Council, they would be commanded, as were peace-keepers, by the Secretary-General.

Neither suggestion was particularly well received by the member states. The conclusion of the Cold War apparently had not increased their appetite for negotiating Article 43 agreements with the Council. Rather, if the Council was entering a period of heightened unity and propensity to under-take enforcement measures, then the sovereignty questions concerning the control of one's forces were, if anything, about to become more acute. Desert Storm, moreover, demonstrated that there were other ways to get the job done. As in Korea forty years before, the Council again turned to a coalition of the willing. Again, its mandate was vague at best. But, with US units doing the bulk of the fighting, the strength and determination of the coalition forces on the ground more than compensated for the looseness of Council drafting or the lack of Article 43 procedures. The notion of peace enforcement units, on the other hand, engendered an unpromising combination of puzzlement and worry. As noted in Chapter 4 above, the range of tasks being undertaken by UN peacekeepers was already beginning to produce a doctrinal muddle. The member states were not looking for further refinements and amendments to existing doctrine or for new reasons for the world body to employ force in the name of peace. If peacekeepers were in constitutional limbo in Chapter VI1/2, would peace enforcement units occupy some unclaimed and uncharted terrain in Chapter VI3/4? Moreover, the thought of the Secretary-General commanding forces in combat led a chorus of skeptics, particularly vocal in the United States, to complain that what was needed was more of a secretary and less of a general.[14]

Three years later, when the Secretary-General produced his sober *Supplement to An Agenda for Peace* – much of which sounded more like a recantation – necessity had apparently become a virtue. While acknowledging that the Charter empowered the world body to take enforcement action, he lamented that "neither the Security Council nor the Secretary-General at present has the capacity to deploy, direct, command and control operations for this purpose, except perhaps on a very limited scale."[15] He continued to see acquiring such capacity as a desirable long-term goal, but argued that "it would be folly to attempt to do so at the present time when the Organization is resource-starved and hard pressed to handle the less demanding peacemaking and peace-keeping responsibilities entrusted to it." He saw advantages and disadvantages in the Council practice of handing over enforcement tasks to groups of member states. On the plus side, he noted the added capacity and a preference for this over unilateral action. On the down side, "the Organization's stature and credibility" would be tarnished and the states involved might claim Council authority for "forceful actions that were not in fact envisaged by the Security Council."[16]

By the time Kofi Annan succeeded Boutros-Ghali as Secretary-General two years later, in January 1997, reliance on self-appointed groups of states to carry out military enforcement had become standard practice. With some understatement, the new Secretary-General declared that "the vision of the Charter of a workable system of collective security has yet to be fully realized."[17] Like his predecessor, he underlined that

> The United Nations does not have, at this point in its history, the institutional capacity to conduct military enforcement measures under Chapter VII. Under present conditions, ad hoc coalitions of willing

Member States offer the most effective deterrent to aggression or to the escalation or spread of an ongoing conflict. As in the past, a mandate from the Security Council authorizing such a course of action is essential if the enforcement operation is to have broad international support and legitimacy.[18]

Though Secretary-General Annan neatly captured the current state of play, troubling questions remained to be resolved. How can the Security Council effectively oversee military operations it does not manage? If those states carrying out an enforcement action do not report back to the Council as fully and frequently as expected on how events are proceeding, what recourse does the Council have? In practice, as in Desert Storm, the tendency of the Council has been to say little and do less in such cases. In authorizing others to do its work, does the Council end up having an uncomfortable degree of responsibility without the authority to correct things that go wrong, as often is the case in large-scale military operations?

The political power of having the Security Council's blessing remains a matter of some debate. Surely it is advantageous, but is it, as the Secretary-General asserts, "essential" to obtaining broad international support and legitimacy? Are legality and legitimacy always on the same side? Hypothetically, if the Soviets had not been boycotting the Council in June 1950, would the defense of South Korea have been less legitimate? Forty years later, the US worked very hard to get Council authorization for the use of force to reverse the Iraqi invasion of Kuwait. However, President George H. W. Bush and his national security adviser, Brent Scowcroft, later wrote that they intended to seek Council backing only for as long as it appeared likely to be forthcoming. "If it became clear we would not succeed, we would back away from a UN mandate and cobble together an independent multinational effort built on friendly Arab and allied participation."[19] Was their vision of a new world order based on an assumption that US views will prevail consistently in the Council? Kofi Annan himself has warned against placing legality before legitimacy in cases of massive human suffering. Regarding Rwanda, he asked the General Assembly in 1999:

> if, in those dark days and hours leading up to the genocide, a coalition of States had been prepared to act in defense of the Tutsi population, but did not receive prompt Council authorization, should such a coalition have stood aside and allowed the horror to unfold?[20]

Three more recent cases of US-led armed intervention suggest that the relationship between legality and legitimacy remains both unsettled and circumstantial. In 1999, when the Council could not agree on the use of force to stop ethnic cleansing in Kosovo, the Western powers decided to bypass the Council and to seek NATO endorsement instead. Most member states accepted the action and few publicly regretted the lack of a Council mandate. Following the terrorist attacks on the United States of 11 September 2001, the Council looked the other way when the US and its partners within Afghanistan fought and overthrew the Taliban regime there. Though the Council passed a number of resolutions on Afghanistan while the fighting was underway, none even mentioned the US-led war.[21] In 2002–3, however, the highly visible and ultimately polarizing efforts of President George W. Bush to gain Council backing for the use of force to compel Saddam Hussein to comply with a dozen years of Council resolutions under Chapter VII met with stiff resistance. A number of member states that had not questioned the legality of the Kosovo and Afghanistan operations fretted that the invasion of Iraq without specific Council authorization would set a dangerous precedent. While the latter was widely condemned as being both illegal and illegitimate, the Kosovo and Afghanistan interventions were generally regarded as legitimate regardless of their ambiguous legal status.

Even if one accepts the Secretary-General's premise that Council authorization is a necessary condition for gaining broad support for military action, the question remains: is it a sufficient condition? The evidence suggests not. Despite Article 25 and other Charter provisions, member states by and large do not seem to feel compelled to participate in Council-authorized military enforcement operations. As of this writing, even those states most vocal about the need to give the UN a central role in rebuilding Iraq have been unwilling to provide forces to protect UN personnel working on the ground there, as called for by Resolution 1546 (2004). Similarly, any number of calls by the Council for troop contributions to Chapter VII missions in dangerous places like Somalia, Haiti, Congo, Liberia, and Sierra Leone met with tepid responses from the member states.

Clearly the notion of the collective use of force, foreseen by the UN's founders to be the glue that would hold the world body together, has, instead, become one of the most divisive and unsettled issues on its agenda. On the surface, most pointedly in the debate over the use of force in Iraq, the key controversies have revolved around the classic tug-of-war between unilateralism and multilateralism, between differing interpretations of the Charter and of international norms and legal requirements. As critical and unresolved as these matters may be, they have tended to mask a layer of practical problems that have complicated the task of resolving the constitutional and legal dilemmas. Indeed, operational considerations would threaten to make any paper resolution of such questions moot in practice. What works best on the level of diplomacy and law may not perform so well on the battlefield, and vice-versa.

While, as Chapter 2 above relates, the UN may not have been conceived initially as a universal or democratic organization, the assumption that it is (and/or should be) both has become commonplace. As Chapter 10 will discuss, much of the membership perceives the Council to be too small and too elitist, with an over-representation of rich and powerful states, and an under-representation of developing ones. This imbalance, it is said, has led the Council to pay too little attention to the recurring security problems of Africa and to devote far greater resources to peace-building in the Balkans – where NATO carries the military burden – than in the developing world. (While the latter is certainly true in terms of per capita investments in peace-building, the Council actually devotes far more time to Africa – around 60 percent of its deliberations – than to any other region.)²² This line of reasoning would seem to infer that UN forces, as well, should look more like the organization they represent, with contingents from a large number of countries from around the world. To some extent, as Chapter 4 pointed out, both in conception and in practice the composition of UN peacekeeping forces has sought to reflect this goal. Over the past decade, however, as developed countries have made smaller troop contributions to UN peacekeeping operations and more of the forces have come from within the region, this goal has proven increasingly elusive.²³

But, should geographical distribution be an objective when it comes to Council-authorized enforcement action? In practice, while UN peacekeepers more and more come from the developing world, enforcers largely come from a handful of wealthy and powerful developed countries, most particularly from the United States. There is a military logic to this, since the fewer the nationalities involved in combat, the easier to coordinate their actions and the smaller the risks to each other and to civilian populations. The fast pace and advanced technology involved in contemporary combat multiply the advantages of a few allies doing the bulk of the fighting, as was true in Desert Storm despite the large number of countries in the coalition to oust Iraqi forces from Kuwait.²⁴ To leave peacekeeping to developing countries and enforcement to the US and its allies, however, has proven to be a politically awkward division of labor, as the debate over the US-led intervention in Iraq underscored. On the one hand, most member states are acutely uncomfortable with the prospect of the Council providing political and legal cover for the assertion of US hegemony around the world. On the other hand, images either of the US bypassing the Council altogether or of the UN sitting on the sidelines when the most dangerous crises arise provide decidedly uncomfortable alternatives.

A big part of the problem can be attributed to the marked, and growing, asymmetries in military effort and capabilities among the member states. It is often said these days that the five permanent members anointed in San

Francisco no longer represent current power realities. This may be true in some respects, but, according to IISS figures, they remain five of the world's six largest defense spenders (with Japan topping the United Kingdom for fifth place).[25] Together, they account for about three fifths of world defense outlays. About two fifths of the global total, however, comes from the US alone. Indeed, it spends more on defense than the next ten countries combined. With the size and growth of its economy, it has managed this as its defense expenditures declined as a portion of its GDP from 6.1 percent in 1985 to 3.3 percent in 2002. More to the point, the US is the only member state capable of projecting large combat forces far from home for an extended period of time. Its capacities for airlift, sealift, logistics, air power, intelligence, communications, mobility, and precision guidance are unparalleled. The gap in military technology, particularly relating to conventional forces, is, if anything, getting broader and deeper.

Such asymmetries matter less for smaller-scale contingencies, of course, but even then UN forces may be dependent on US airlift and logistical support. More subtly, but profoundly, both the realities and perceptions of shifts in power relationships have affected the politics of Council deliberations and choices. As they become more dependent on the US as the ultimate enforcer, other member states will also become more wary of US dominance of the Council and, through it, of the UN. American policy-makers, on the other hand, may believe that they have military options in crisis situations that are not open to other member states. Going through the Council may be seen, as so often in the past, as an option rather than as an obligation.[26] Others may be increasingly likely to insist on the latter, as they did during the debate over Iraq, but with decreasing leverage as they become less relevant to the military equation. Maintaining the Council's credibility, relevance, and reputation on issues of military enforcement, in short, is going to be no simple task in the demanding days ahead.

6 Economic sanctions, arms embargoes, and diplomatic instruments

More theory than practice before 1990

Policy-makers, diplomats, and scholars have long sought a middle way – between words and war – to influence those who would disturb the peace. Prior to the First World War, it was widely believed that growing economic interdependence would make it financially and commercially suicidal for any of the major Western powers to resort to war. The threat of economic sanctions, therefore, was seen as a uniquely persuasive tool to back up non-coercive techniques of arbitration and judicial settlement to resolve international disputes. As William Howard Taft, former US President and an ardent supporter of the League of Nations, put it, an economic boycott could serve as "a powerful deterrent weapon and probably make resort to force unnecessary."[1]

The League Covenant, reflecting this perspective, placed greater emphasis on economic than military tools of coercion. Under Article 16(1), "the severance of all trade and financial relations" with a member that had violated its Covenant obligations and resorted to war was mandatory. The Council, on the other hand, was only to recommend possible military steps for the members to take (16(2)). The failure of key League members to sanction Japan over its invasion of Manchuria in 1931 or to cut off oil shipments to Italy after its assault on Abyssinia (Ethiopia) in 1935, however, severely undermined this faith in economic leverage as a reliable deterrent to aggression.[2]

Economic statecraft, like the League itself, fell into disrepute with the outbreak of the Second World War. Both in planning and in negotiating the postwar security system, non-military measures took a decided back seat to the consideration of more forceful means of enforcement. The Charter, reversing the priorities in the Covenant, makes no reference in Article 41 to how steps not involving armed force might be assembled and coordinated, in contrast to its detailed provisions on organizing a military response. In terms of possible measures, it refers to "complete or partial interruption of economic relations and of rail, sea, air, postal, telegraphic, radio, and other means of communication, and the severance of diplomatic relations." Recognizing that third parties – whether trading partners or neighbors of the target of sanctions – could be "confronted with special economic problems arising from the carrying out of these measures," Article 50 gives such states, whether members of the UN or not, "the right to consult the Security Council with regard to a solution of those problems." The Council, of course, is not obligated to remedy such hardships and rarely has asked the member states to do so.[3]

True to form, when the Council – with the Soviet delegation boycotting the session over who should represent China in the Council – voted in 1950 for an international force to resist the North Korean invasion of South Korea, it failed to impose any form of economic sanctions on the North. It took the Council two decades and more than 200 resolutions before it first invoked economic sanctions. Initially, moreover, these were not taken under Chapter VII, with its binding character. Rather, Resolution 217 (1965) called on all states "to do their utmost in order to break all economic relations with Southern Rhodesia [now Zimbabwe], including an embargo on oil and petroleum products." Taken in response to the claim of independence by the white racist regime of Ian Smith, the Council's call for economic measures followed its earlier appeal to all states not to recognize or assist that regime (Resolution 216 (1965)). Concerned by the spotty implementation of the sanctions, the Council passed a series of resolutions seeking to strengthen them (221 (1966), 232 (1966), and 253 (1968)). Resolution 232 invoked Articles 39 and 41 of the Charter and reminded member states of their obligations under Article 25. Resolution 253 – the first in the series to be adopted unanimously – made specific reference to Chapter VII and established the Council's first committee to be tasked with monitoring the implementation of a sanctions regime.[4]

This turned out to be the only case in which the Security Council managed to adopt economic sanctions during its first forty-five years, or until the end of the Cold War.[5] In 1960, the Council recognized that the violence in apartheid South Africa could endanger international peace and security (Resolution 134). Wary of likely British and French vetoes, however, the Council never attempted to apply economic sanctions against the apartheid regime, despite passing dozens of resolutions condemning its actions and policies. The General Assembly, on the other hand, did so under Resolution 1761 (XVII) of 1962, though it was a request without binding authority.

The Council, even during the Cold War years, took much more readily to arms than trade embargoes.[6] The political appeal of imposing arms rather than economic sanctions is clear enough, given the former's focus on the means of violence and the lack of negative humanitarian impacts. Being appealing and effective, of course, may be two different matters. There is substantial evidence that curbs on small arms flows, in particular, are very difficult to monitor and enforce. Nevertheless, the first Council-imposed arms embargo, of a voluntary nature, came in 1948 (Resolution 50) and was related to the conflict in and around Palestine. A second call for a voluntary arms embargo, this time related to the growing conflict in the Congo, was passed in 1961 (Resolution 169). Two years later, the Council requested all states to refrain from supplying the Portuguese government any arms or military equipment that might be used to suppress the peoples in its territories (Resolution 180 (1963)). Just eight days later, the Council called on all states to cease the "sale and shipment of arms, ammunition of all types and military vehicles to South Africa" (Resolution 181). In Resolution 217 (1965), noted above, the Council called on states to "desist from providing" the breakaway white regime in Southern Rhodesia "with arms, equipment and military material." Like the economic sanctions, the military ones on the Ian Smith regime were initially of a voluntary character. Resolutions 237 (1966) and 253 (1968), also noted above, confirmed that the arms, as well as economic, measures would henceforth be mandatory.

The arms ban on South Africa followed a similar evolution. In 1970 and 1972, in resolutions 282 and 311 respectively, the Council lamented violations of the arms embargo it had declared in 1963, but it was not until 1977 (Resolution 418) that it imposed its first mandatory arms cut-off on South Africa. A month later, the Council, in Resolution 421, established the South Africa Sanctions Committee – the Council's first such arms monitoring mechanism – to assess the implementation of the arms embargo and to consider ways of strengthening it. As has since become the standard pattern for Council subsidiary bodies, the Committee included all fifteen members of the Council. As had been the case for Southern Rhodesia, these two 1977 resolutions on South Africa – the toughest and farthest reaching to date – proved to be the first of the series to be adopted unanimously by the Council.[7]

In addition to the blunter instruments of economic sanctions or arms embargoes, the Council began to experiment as well with diplomatic and political measures during the Cold War years. It urged the member states not to recognize the racist regime in Southern Rhodesia (217 (1965)), South Africa's illegal occupation of Namibia (283 (1970)), or Pretoria's new constitution (554 (1984)). It never employed, however, its power under Article 6 of the Charter to recommend to the General Assembly the expulsion of any member state for having "persistently violated the Principles contained in the present Charter." Nor did it recommend suspension, under Article 5, of any members "against which prevention or enforcement action has been taken."[8] Cold War politics frequently impinged during those years on the Council's choices about which states to recommend for admittance to the Organization, increasingly seen as the clearest sign of acceptance by the world community.

For former enemy states, as defined by the Charter, such a step could be held out as an inducement for internal as well as external reform.

Practice, practice, and reform since 1990

In the realm of sanctions, as with the tools of peace operations and military enforcement addressed in the preceding chapters, the 1990s became an era of high activity and bold experimentation, followed by considerable disillusionment and retrenchment. The decade began with the Council mandating comprehensive sanctions on Iraq for its invasion and occupation of Kuwait (661 (1990)).[9] Sixteen related resolutions later, the Council was still debating at decade's end how to package and implement an effective and humane sanctions regime to quell Saddam Hussein's ambitions. In the interim, the Council managed to mount far more sanctions, of wider variety, against more targets, for a broader spectrum of reasons than ever before.[10]

- Among the targets were armed groups in Angola (UNITA), Cambodia (Khmer Rouge), Sierra Leone (RUF), and Somalia, and governments or quasi-governments in Afghanistan, Haiti, Liberia, Libya, Rwanda, Sudan, and the former Yugoslavia.
- Arms embargoes were the most popular tool, having been applied to Iraq in Resolution 661 (1990), to the former Yugoslavia in Resolution 713 (1991) (terminated in Resolution 1074 (1996)), to Somalia in Resolution 733 (1992), to Libya in Resolution 748 (1992) (suspended in Resolution 1192 (1999)), to Liberia in Resolution 788 (1992), to Haiti in Resolution 841 (1993) (terminated in Resolution 944 (1994)), to Angola (UNITA) in Resolution 864 (1993), to Rwanda in Resolution 918 (1994), to Sierra Leone in Resolution 1132 (1997) (terminated in 1171 (1998)), and again to the former Yugoslavia in Resolution 1160 (1998). In 2000, arms bans were also imposed on Eritrea and Ethiopia (Resolution 1298) and on Afghanistan (Resolution 1333).
- Bans on air links or the travel of elites were imposed on Iraq, the former Yugoslavia, Libya, Haiti, Angola, Sudan, Sierra Leone, and Afghanistan (Taliban).
- The financial assets of governments or particular individuals were targeted in Iraq, the former Yugoslavia (twice), Libya, Haiti, Angola, and Afghanistan.[11]
- Trade was banned in specific commodities, such as oil in Cambodia, Haiti, Angola, and Sierra Leone, so-called "conflict diamonds" in Angola, Sierra Leone, and Liberia, and timber in Cambodia.[12]
- Sudan faced a scaling back of its diplomatic presence abroad.

- Naked aggression triggered sanctions against Iraq, transnational or internal conflict in the cases of the former Yugoslavia, Somalia, Liberia, Angola, and Rwanda, overthrowing governments in Haiti and Sierra Leone, and assisting terrorism in Libya, Sudan, and Afghanistan. In the case of Eritrea and Ethiopia, they were applied to both sides of a costly inter-state conflict.
- With its readiness to impose potentially damaging sanctions well established, by mid-decade the Council found that just threatening the use of sanctions had some value as a deterrent, as in resolutions 1040 (1996) and 1072 (1996) on Burundi.

As the decade progressed, the kind of comprehensive sanctions imposed on Iraq, the former Yugoslavia, and Haiti began to fade in the face of associated humanitarian calamities in favor of more carefully targeted sanctions aimed at governing elites or specific armed groups.

The retreat from comprehensive sanctions testified less to doubts about their effectiveness – some studies had contended that blunter sanctions actually tended to pack more clout[13] – and more to humanitarian, political, and sustainability concerns. If comprehensive sanctions are applied quickly and implemented rigorously, the targeted economy has less opportunity to adjust through indigenous production, substitution, or circumventing international controls. In their review of UN sanctions imposed in the 1990s, David Cortright and George A. Lopez found that two of the three sanctions regimes they rated as most effective in bringing pressure to bear on the target regime – those on Iraq and the former Yugoslavia – were comprehensive in scope. The third relatively effective case, against Libya, used more selective and targeted measures over an extended period of seven years, backed by pressure from several major powers. In Haiti, on the other hand, comprehensive sanctions accomplished relatively little other than to further impoverish the beleaguered society.[14]

The growing concern about the collateral costs of sanctions could be seen in successive commentaries by secretaries-general Boutros Boutros-Ghali and Kofi Annan. In his 1992 *An Agenda for Peace*, Boutros-Ghali had little to say about sanctions, other than urging the Security Council to "devise a set of measures involving the financial institutions and other components of the United Nations system that can be put in place to insulate States" from the kind of special economic problems contemplated under Article 50 of the Charter.[15] His *Supplement to An Agenda for Peace* three years later, however, fretted that "the Security Council's greatly increased use of this instrument has brought to light a number of difficulties, relating especially to the objectives of sanctions, the monitoring of their application and impact, and their unintended effects."[16] Warning that sanctions "are a blunt instrument," he cautioned that:

They raise the ethical question of whether suffering inflicted on vulnerable groups in the target country is a legitimate means of exerting pressure on political leaders whose behaviour is unlikely to be affected by the plight of their subjects. Sanctions also always have unintended or unwanted effects. They can complicate the work of humanitarian agencies by denying them certain categories of supplies and by obliging them to go through arduous procedures to obtain the necessary exemptions. They can conflict with the development objectives of the Organization and do long-term damage to the productive capacity of the target country. They can have a severe effect on other countries that are neighbours or major economic partners of the target country. They can also defeat their own purpose by provoking a patriotic response against the international community, symbolized by the United Nations, and by rallying the population behind the leaders whose behaviour the sanctions are intended to modify.[17]

His successor, Kofi Annan, noted in 1997 both the increasing frequency with which the Council had been invoking economic sanctions under Chapter VII and that "the universal character of the United Nations makes it a particularly appropriate body to consider and oversee such measures."[18] Echoing the concerns of many member states, he urged greater attention to effectiveness "in modifying the behaviours of those targeted, while limiting collateral damages" and to developing "objective criteria in their application and for their termination."

Responding to the growing clamor about the unintended consequences of economic enforcement measures, the five permanent members of the Security Council presented the President of the Council with a joint non-paper on the humanitarian impact of sanctions in April 1995.[19] It invited the Department of Humanitarian Affairs to coordinate the supply of information to the Council on the humanitarian situation in these cases, called for the development of expedited procedures for exempting humanitarian supplies – such as foodstuffs and medicine – destined for civilian populations, suggested that its various sanctions committees learn from each other's experience, and urged targeted regimes to allow their people unimpeded access to humanitarian aid. This statement, in essence, opened the doors politically to a wide-ranging effort to rationalize and reform the way the Council and the rest of the world body would go about designing, implementing, and overseeing the employment of sanctions for enforcement purposes.[20]

Without significant reforms, they recognized, there would not be sufficient public and member state support to sustain sanctions in cases, like Iraq, in which a targeted government chose to manipulate international opinion by withholding or diverting humanitarian assistance from its beleaguered citizens.

And it was just such repressive governments, not accountable, transparent and democratic ones, that were the most likely candidates to be sanctioned. The imposition of sanctions, moreover, may present corrupt leaders with golden opportunities to profit from the likely growth of black markets and artificial pricing mechanisms, while finding convenient external scapegoats to blame for humanitarian setbacks and for their domestic failings.[21] As discussed below, in attempting to address the latter problem with the sanctions on Iraq, the Security Council's ill conceived oil-for-food program opened enormous new avenues for corruption not only by Saddam Hussein's regime, but also by neighbors, trading partners, private firms, and, to a lesser extent, the UN secretariat itself.

As a decade of unprecedented activism was coming to a close, it seemed as if the Council was at risk of witnessing its second major enforcement tool lose much of its political viability – not unlike the growing disillusionment with military instruments of collective coercion. To many in the UN community, the answer appeared to lie in a broad-based reform of the way the Council went about its sanctions business. The UN Department of Humanitarian Affairs, now the UN Office for Coordination of Humanitarian Affairs (OCHA), was tasked with producing a series of humanitarian assessment reports for specific sanctions regimes. The Council began to hear more frequently from individuals and agencies with direct experience in and knowledge of the conditions in sanctioned countries. While the Council had already adopted the practice of convening a dedicated subsidiary body to oversee each new sanctions regime, the effectiveness of these sanctions committees varied markedly, with few of them receiving high marks. As a result, in January 1999 the President of the Council announced a long list of rules and standards to guide the work of the sanctions committees.[22] In light of concerns about the spotty oversight of the implementation of arms embargoes, expert monitoring groups were established to report on how follow-up was faring in several of the more troubling cases.[23]

The most fundamental and far-reaching renovation, however, related less to process than to substance, i.e. to what and whom would be sanctioned. If the restraints imposed by the Council could be carefully targeted on those decision-makers most responsible for the behaviors or policies of concern to the Council, then the collateral damage to civilians, neighbors and trading partners could presumably be limited. This, in turn, would make the sanctions both more effective and more sustainable politically. Over a five-year period, from 1998 to 2003, three rounds of policy research and expert/practitioner consultations, sponsored by interested member states, were held to explore ways of sharpening the UN's sanctions tools. The first, the Interlaken process sponsored by Switzerland, focused on financial measures.[24] Next, the Bonn-Berlin process addressed arms embargoes, travel and aviation-related steps.[25]

Finally, the Stockholm process considered the generic problem of developing effective means of implementing targeted sanctions.[26]

While these studies and dialogues undoubtedly spurred some degree of convergence of thinking on the conceptual and analytical planes, the political terrain for pursuing a more effective sanctions strategy remains uncertain and unpredictable.[27] The Council's performance in designing and overseeing sanctions regimes has varied markedly from case to case, as the contrasting experiences with Angola and Iraq illustrate. On Angola, the Security Council took a step forward by finding creative ways to bolster a sagging sanctions regime. On Iraq, on the other hand, its internal divisions and unwillingness to exercise proper oversight of its poorly structured oil-for-food program opened the door to the largest scandal in UN history.[28]

In Angola, the Council demonstrated a welcome capacity to learn from its mistakes. Beginning in 1993, the Council invoked a series of escalating sanctions, involving arms, petroleum, travel, and diamond sales and exports, on UNITA, the guerilla force in Angola that had been disrupting the UN-brokered peace process. This was the first time that the Council had chosen to sanction an armed group, as opposed to a government. Sanctions, however, are hardly self-enforcing. Compliance with these measures was poor for their first six years, given the oil and diamond wealth of Angola and the considerable stakes involved in the civil war. When Canada assumed the chair of the Angolan sanctions committee in January 1999, it was determined to reverse this decline through extensive visits to member state capitals, building a broad-based coalition with regional groups, Interpol, diamond trade associations, and activist NGOs, launching expert panels and reports, establishing a monitoring mechanism, and threatening enforcement action against states that had violated the sanctions.[29] The new-found determination to enforce the sanctions, maintained when Ireland succeeded Canada as chair, undoubtedly managed to increase the pressure on UNITA and the long and costly conflict was brought to a close once UNITA's long-time leader, Jonas Savimbi, was killed in 2002 during the fighting.

When sanctions were first imposed by the Council on Iraq in August 1990 to try to compel its forces to abandon Kuwait, they were not notably controversial. The vote on Resolution 661 was 13–0–2, with only Cuba and Yemen abstaining. Some members probably saw this as a step away from war, and others as a means of building a broader coalition in support of the eventual collective use of force. Likewise, there was broad support in the Council eight months later for Resolution 687, laying out the conditions for a ceasefire, an end to hostilities, and the lifting of the comprehensive sanctions. Cuba this time voted against the "mother of all resolutions," while Ecuador and Yemen abstained. Operational paragraph 22 stipulated that the measures imposed in 661 "shall have no further force or effect" once the Council had approved of a compensation fund and agreed that Iraq had taken a long list of steps (operational paragraphs 8–13) to eliminate its weapons of mass destruction and their delivery systems. This plan sounded sensible enough, but it did not take into account the depth of Saddam Hussein's determination to flout the Council's edicts and undermine both its 661 sanctions and the disarmament regime established under 687.

For the next dozen years, until deposed by the US-led coalition's intervention in March 2003, Saddam proved his mastery of tactics to divide the permanent members of the Council and to exploit the misery of the Iraqi people in order to gain broad international sympathy for lifting the sanctions.[30] While the permanent members were united in their determination to reverse the Iraqi invasion and occupation of Kuwait, their sense of common purpose began to fray when, in subsequent years, it came to matters of how far to push a supposedly still sovereign Iraq on the implementation of the 661 sanctions and 687 arms inspection and destruction regimes. Again and again, the US and United Kingdom pushed to tighten these controls, while China, France, and Russia sought to ease them.[31] Though 661 contained humanitarian exemptions, officials in Baghdad found that allowing their citizens to suffer in front of the global media was an excellent way to weaken international support for the sanctions regimes and, subsequently, for the UN weapons inspectors.[32] As a major oil producer, moreover, Iraq had some economic leverage for dividing the Council and for influencing some of its members to the extent it was allowed to resume its oil exports.

As a way out of this quandary, the Council developed the oil-for-food (OFF) program, under which Baghdad would be permitted to export specified quantities of oil under international supervision as long as the proceeds were largely used for civilian and humanitarian purposes in Iraq.[33] First authorized in Resolution 706 (1991) but rejected by Iraq, the program was significantly expanded four years later, in Resolution 986 of 14 April 1995, with a portion of the revenues now to go, as well, to cover the costs of the UN's Special Commission (UNSCOM) working to disarm Iraq. Again, Saddam demonstrated how a determined, wily, and authoritarian regime can work to undermine sanctions imposed by the Council. As designed by the Council, or more accurately as an unfortunate compromise among its divided members, the oil-for-food program allowed Baghdad to choose to whom to sell oil and from whom to purchase humanitarian goods. As noted earlier and exhaustively documented by the Independent Inquiry Committee, headed by Paul Volcker and commissioned by the Secretary-General and the Council, this provision, plus lax management by the UN secretariat and absent oversight by the Council, permitted the corruption for which Saddam's regime had long been infamous to seep through a dismaying range of international channels and actors.[34] What lessons the membership will draw concerning the viability of sanctions as a tool for maintaining international peace and security remains to be seen, though the force of future events may well dictate that the answer lies in sharpening this instrument and how and when it is employed, rather than abandoning it altogether.

These two cases illustrate that for sanctions, as for military enforcement or peace operations, the critical factor is the willingness and capacity of member states to implement the Council's decisions. In each case, to understand the results, analysts and students alike should first probe the depth of commitment among key actors to translating the Council's words into action. Political will is not an independent variable, as it will be affected by perceptions of the stakes involved, the likelihood of success, and the motivations of others. It should not be assumed, in that regard, that a vote for a sanctions resolution necessarily indicates either an unalloyed commitment to its implementation or a conviction that sanctions alone will compel parties to a conflict to do as the Council demands. In some cases, when words alone have proven insufficient and military enforcement is deemed infeasible and/or undesirable, sanctions – even if they too may prove inadequate – may nevertheless appear to be the only option on the table. Because sanctions come in so many graduated shapes and sizes, they can be an enormously flexible and individually tailored tool for signaling intent. They can, in most cases, be escalated or deescalated, or even coupled with incentives, as conditions change.

Members of the Council, moreover, may employ sanctions either to build support for stronger measures when the former "fails" (as in Iraq after its invasion of Kuwait) or to convince domestic constituencies that something is being done when the will is lacking to take more potent steps (as in the feckless arms embargo on Rwanda). Because this is such a nuanced instrument of international and domestic politics, it has proven difficult to gauge with any certainty whether sanctions have proven, on balance, to be a successful tool in the Council's arsenal, and conclusions vary widely.[35] One thing is evident, however: in most cases the chances of being persuasive with sanctions are much higher with multilateral than unilateral ones, since the broader the international cooperation the less likely that they will be circumvented or undermined by others. So, despite the many episodes of faulty implementation and painful humanitarian consequences noted above, sanctions appear to be here to stay.

7 Enlisting and empowering partners

The architects of the United Nations had the considerable advantage of being able to learn from the miscues of their predecessors, the founders of the League of Nations. Nowhere is this as evident as in the edifice and machinery of the Security Council. In part, as related in previous chapters, this learning process can be seen in the unique enforcement powers and tools provided in the Charter, along with the limited circle of permanent members possessing veto power over Council actions. They also understood, somewhat paradoxically, that a Security Council with unprecedented powers should be embedded – much more than the League's Council had been – in a web of cooperative relationships with other UN principal organs and with regional organizations and arrangements. Over time, as the Council's attention turned increasingly to intra-state and transnational conflict, it became clear that it would need to learn to deal with non-state actors as well.

Other UN principal organs

The Covenant failed to make a clear differentiation of the respective roles of the League's Council and Assembly. Each was to deal "with any matter within the sphere of action of the League or affecting the peace of the world" (Articles 4(4) and 3(3) respectively).[1] Under the Charter, in contrast, the Council is given "primary responsibility for the maintenance of peace and security" (Article 24(1)). According to Article 12(1),

> while the Security Council is exercising in respect of any dispute or situation the functions assigned to it in the present Charter, the General Assembly shall not make any recommendation with regard to that dispute or situation unless the Security Council so requests.

While the Assembly, under Article 11(2), may "discuss" any security matters and can make "recommendations" on those not covered by Article 12, in practice the Council maintains such a long list of issues with which it remains seized as to leave little room for Assembly action. The Assembly, like the Secretary-General (Article 19), "may call the attention of the Security Council to situations which are likely to endanger international peace and security" (Article 11(3)).[2] It is rare, however, either for the Assembly or the Secretary-General to make use of this provision.[3]

While its small size, core of permanent members, and authority to take binding decisions have made the Security Council the most active, dynamic, and influential of the principal organs, its relationship with the General Assembly is far from being just a one-way street.[4] As the convening powers were quick to point out during the debates at San Francisco about the inequities of the veto, the five permanent members could not pass any Council resolution without the support of at least two (now four) of the non-permanent members elected directly by the Assembly.[5] In a nod to the general membership, the convening powers agreed that the Assembly should select the majority of the Council's members, its original six and now ten non-permanent members. While these elected members individually do not possess veto power, any seven of the ten can block Council action by denying the attainment of the super-majority of nine votes needed to pass a resolution on either a procedural or non-procedural matter (Articles 27(2) and (3) respectively). While the permanent members can veto the admission of a new member to the UN – or the appointment of the Secretary-General, for that matter – the election of non-permanent members to the Council itself is veto-proof.

For all of its powers, moreover, the Council has no authority over budgetary matters, which are to be considered and approved by the Assembly (Article 17(1)). So, for example, while only the Council has the authority to mandate the creation of a new peacekeeping mission, only the Assembly can either appropriate the funds or assess member states for the costs of mounting and running it.[6] Generally the two bodies have worked together on such matters fairly smoothly,[7] but, with the costs of peacekeeping currently running at more than double the UN's regular budget, the risk of a constitutional crisis over such matters remains. Indeed, two of the UN's deepest financial crises, in the early 1960s and the late 1990s, stemmed from the refusal of key member states to pay their assessments for peacekeeping operations.[8]

Despite the best efforts of the Charter's architects to draw a clear division of labor between the Council and the Assembly, the divisive politics of the Cold War conspired to blur some of these distinctions. As noted earlier, the Soviet boycott of the Council (over the continued seating of the Taipei government as the representative of China) permitted the initial Council authorization of the use of force to resist the invasion of South Korea. When the chastened Soviet delegates returned, however, further action was blocked by Moscow's veto. Washington, against London's advice,[9] pushed for a new and creative constitutional wrinkle: a "uniting for peace" resolution in the Assembly giving that body authority to recommend "collective measures" and to convene an "emergency special session" when the Council, "because of lack of unanimity of the permanent members, fails to exercise its primary responsibility for the maintenance of international peace and security."[10] (For a fuller description of the "uniting for peace" option, see Chapter 5 above.) Though somewhat out of favor these days, when the use of the veto is not so prevalent or disruptive, by the end of the Cold War nine such emergency special sessions of the Assembly had been called under this rubric.[11] None of these called for collective coercive military measures, and decisions of the Assembly remain non-binding in any case. Yet they addressed a number of major crises, such as the Suez crisis of 1956, the Soviet intervention in Hungary that same year, the dispatch of peacekeepers to the Congo in 1960, and the Soviet invasion of Afghanistan in 1979–80. Though the constitutionality of the uniting for peace procedure is somewhat dubious, it has been used – at least over the last four decades – primarily to make a political point rather than to authorize the kinds of specific actions that the Charter clearly intended be left to the Council. For example, this option was reportedly considered and rejected in the cases of massive human rights violations in Kosovo in 1999 and in Darfur, Sudan in 2005, when Council action was blocked by one or more permanent members.

The Assembly and Council have equal status under the Charter as principal organs. To encourage some degree of accountability to the larger membership, the Council is required under Article 24(3) to "submit annual and, when necessary, special reports to the General Assembly for its consideration." As discussed more extensively in Chapter 10 on reform issues, a number of delegations have complained that the Council's annual report to the Assembly has not been sufficiently detailed and analytical. Given the substantial growth in Council activities over the past fifteen years, however, the last annual report reached 235 pages, even without much substantive content. As detailed in Chapter 3 above, much of the Council's work is now carried out through a growing array of about two dozen subsidiary bodies, whose transparency and openness to the larger UN membership varies.

A range of modifications in Council working methods, again detailed in Chapter 10 below, have been adopted over the past decade to reach out more regularly and fully to the membership as a whole, given that less than 8 percent of the members can serve on the Council at any given point. Though the members agree, under Article 25, "to accept and carry out the decisions of the Security Council in accordance with the present Charter," the degree to which they readily provide troops, civil police, and civilian experts to peacekeeping missions or fully implement sanctions or counter-terrorism mandates from the Council will depend, in part, on their perceptions of the legitimacy of the relevant Council decisions and their understanding of their purposes. In this sense, the Council needs to be accountable if not to the General Assembly in a formal, hierarchical way, then to the larger membership that expresses its voice through the Assembly.

The Security Council's relationship to the Economic and Social Council (ECOSOC) is more distant. The four chapters of the Charter focused on security and the work of the Security Council – V, VI, VII and VIII – make no reference to ECOSOC, while chapters V and VI, at least, cite the General Assembly five times.[12] Like the General Assembly, ECOSOC's decisions are not binding. Twice enlarged, from 18 to 27 to 54 members, ECOSOC is too large for ready action and too small to represent the membership as a whole. According to Article 65, ECOSOC "may furnish information to the Security Council and should assist the Security Council upon its request." The latter, however, has found relatively few occasions to make such a request.[13]

During the Cold War years, when the Security Council rarely ventured far from traditional guidelines for peacekeeping (see Chapter 4 above), the relatively sharp distinction between the work of the two councils was understandable. ECOSOC, for its part, tended to address global development issues, particularly the generic ones dividing North and South that it could do little about, rather than the economic and social problems within countries or regions facing acute security challenges. As UN peace operations turned more and more to the daunting task of nation-building over the course of the 1990s, however, the rationale for integrating economic, social, and security policy became increasingly compelling. Persistent doubts about whether ECOSOC is structured or oriented to provide such expertise and insights nevertheless remain a major stumbling block to closer ties between the councils.

During the 2005 reform process, Secretary-General Kofi Annan and his High-level Panel on Threats, Challenges and Change highlighted several ways in which closer cooperation between the Security Council and ECOSOC might help the world body to address a changing security environment. The Secretary-General, based on a historically dubious understanding of the founders' intent, argued for a restoration of the balance among those two councils and a new one devoted to human rights.[14] ECOSOC, he suggested, should "reinforce its links with the Security Council in order to promote structural prevention."[15] The High-level Panel called on ECOSOC to "establish a Committee on the Social and Economic Aspects of Security Threats," to commission research on the economic and social aspects of a range of threats, including terrorism and organized crime, and to regularize the exchange of information and meetings between the presidents of the two councils.[16] One of the few major institutional innovations proposed by the Secretary-General and his High-level Panel that generated sufficient interest among the member states to be adopted was for the establishment of the new Peacebuilding

Commission. As described in more detail in Chapter 4 above, the Commission will address the wide range of issues facing a country emerging from conflict and intent, with the help of international partners, on rebuilding its society and economy.[17] Since these matters tend to fall between the respective competences of ECOSOC and the Security Council, the Commission's membership will draw from both bodies, as well as from leading financial and troop contributors.[18] Representatives of the Bretton Woods institutions, UN agencies, and other stakeholders will be involved in the country-specific discussions of this new advisory body. Though neither the Secretary-General nor his High-level Panel flagged this issue, another area in which the work of the Security Council might benefit from more economic and social analysis is sanctions, as the account in Chapter 6 above would indicate.

Another principal organ with which the Security Council has had a distant relationship is the International Court of Justice (ICJ). In this case, however, the Charter and the ICJ Statute lay out a number of procedural and substantive linkages. The most important procedural tie is that the Security Council and the General Assembly, proceeding "independently of one another" (Article 8 of the Statute), elect the members of the Court (Article 4 of the Statute), who are to be "independent judges" (Article 2 of the Statute).[19] Substantively, the Charter includes two potentially important ways that the Council could make use of the Court: by referring disputes to the ICJ or by seeking its advisory opinion. Under Chapter VI, the Council is given wide authority for seeking means to achieve a pacific settlement of disputes, though Article 36(3) stipulates that "legal disputes should as a general rule be referred by the parties to the International Court of Justice in accordance with the provisions of the Statute of the Court." According to Article 96(1), either the Assembly or the Council "may request the International Court of Justice to give an advisory opinion on any legal question." The Council, however, has made little use of either option, only once seeking an advisory opinion (on Namibia in 1970–1) and twice referring a legal dispute to the court.[20] Given the highly political nature of the Council's work and the reluctance of its members, especially the permanent ones, to submit to judicial review, there is no reason to expect this relationship to blossom anytime soon.

Regional and sub-regional arrangements

The architects of the Charter gave regional solutions to security challenges far greater prominence than had their predecessors with the League. In a bow to the Monroe Doctrine – and to the US Senate – Article 21 of the Covenant pledges that nothing in the document would invalidate existing "treaties of arbitration or regional understandings" aimed at securing the peace. Nothing is said about the relationship of the Council to regional actors. The Charter, on the other hand, devotes a whole chapter (VIII) to regional arrangements. Indeed, a clear preference is voiced for going the regional route first. As Article 52(2) advises, member states "shall make every effort to achieve pacific settlement of local disputes through such regional arrangements or by such regional agencies before referring them to the Security Council." The Security Council, as well, according to Article 52(3), "shall encourage the development of pacific settlement of local disputes through such regional arrangements or by such regional agencies." Even in the case of enforcement, "the Security Council should, where appropriate, utilize such regional arrangements or agencies for enforcement action under its authority" (Article 53(1)). An important caveat follows, however: "no enforcement action shall be taken under regional arrangements or by regional agencies without the authorization of the Security Council, with the exception of measures against any enemy state."

The Charter, therefore, envisions more than a global-regional division of labor. It expresses a clear preference for an ongoing, symbiotic, working relationship based on a legal hierarchy when it comes to enforcement and on a subsidiarity principle for peaceful settlement. As the Council's agenda and ambitions have grown in recent years, the logic of such a working relationship seems increasingly attractive, even compelling. In practice, of course, these global-regional partnerships have not been so easy to initiate or sustain, particularly in areas where efforts to develop regional political and security institutions are underdeveloped. As a result, the track record has been uneven in some regions – Africa, Europe, Central America, and the Caribbean – and virtually non-existent in some others, such as the Middle East, South Asia, and Northeast Asia. Often, intra-regional cooperation is least developed where most needed. Even where regional organization is relatively well developed, putting the Charter principles for global-regional cooperation into practice has proven to be a challenging enterprise, with lessons varying markedly from place to place and case to case.[21]

As on so many matters, expectations for enhanced Security Council-regional cooperation on peace operations soared with the end of the Cold War. In his seminal *An Agenda for Peace* report in 1992, UN Secretary-General Boutros Boutros-Ghali commented that

> the cold war impaired the proper use of Chapter VIII . . . but in this new era of opportunity, regional arrangements or agencies can render great service if their activities are undertaken in a manner consistent with the Purposes and Principles of the Charter, and if their relationship with the United Nations, and particularly the Security Council, is governed by Chapter VIII.

While noting that the Council would continue to have primary responsibility, he asserted that "regional actions as a matter of decentralization, delegation and cooperation with United Nations efforts could not only lighten the burden of the Council but also contribute to a deeper sense of participation, consensus and democratization in international affairs."[22] Thirty months later, his *Supplement to An Agenda for Peace* retreated on enforcement matters, but mostly added nuances to the question of regional cooperation. While the UN does not have "a monopoly" on peace "instruments," he suggested that the UN was "better equipped than regional organizations or individual Member States to develop and apply the comprehensive, long-term approach needed to ensure the lasting resolution of conflicts." Given the varied experiences and variety of forms of such cooperation, he cautioned against trying "to establish a universal model" for such relationships, preferring to lay out a series of principles to guide them instead.[23]

As enthusiasm for UN-led peacekeeping ebbed in the mid-1990s following setbacks in Somalia, Rwanda, and Bosnia-Herzegovina, participation in non-UN peacekeeping surged. According to a table prepared by Brian L. Job, in 1993 only 14 percent of total peacekeepers deployed worldwide served in non-UN missions, but from 1996 through 2001 the portion had swelled to an average of over 70 percent.[24] In the early years of the new millennium, the demand for both UN and non-UN peacekeepers has grown. In several large and strategically sensitive operations, such as Afghanistan, Bosnia, and Kosovo, NATO has been delegated operational command of the forces, while the UN oversees the rebuilding of much of the political, economic, and social infrastructure. It appears, as well, that the political authority of the Security Council still matters for many troop contributors, as the four largest non-UN peacekeeping missions (KFOR in Kosovo, SFOR in Bosnia, EUFOR in Bosnia, and ISAF in Afghanistan) have all been authorized by the Security Council.[25] For developed countries with long traditions of contributing forces to peacekeeping, the model of NATO command and Security Council authorization appears to be the most comfortable mix at this point.

Some UN veterans, on the other hand, have begun to question whether the tail is not beginning to wag the dog. James O. C. Jonah, a former Permanent Representative of Sierra Leone and UN Under-Secretary-General with long peacekeeping experience, sees the need to go "from burden shedding to burden sharing."[26] To Sir Marrack Goulding, who headed the UN departments of peacekeeping and then of political affairs from 1986 to 1997, "the arguments for regionalization are specious and the arguments against it strong." Of the latter, he contends that only NATO "has the administrative, logistical and command structures needed to deploy and manage multinational military operations" and that it is unethical in a universal organization "to insist that member states in a particular region should receive only the level of peacekeeping that their regional organization can provide."[27] Under such circumstances, Professor Job cautions that "the vision of the Charter to support the roles and responsibilities of regional organizations and simultaneously sustain the hierarchical position of the UN vis-à-vis regional organizations is in danger of unraveling."[28] Certainly the ongoing conversation between the UN and the African Union about their respective roles in peace operations in Darfur underlines the risks and uncertainties involved in the search for a sustainable global-regional division of labor. On the other hand, those who assert the need to respect the relationships laid down in Chapter VIII of the Charter should recognize that in tough cases, like Darfur, the immediate policy question is whether any international body – global, regional, or sub-regional – has the will and capacity to try to fill the local security vacuum.

These trends have contributed to a marked shift in the composition of UN peacekeeping units, as noted in Chapter 4 above. In 1993, the four largest troop-contributing countries were France, United Kingdom, Canada, and the Netherlands.[29] By 2003, the nine top contributors were all developing countries.[30] UN and non-NATO regional peacekeeping, therefore, are facing similar strains in terms of training, equipment, logistics, and funding. In response, the G-8 countries have offered a plan to train 75,000 peacekeepers, initially from Africa, through a Global Peace Operations Initiative.[31] In his 2005 reform plan, UN Secretary-General Kofi Annan announced that he was inviting regional organizations to participate in relevant meetings of UN system coordinating bodies and introducing "memorandums of understanding between the United Nations and individual organizations, governing the sharing of information, expertise and resources, as appropriate in each case." He called upon donor countries to "pay particular attention to the need for a 10-year plan for capacity-building with the African Union." More controversially, he proposed amending current rules "to give the United Nations the option, in very exceptional circumstances, to use assessed contributions to finance regional operations authorized by the Security Council, or the participation of regional organizations in multi-pillar peace operations under the overall United Nations umbrella."[32] However these particular recommendations fare, the issue of developing more productive and regular relations between the Council and regional and sub-regional arrangements will remain a perennial challenge for the world body.

Non-state actors

Despite the ringing "we the peoples" phrase that opens the Preamble, the Charter's four chapters devoted to security matters (V through VIII) make no reference to non-state actors. This omission is particularly striking given the hundreds of non-governmental organizations (NGOs) that the Roosevelt and Truman Administrations brought to San Francisco to help build US public support for the new enterprise.[33] Unlike the Covenant, the Charter at least offers civil society an entryway into its predominantly inter-governmental process. The route, however, is through the Economic and Social Council (ECOSOC) which, under Article 71, "may make suitable arrangements for consultation with non-governmental organizations which are concerned with matters within its competence." Those focused on security need not apply. This segregation is especially remarkable in light of the extent to which non-state actors have become both partners (civil society) and targets (uncivil society) of Security Council action, even of sanctions. At headquarters, the Council frequently consults informally with or hears from independent experts and NGOs that have experience, expertise, or analysis that could inform its deliberations. In the field, private groups – national and international – play central roles in the delivery of humanitarian assistance, the monitoring of human rights, the provision of local knowledge, and economic and social development.[34]

Both the breadth and depth of Security Council involvements following the Cold War dictated closer attention to the ways in which non-state actors were assisting or hindering the achievement of Council objectives. Some of the most demanding and frustrating crises were in failed or failing states in which there was no-one but non-state interlocutors with whom the Council could deal. Rebuilding collapsed societies in such cases was the sine qua non for peace and stability. Civil society groups sometimes offered the only fragments of a social-political foundation on which to build, as well as a vehicle for disseminating the messages the Council members hoped to project to civilian populations and armed elements alike. The UN, not unlike interventionist military powers, had to be concerned with "winning hearts and minds" whenever it became involved on the ground in situations of risk and uncertainty.

The deeper the UN became immersed in the task of responding to complex humanitarian emergencies, moreover, the more the world body had to depend on the operational experience and reach of humanitarian-oriented NGOs. The UN side of this "marriage of convenience," as Andrew S. Natsios has described it, however, was largely confined to specialized UN agencies, programs, and departments during the 1990s.[35] Yet it was the Security Council that played the central role in defining the political, security, and strategic parameters within which these relationships could develop. Only in the last few years has the Council begun to deal directly and formally with the UN's humanitarian and independent sector partners on a regular basis.

Today, these Security Council-civil society interactions take place in several forms and places. At headquarters, the first important innovation came in

1992, when the Venezuelan Permanent Representative to the UN, Diego Arria, invited fellow members of the Council to meet away from the Council's chambers with independent experts, initially on the unfolding tragedy in the Balkans, to get fresh perspectives and to spur informal conversation. Through the years, various members of the Council have found it useful to convene such "Arria Formula" meetings on a wide range of issues facing the Council. In recent years, there have been reports of declining enthusiasm among the Council members for this format, perhaps in part because it has been invoked so often and there are now a number of alternative routes for meeting with civil society partners.[36]

Since 1995, a group of NGOs, led by the Global Policy Forum, has met with Council members periodically to discuss reform issues. Several New York-based think tanks, led by the International Peace Academy, and university research centers (Columbia, New York University, and CUNY Graduate Center) have frequently convened, at the request of members of the Council and/or the UN secretariat, meetings to explore emerging or difficult topics on the Council's agenda. Sometimes these have taken the shape of retreats at which the Council members can meet with the Secretary-General, other top UN officials, and leading independent experts. The frequency of having non-governmental representatives meet with the Council or one of its subsidiary bodies at formal meetings has also increased.[37] In addition, the Council's recent practice of undertaking missions to regions of interest, whether for fact-finding, monitoring implementation, or relaying messages to parties to a conflict, has opened up new opportunities to meet with local civil society leaders and experts in the field, as well as to consult with regional specialists in New York prior to such trips.

By and large, the Council has been given high marks for its efforts to open up to independent views and voices since the end of the Cold War. In its June 2004 report, the Secretary-General's Panel of Eminent Persons on United Nations Civil Society Relations noted that "the Security Council, the most politically sensitive organ of the United Nations, has greatly enhanced its informal relations with civil society."[38] While the panel recommended little beyond a continuation of present trends, it did note that some interlocutors had complained that the Council – like other UN bodies – tends to interact more frequently with Northern- than Southern-based groups.[39]

Dealing with armed groups, on the other hand, has proven both challenging and frustrating for the Council. Very often, as Stephen John Stedman has documented, these groups act as spoilers, since they may have more to gain through continuing a conflict than through an internationally imposed peace process.[40] The Security Council may find it difficult to identify the spoilers in a given conflict and then to act in a unified and timely manner to manipulate their incentives and disincentives. In some cases, of course, one or more members of the Council may have ties to or sympathies for them.[41] As pointed out in Chapter 6 above, the Council's experience in imposing sanctions on non-state actors has been mixed: relatively strong in the case of UNITA in Angola and the RUF in Sierra Leone; relatively weak in terms of arms embargoes in Rwanda, Somalia, Congo, and elsewhere; and too soon to tell in efforts to restrict terrorist access to finance, arms, and weapons of mass destruction.[42] Certainly the founders had not expected that the Council would need to become so deeply concerned and engaged with armed groups at below the national level. But, as Chapters 2 and 3 above documented, there is nothing in the Charter to prevent the Council either from investigating such groups or enforcing Chapter VII resolutions against them, when the Council determines that they represent a threat to international peace and security.

Such groups, however, by definition are neither members of the world body nor parties to the norms and conventions it produces to help guide the behavior of states and the interactions among them. As Jeffrey Herbst has emphasized, this anomaly poses difficult choices both for norm entrepreneurs – be they advocacy NGOs or UN member states – and for the Council and others charged with enforcing those norms.[43] In terms of humanitarian norms and the laws of war, he asks, can states be expected to live up to norms their non-state adversaries ignore? Likewise, as Chapter 10 below discusses, how can the Security Council equip itself to take into account the probable effects on human rights within societies of the counter-terrorism policies it has called on member states to carry out? These, and similar, dilemmas cannot be resolved easily and are unlikely to fade away in an era when some of the prime threats to security – and hence the Council's business – stem from terrorists, armed groups, and the breakdown of civil society and the state in critical regions of the world.

Part III

Challenges

8 The humanitarian imperative

Humanitarian concerns are rarely at the top of the action agendas of major capitals. They are, however, anything but new to the Council. They are listed among the third of the four sets of purposes for the United Nations laid out in Article 1 of the Charter. The stirring opening words of the Preamble – "to save succeeding generations from the scourge of war, which twice in our lifetime has brought untold sorrow to mankind" – invoked the humanitarian imperative that had spurred the creation of the world body as an alternative to the carnage and horrors of unrestricted warfare. As Secretary-General Kofi Annan put it, "unless the Security Council can unite around the aim of confronting massive human rights violations and crimes against humanity . . . then we will betray the very ideals that inspired the founding of the United Nations."[1]

Constitutional and political dilemmas

For the architects of the UN, the question of how to go about insuring the security and well-being of individuals and groups in the nation state era posed some difficult dilemmas. States, not people, were to be represented in the world body. Their sovereign equality before international law was to be respected. On the one hand, the member states undertook a series of responsibilities and obligations under the Charter that they ratified. But on the other hand, their domestic political processes and constitutional restraints remained in place. The Charter, of course, charged the organization it established, and primarily its Security Council, with the maintenance of international peace and security as its first purpose (Article 1(1)). While this was a much more ambitious mandate than that given the League, it was generally accepted that the protection of people could only be accomplished through states and through their peaceful relations. As two world wars in the first half of the century had amply and tragically demonstrated, humanitarian principles were among the first casualties of inter-state warfare.

Fair enough, nations at war are often ill equipped to provide proper protection to their people. But what if states that are at peace with their neighbors act as if they are at war with segments of their own people? If a state practices ethnic cleansing but the resulting refugees fail to cross international boundaries, should this be of no concern to other governments and inter-governmental institutions?[2] Who is to enforce domestic peace when the human rights of individuals or groups within a society are persistently and flagrantly violated by the very government that is responsible for their protection? Is the UN, and its Security Council, ultimately accountable to member state governments or to "we the peoples"? According to Secretary-General Kofi Annan, "the Charter protects the sovereignty of peoples. It was never meant as a license for governments to trample on human rights and human dignity. Sovereignty implies responsibilities, not just power."[3]

Not surprisingly, however, the disparate delegations at the founding conference in San Francisco had a range of views on such matters. As a result, the Charter lacks consistency. Under Article 1's purposes, it includes references to humanitarian, self-determination, and human rights concerns, as well as to "fundamental freedoms for all without distinction as to race, sex, language, or religion." On the other hand, Article 2's principles include a non-intervention clause, except for Chapter VII enforcement purposes, "in matters which are essentially within the domestic jurisdiction of any state or shall require the Members to submit such matters to settlement under the present Charter" (Article 2(7)). As noted in Chapter 3 above, the Council's investigations under Article 34, determinations under Article 39, and enforcement actions under Articles 41 and 42 need not be limited to the international level. Yet the Charter implies that any such actions by the Council should be justifiable as necessary for the fulfillment of its mandate to maintain international peace and security, not human rights or domestic tranquility.

In other words, if the Council determines that a situation within a state could threaten the maintenance of international peace and security at some point, then it can take non-coercive action under Chapter VI or coercive steps under Chapter VII. The Charter neither offers guidelines that the Council should take into account in making such a determination nor suggests that it should develop such rules to guide its decision-making, other than the Article 24(2) admonition that "in discharging these duties the Security Council shall act in accordance with the Purposes and Principles of the United Nations." As an innately political body composed of member states with individual national interests as well as some degree of shared or collective values and interests, the Council's determinations about such things – whether a government's lack of control of its territory, suppression of some of its population, or harboring of armed groups or terrorists threaten its neighbors or more distant states – may often be controversial. Nowhere is this more pronounced than when the Council deals, or, more often, fails to deal with, humanitarian problems. As noted earlier, these dilemmas illustrate why the founders were wise not to link Council decision-making to measurable standards and universal principles. Given the dynamic nature both of its changing membership and of domestic and international politics, as well as the often inelastic nature of capacity and will, the Security Council has displayed little consistency in applying humanitarian standards to its decisions and actions. But, presumably, inconsistency is to be preferred to disinterest.[4] Over time, the Council's interest in humanitarian affairs has certainly grown, even if its willingness to act has expanded at a slower rate. The Council, moreover, has had no monopoly on inconsistent and politically skewed decision-making. For instance, while there are few constitutional restrictions on the Council's freedom to choose and decide, the degree to which other states and actors pay heed to the Council's decisions, or respect its political and legal authority, varies from case to case and resolution to resolution. The same inconsistencies can be seen in how regional bodies decide when and how to act, as well as in the variable responses of their member states. When faced with man-made humanitarian calamities, the Council may well find itself caught between cross-pressures from publics and governments. The former, moved by media accounts of gross violations of human rights, ethnic cleansing, and refugee flows, are likely to press for quick and decisive action.[5] As Boutros Boutros-Ghali acknowledged, graphic media coverage of humanitarian suffering can be a double-edged sword: "while such images can help build support for humanitarian action, such scenes also may create an emotional environment in which effective decision-making can be far more difficult."[6]

Member state governments, on the other hand, reluctant to pay the costs and take the risks of intervention, may be all too ready to delegate the tasks to the Security Council or to regional organizations and arrangements. Member states, therefore, have been known to quietly discourage forceful Council action in places like Rwanda, Srebrenica and Darfur, while publicly bemoaning the lack of an effective international response. As Secretary-General Kofi Annan bluntly put it in his *In Larger Freedom* report, "nowhere is the gap between rhetoric and reality – between declarations and deeds – so stark and so deadly as in the field of international humanitarian law."[7] By acting as a political lightning rod, the Council and the UN more generally may end up providing a valuable political service for recalcitrant and free-riding member states, while doing little to relieve the suffering on the ground. In such cases, the service, while real enough, is a political one for states, rather than a humanitarian one for the people in need.

The evolution of doctrine

As Thomas G. Weiss has noted, "the Security Council was largely missing in action regarding humanitarian matters during the Cold War."[8] It did not rush to embrace the humanitarian imperative, moreover, with the demise of the Cold War. When the Council members met in January 1992, for the first time at the summit level, to address the Council's expanding horizons, they barely mentioned humanitarian concerns. Their consensus presidential statement noted that "the non-military sources of instability in the economic, social, humanitarian and ecological fields have become threats to peace and security."[9] But these, in their view, were to be addressed not by the Security Council, but by "the United Nations membership as a whole, working through the appropriate bodies." They also did not appear among the topics the new Secretary-General, Boutros Boutros-Ghali, was asked to review in what was to become his *An Agenda for Peace* report. In it, the Secretary-General did acknowledge that "humanitarian assistance, impartially provided, could be of critical importance" to efforts to prevent conflict.[10] Yet he went on to stress the "need to respect the sovereignty of the State" and to enumerate several caveats to that effect. The latter had been included among the guiding principles that the General Assembly had attached to its resolution 46/182 on the humanitarian work of the world body.[11] Among these conditions was "the consent of the affected country and, in principle, on the basis of an appeal by that country."

Two and a half years later, in his *Supplement to An Agenda for Peace*, the Secretary-General recognized that developments on the ground had compelled a "qualitative change" in terms of "the use of United Nations forces to protect humanitarian operations."[12] Warring parties, he noted, had repeatedly either prevented the delivery or diverted humanitarian assistance away from those in need in places like Somalia and Bosnia-Herzegovina. "This had led," in his view, "to a new kind of United Nations operation. Even though the use of force is authorized under Chapter VII of the Charter, the United Nations remains neutral and impartial between the warring parties."[13] The example he cited, "the 'safe areas' concept in Bosnia and Herzegovina," however, proved to have tragic consequences when the members of the Council rebuffed his appeals for a more robust force to defend Srebrenica and the other mislabeled safe havens.

In *An Agenda for Peace*, Boutros Boutros-Ghali commented that "the time of absolute and exclusive sovereignty . . . has passed; its theory was never matched by reality."[14] Yet, as noted above, the political winds of the time discouraged him from drawing any major doctrinal conclusions from this observation. His successor, Kofi Annan, decided to test these limits again, but in a bolder and more concerted way. In a series of speeches in 1998 and 1999, the new Secretary-General asked officials and publics alike to reconsider the rules and principles that should guide the world body's approach to humanitarian intervention.[15] As he told the General Assembly in September 1999, "the choice . . . must not be between Council unity and inaction in the face of genocide – as in the case of Rwanda, on the one hand; and Council division, and regional action, as in the case of Kosovo, on the other."[16] He succeeded admirably in spurring a lively debate among the member states about what he termed "this developing international norm in favour of intervention to protect civilians from wholesale slaughter." It became abundantly clear, however, that there was nothing close to a consensus or even convergence of views on the subject, as a number of countries, particularly from the developing world, continued to fret that such a doctrinal development could provide a cover for interventions with other motivations or effects.[17]

The next year, in an effort to identify fresh approaches to these issues and to open new possibilities for building a wider international consensus on how to proceed, the Canadian government established an International Commission on Intervention and State Sovereignty. The Commission concluded that state sovereignty entails a responsibility to protect, i.e. that "the primary responsibility for the protection of its people lies with the state itself."[18] It is only when a state is unwilling or unable to halt or avert serious humanitarian suffering by its population that "the principle of non-intervention yields to the international responsibility to protect." In the Commission's view, a range of preventive and non-coercive measures should be considered before the Security Council addresses the possibility of authorizing a military intervention. In such cases, moreover, the permanent members should, the group contended, agree not to employ their veto power.[19] The findings of the Commission were strongly endorsed by the Secretary-General in his March 2005 reform report.[20] Earlier, he had appointed a Special Adviser on the Prevention of Genocide.[21]

Though the humanitarian imperative is not yet a well established norm, it is much more widely accepted now than when Secretary-General Annan espoused it so boldly in the late 1990s.[22] "Each individual State has the responsibility to protect its population from genocide, war crimes, ethnic cleansing and crimes against humanity," declared the September 2005 UN summit.[23] The gathered heads of state and government pledged that "we accept that responsibility and will act in accordance with it." They went on to assert that:

> We are prepared to take collective action, in a timely and decisive manner, through the Security Council, in accordance with the Charter, including Chapter VII, on a case-by-case basis and in cooperation with relevant regional organizations as appropriate, should peaceful means be inadequate and national authorities manifestly fail to protect their population from genocide, war crimes, ethnic cleansing and crimes against humanity.[24]

Though heavily caveated for all of the political and material reasons discussed above, this declaration marks a substantial step forward when viewed from a historical perspective.[25] At the very least, such a global summit declaration shifts the burden of proof when the Council is considering possible measures to respond to humanitarian emergencies. There is still no guarantee, of course, that the Council's deeds will match its words, as the unfolding debacle in Darfur confirms.

Strategic context

Since the end of the Cold War, strategic, technological, and normative developments have conspired to push humanitarian concerns towards the upper reaches of the Council's agenda.[26] On the strategic side, changing geopolitical relationships have produced shifts in the nature of armed conflict and, consequently, of the Council's involvement in trying to prevent, contain, and resolve it. Wars between and among states unfortunately have not disappeared from contemporary history, but in recent years there have been fewer of them and they have produced, on average, far fewer casualties. The end of the East-West competition for strategic supremacy has lessened the tendency for the great powers to fuel and sustain local wars fought by their proxies. The United States, as the last power with global defense obligations and with the capacity to project and sustain substantial military power far from home, does, of course, continue to exercise its military muscle from time to time, especially in relation to its declared global war on terrorism. However, its technological dominance and precision targeting have insured that the battlefield casualties produced by the wars it has engaged in have been remarkably low by historical standards.

The 2005 *Human Security Report*, for example, cites a study by Bethany Lacina and Nils Petter Gleditsch that found that there were 38,000 deaths per conflict in 1950 compared to only 600 in 2002.[27] Drawing data from a study by Meredith Reid Sarkees *et al.*, the *Report* concludes that, in terms of global battlefield deaths as a portion of world population, "war in the 1990s was only one third as deadly as in the 1970s."[28] Tellingly, it appears likely that the guerilla style struggles within Afghanistan and Iraq following the rapid battlefield successes by US-led coalitions will produce greater casualties than the initial phases of the wars, when US firepower and technological advantages could be brought to bear more effectively with lower levels of collateral civilian losses.

As the strategic rationales for war have faded – other than counterterrorism or counter-proliferation – the most prevalent form of organized violence since the end of the Cold War – by far – has come to be the intrastate and transnational variety. According to the database assembled and regularly updated by the Uppsala Conflict Data Program (UCDP), of the 119 conflicts from 1989 through 2004, ninety were intrastate, twenty-two were "internationalized intra-state" (i.e. one or both sides received military support from other governments), and only seven (6 percent) were between states.[29] According to UCDP data, in 2004 the number of armed conflicts around the world was "lower than at any time since the early 1970s" and the sub-total for each category had fallen from 1989 to 2004.[30] As the Secretary-General's High-level Panel points out, "since 1992, civil wars have declined steadily, and by 2003 had dropped by roughly 40 per cent."[31] In contrast, in the unsettled years of the early 1990s, following the end of the Cold War, the number of intrastate conflicts grew, as did the pace of Security Council-authorized peace operations seeking to quell the violence (see Chapter 4 above). As the international efforts to resolve the multiple conflicts in the Balkans began to take hold, the Council's attention shifted increasingly to Africa, which has occupied about two thirds of its time in recent years. The *Human Security Report 2005* notes that "at the beginning of the new millennium the battle-death toll in sub-Saharan Africa was greater than the toll in all other regions combined," though the number of conflicts there has subsided somewhat since 2002.[32] Africa has witnessed one major inter-state war in recent years, between Ethiopia and Eritrea, but it began as an internal conflict leading to Eritrea's secession.[33]

Operational hurdles

The humanitarian toll of intrastate and transnational (or internationalized intrastate) conflicts has tended to be disproportionately high, compared to traditional inter-state wars with their more clearly defined battlefields and combatants. The encouraging decline in battlefield casualties masks the incalculable danger done to fragile societies and vulnerable people when wars are not confined to geographically delineated fields of battle and to contests between professional and, hopefully, disciplined military units. As Secretary-General Boutros Boutros-Ghali lamented in 1995, in the uncivil conflicts of the post-Cold War era, civilians too often have been both the targets of and the participants in acts of extreme, if localized, violence.[34] The wars in the Balkans made "ethnic cleansing" one of the sorrier household words, as well as helping to waken the Council's eyes to the often tragic interface among humanitarian and human rights violations, intrastate violence, and international peace and security. Among the more grotesque dimensions of such intensive struggles have been sexual violence as a tactic, child soldiers as an instrument, the spread of HIV/AIDs as a byproduct, and displaced people as an often intentional consequence of contemporary warfare. Though true for much of the world, these trends have been seen most sadly and frequently in sub-Saharan Africa, where HIV/AIDs has become the most common cause of death, wreaking havoc on both armed forces and the civilians they interact with or intimidate.[35] In 2000, led by a Clinton administration initiative, the Security Council declared HIV/AIDs to be a threat to international peace and security.[36]

In failed or failing states, the imploding security environment and declining government services encouraged a breakdown in respect for international norms, as well as for domestic institutions and societal values. Armed groups often felt little obligation to abide by international human rights and humanitarian conventions to which they were not party.[37] Preying on the most vulnerable elements of society, such groups and, less often, desperate government forces, engaged in the forced recruitment of child soldiers with such frequency that the practice reached epidemic proportions and gained vast publicity in the early to mid-1990s. In her landmark August 1996 study of the phenomenon commissioned by Secretary-General Boutros Boutros-Ghali, Graça Machel presciently commented that "children present us with a uniquely compelling motivation for mobilization."[38] Indeed, the publication was followed by the establishment of the Office of the Special Representative of the Secretary-General for Children and Armed Conflict; various interagency task forces; the inclusion of child protection advisers in peacekeeping operations, plus efforts to encourage similar efforts by regional groups; the addition of an Optional Protocol to the Convention on the Rights of the Child on the Involvement of Children in Armed Conflict; the institution of annual reports by the Secretary-General to the Assembly and Council, including assessments of developments in specific member states; and the establishment of a Security Council working group to review, at the Council's annual debate on the topic, these reports and progress on action plans to be prepared by each of the named states.[39] Though such norm building, reporting, and cajoling lack the immediate teeth of Chapter VII enforcement measures, they are far more sustainable and appropriate tools given that the worst violators are often non-state actors in situations where government authority is crumbling or being contested by armed groups.

Sexual violence has proven to a more problematic issue for the Council and the peacekeeping operations it mandates. Like child soldiers, though somewhat later, the issue of rape and sexual exploitation as a tactic and perversion of contemporary warfare generated broad media coverage before action was taken in the Council. In Resolution 1325 of October 2000, the Council called "on all parties to armed conflict to take special measures to protect women and girls from gender-based violence, particularly rape and other forms of sexual abuse" and emphasized the need "to put an end to impunity and to prosecute those responsible for genocide, crimes against humanity, and war crimes, including those relating to sexual and other violence against women and girls."[40] Earlier, in 1994, the Council had included rape as one of the crimes against humanity that would be prosecuted by the International Criminal Tribunal for Rwanda (ICTR).[41] In its series of deliberations, resolutions, and presidential statements on the protection of civilians in armed conflict, the Council recognized that women were not only victims of violence, they could be important players both in efforts to prevent conflict and to heal the wounds and rebuild society afterwards.[42] According to the Secretary-General, between 2000 and 2004 almost one sixth of all Council resolutions paid attention "to women or to gender concerns."[43] Gender advisors were included in peacekeeping operations, training materials and tools were provided on gender issues, HIV/AIDs, and human trafficking, and units to assist the victims of sexual violence were added to local police stations in a number of peacekeeping operations.[44]

Over these same years, however, there was a growing awareness in the Council – once again fueled in part by media coverage and commentary – that the UN itself had become part of the problem it was seeking to solve. The UN's Office of Internal Oversight Services (OIOS) confirmed reports of sexual exploitation by aid workers in West Africa, where refugees and internally displaced had been abused despite the Secretary-General's policy of zero tolerance for such abuse.[45] With increasing reports of such abuses by UN peacekeepers as well, the President of the Council urged troop-contributing countries "to prevent and remedy situations of sexual abuse and exploitation, when their nationals are involved in such cases."[46] Among other steps, complaint mechanisms were improved, resulting in a jump in abuse reports from the Democratic Republic of the Congo (DRC) in 2004.

In early 2005, with encouragement from the Assembly's Special Committee on Peacekeeping Operations, the Secretary-General enlisted a former civilian peacekeeper and Jordanian Permanent Representative to the UN, HRH Prince Zeid Ra'ad Zeid Al-Hussein, to prepare a detailed report on the situation. After visiting the region, he called for a sweeping series of reforms in UN rules, investigations, and accountability, and in individual disciplinary, financial, and criminal accountability.[47] As the report recognized, the urgency of eliminating this scourge on the reputation and integrity of the UN's blue helmets is matched by the difficulty of enforcing rules when it is often hard to find countries to contribute forces to such missions, and when they ultimately must be responsible for overseeing and disciplining their troops. In the less frequent case when UN civilian personnel are involved, it should be easier to insure that UN rules and international norms are fully respected and enforced. In response to the report, the Special Committee held a week of meetings to consider its findings, which it largely endorsed and echoed in its follow-up report.[48] In more general terms, the Security Council added its consent as well.[49]

As Arthur C. Helton ruefully acknowledged, the conditions that fostered such a decline in respect for humanitarian norms made the 1990s "a decade of extraordinary human displacement."[50] Whether motivated by greed, grievance, or a combination of the two, wars that pit different segments of a society against each other tend to produce large numbers of internal and external refugees.[51] From 1987 to 1994, the number of external refugees worldwide doubled from 13 to 26 million.[52] While the flow of refugees crossing borders declined markedly after peaking in the early 1990s, the number of internally displaced appears to have remained at a high level.[53] By 2000, there were more than 20 million internal refugees.[54] These trends roughly correspond to the shift from wars between states to wars within states. With tens of millions of civilians displaced, even if the fighting is localized, the spillover effects in terms of regional or sub-regional stability may not be. A government faced with an armed uprising, for example, may have reason to believe that one or more of its neighbors are providing sanctuary, arms, or financing to the rebel group(s). When borders are relatively porous, as in much of the developing world, few conflicts – even so-called civil ones – can be contained entirely within one country. This disruptive process could be seen in places as diverse as Iraq, West Africa, Kashmir, the Democratic Republic of the Congo, Afghanistan, the Balkans, El Salvador, and Rwanda. For the Council, these dynamics have required acute attention to insecurity within, as well as between, countries.

The savagery of the internecine conflicts of the 1990s posed a related challenge for the Council: how to insure some degree of personal accountability for atrocities perpetrated during those strikingly uncivil "civil" wars. International law, like the founding mandate for the Council itself, was largely developed to codify a set of relationships among sovereign states. As Luc Côté points out, international humanitarian law has traditionally been short on implementation, much less enforcement, mechanisms. The near universality of these normative regimes, he notes, may in part be due to how unlikely it has been that violators would ever be punished.[55] International humanitarian law, of course, has a long and distinguished history, but its focus, until recently, has been on wars between, not within, states and on how states treated enemy populations and combatants, not their own.[56] There is nothing in the Charter, moreover, to suggest that the Security Council is tasked with enforcing humanitarian law, or any other set of norms beyond the Charter, for that matter.

However, over the course of the turbulent post-Cold War years, it became increasingly apparent that the Council could not fulfill its responsibility to maintain international peace and security if state and non-state actors could blatantly abuse humanitarian standards with complete impunity. The unraveling of the normative regime was making the Council's job – as well as the lives of innocent civilians and UN peacekeepers and humanitarian workers – that much harder. If those leaders encouraging ethnic cleansing, systematic sexual abuse, and even genocide could not be held accountable, then others would not be deterred from committing such acts in the future. Each round of violence would simply sow the seeds for the next one. So postwar justice became an integral part of the Council's expanding agenda. Understandably, the Council chose to experiment with the establishment of the UN's first international criminal tribunals in two places – the former Yugoslavia and Rwanda – where it had been unable or unwilling to make much of a difference on the ground as atrocities multiplied.

By the summer of 1992, there were widespread media accounts of serious human rights abuses in Bosnia-Herzegovina despite the deployment there of the misnamed UN Protection Force (UNPROFOR) earlier that year. On 13 August 1992, the Security Council passed two resolutions, 770 and 771, under Chapter VII calling for cooperation in the delivery of humanitarian assistance, demanding access to camps and prisons, and condemning ethnic cleansing.[57] Frustrated by the lack of response from the parties yet unwilling to add teeth to the enforcement provisions of those resolutions, the Council took the unprecedented step in May 1993 of establishing an international tribunal to prosecute those responsible for serious violations of international humanitarian law in the former Yugoslavia. Adopted unanimously under Chapter VII, resolution 827 stipulated that the International Criminal Tribunal for the former Yugoslavia (ICTY) was to be a subsidiary body of the Council under Article 29 of the Charter.[58] The court, situated in The Hague, got off to a slow start, hampered by its distance from the affected populations, by the initial difficulty having prime defendants turned over for trial, and by charges that it was just an expression of victor's justice. In recent years, however, its reputation has improved, particularly in its efforts to document systematic sexual abuse, to prosecute those accused of crimes from each side of the conflict, and to bring some of the major figures to trial, including Slobodan Milosevic, the former president of the Federal Republic of Yugoslavia.[59]

In Rwanda, the Council established a small and lightly armed peacekeeping mission in October 1993 – under Chapter VI, not VII – to help implement the Arusha Peace Agreement.[60] As has been widely documented in numerous press accounts, studies, and even a popular film, this UN Assistance Mission for Rwanda (UNAMIR) was neither mandated nor equipped, nor even encouraged, to try to stem the genocide of the following spring, though the Council then added the task of assisting humanitarian relief operations "where feasible" to its tragically unfulfilled mission.[61] As in the former Yugoslavia, the Council followed its failure to take timely action with resolutions establishing (1) a commission of experts to gather evidence and report on grave violations of humanitarian law, and (2) an international criminal tribunal – the International Criminal Tribunal for Rwanda (ICTR) – to prosecute those responsible for genocide and other serious violations of international humanitarian law in Rwanda.[62] It, too, was established under Chapter VII, with its enforcement powers, and as a subsidiary organ of the Council. Like the ICTY, it has suffered from being based in Arusha, far from the victims, and it faced debilitating financial and bureaucratic problems, along with charges of mismanagement, early on. As observers from the region have pointed out, however, the pace of referrals to the Tribunal accelerated from 1996 on and by 2003 seventeen states had arrested and transferred to the ICTR sixty-five individuals to stand trial.[63] Though the subsequent creation of the International Criminal Court was intended to obviate the need for such regional, conflict-specific tribunals in the future, the ICTY and ICTR represent both an important chapter in the ongoing saga of the Council's development of tools for addressing the humanitarian agenda and possible precedents for similar action in particularly egregious cases in the future.[64]

None of these innovations in doctrine and in machinery, of course, have succeeded in removing persistent doubts about the Council's effectiveness in meeting man-made humanitarian emergencies. "The core challenge to the Security Council and to the United Nations as a whole in the next century," according to Secretary-General Kofi Annan, is "to forge unity behind the principle that massive and systematic violations of human rights – wherever they may take place – should not be allowed to stand."[65] Fair enough, the Council's track record in such situations is mixed even when it does get involved, and too often it looks the other way. But when compared to its earlier years or to other international bodies, the Council's performance does not look so anemic. Indeed, why should it be expected that member states will choose to send their relief workers and armed forces into harm's way, far from home, when the risks and costs are high and the benefits for their national interests, narrowly conceived, are low?[66] The fact that the humanitarian imperative shows signs of taking hold in national decision-making processes, however slowly and unevenly, and that public acceptance of a shared responsibility to protect is becoming commonplace, is remarkable in historical and political terms. As the developments in the Council's doctrine and repertoire described above suggest, the Security Council has both been affected by and, quite often, been a proponent for the progressive development of the humanitarian imperative.

9 Terrorism and weapons of mass destruction

As Chapter 3 related, during the deliberations at San Francisco the founders were determined to preserve for the Security Council as much flexibility as possible to determine what might constitute a threat to international peace and security under Article 39. Moreover, Article 34 gives the Council wide latitude to investigate any dispute or situation that could "endanger the maintenance of international peace and security." They understood that any attempt to list the proximate causes of conflict would be a fruitless and controversial exercise, subject to misinterpretation, debate, and delay when collective action was most urgently needed. With due modesty, they realized, as well, that geopolitical and technological conditions were likely to change in unpredictable ways in the years ahead. Most of all, the founders were determined to fashion a Charter and a Council for the ages. So they would not be the least bit surprised, or chagrined, to learn that two of the most worrisome threats six decades later – the proliferation of weapons of mass destruction (WMD) and global terrorism – had not been mentioned in the Charter.

Convened while the war in the Pacific was still raging and the battle for Europe was in its final weeks, the San Francisco Conference was understandably and properly focused on developing instruments to prevent or contain conflict between states. Having witnessed the horrific destruction of two world wars in two generations, as well as the utter failure of the League to head off the second, the delegates were determined to tame aggressive states through the collective action of the "peace-loving" countries. Terrorism was far from their minds. Less than a decade before, as aggression unfolded and a world war loomed, the League of Nations, with characteristically poor timing, had chosen to tackle terrorism. In what appeared to be a classic case of fighting – or, in this case, seeking to deter – the last war, the League drafted an anti-terrorism convention in 1937 to address political assassinations, as if it was 1914 all over again. A companion convention would have established an International Criminal Court to try those accused of such crimes.[1] Neither convention took effect in the end, but many of the topics raised in the debate – globalization, mass communication, counterfeiting, and narcotics trafficking – are unfortunately still in play.[2]

Postwar adjustments

The Charter was a pre-atomic document. Signed before the first test of an atomic weapon, much less its actual use on Hiroshima and Nagasaki, the Charter could not have anticipated the reordering of global security and world politics that would be caused by the introduction of nuclear weapons, the strategic arms race, and the Cold War. It would be decades before the three multilateral treaties to curb the proliferation of nuclear (1968), biological (1972), and chemical weapons (1993) could be negotiated.[3] Nevertheless, the need to address the dangers posed by weapons of mass destruction (WMD) was high on the UN's agenda from its earliest days. The General Assembly's first resolution, in January 1946, in fact, called for "the elimination from national armaments of atomic weapons and of all other major weapons adaptable to mass destruction."[4] Two months earlier, the United States, the United Kingdom and Canada had proposed the creation of a UN Atomic Energy Commission with the goal of "entirely eliminating the use of atomic energy for destructive purposes."[5]

For the Security Council, however, the implications of the atomic age were more troubling. On the one hand, Article 26 of the Charter gives the Council the responsibility "for formulating," with the assistance of its Military Staff Committee, "plans to be submitted to the Members of the United Nations for the establishment of a system for the regulation of armaments."[6] On the other hand, the acquisition of weapons of mass destruction was as likely to divide the veto-wielding permanent members as to unite them. Rather than presenting a threat from former enemies outside of the UN circle, the proliferation of WMD threatened to alter the security relationships among the members of the United Nations itself. Bernard Baruch, author of a very ambitious plan for the international control of atomic energy, in June 1946 voiced the dilemma as follows:

> There must be no veto to protect those who violate their solemn agreements not to develop or use atomic energy for destructive purposes. The bomb does not wait upon debate. To delay may be to die. The time between violation and preventive action or punishment would be all too short for extended discussion as to the course to be followed.[7]

Even without a veto, the enforcement of Council measures could become problematic if a nuclear power or one of its clients was involved. Nuclear deterrence may have brought an added layer of stability to bilateral relations between the superpowers and between their alliances, but it also threatened to bring the Council's enforcement powers into question in many cases. At the very least, such strategic factors and asymmetries would soon raise questions about the consistency of the Security Council's decisions and implementation efforts.[8]

The Cold War years

During four decades of Cold War, the Security Council never grappled seriously with the threats posed either by terrorism or by weapons of mass destruction. The thought of addressing them together came much later. In the case of terrorism, political factors largely explained the Council's tendency to look elsewhere for threats to international peace and security, but strategic and institutional factors also contributed. Even as the pace of terrorist bombings and airline hijackings accelerated in the late 1960s and early 1970s, the Security Council tended to look the other way.[9] It did manage to adopt, without vote, its first resolution on terrorism in September 1970. Resolution 286 made a generic appeal for the release of passengers and crews held from hijackings and called on states "to take all possible legal steps to prevent further hijackings or any other interference with international civil air travel."[10] While a step forward, such a general appeal could not compensate for the Council's inability to address specific terrorist strikes or to organize a collective response to the generic problem.

Most of the incidents were aimed against Western or Israeli targets and took place in the Middle East or Western Europe. In some cases, allies or client states of the Soviet Union were suspected of aiding or abetting some of the shadowy groups that employed terrorist tactics. In the midst of the Cold War competition for influence in Europe as well as in the Third World, Moscow had little interest in seeing the Security Council take up these matters and Washington was largely preoccupied with what were deemed to be more pressing state-to-state security concerns.

With the influx of scores of newly independent countries from Asia and Africa into the UN in the 1960s and 1970s, moreover, the political and substantive orientation of the world body shifted in ways that put the Western countries on the defensive on issues as varied as South Africa, the Middle East, development, and disarmament. In the General Assembly, and to a lesser extent the Security Council, there was some tendency in those years to view terrorism as one of the unfortunate but necessary tactics of struggles for national liberation.[11] Given the unfavorable politics of the UN and what was perceived to be the localized nature of most terrorist threats, most countries experiencing terrorist violence were reluctant to see the Council take up their cases.[12] This was true not only for Western European states such as the

United Kingdom, Italy, France, Germany and Spain, but also for Sri Lanka, India, and later Japan. States facing violent irredentist movements were particularly resistant to having these sensitive domestic or sub-regional issues addressed by global political bodies, such as the Assembly or Council. At that point, in any case, the Council had demonstrated scant will to employ its Chapter VII enforcement powers except on rare occasions. So referring such matters to the Council would have entailed high political risk for little substantive gain.

The divisive politics of the Middle East cast a shadow over the Council's infrequent attempts to address terrorism.[13] Throughout the Cold War years, the Council seemed more concerned about the alleged excesses of Israeli and American counter-terrorism measures than about the terrorist acts that preceded them. Nothing captured the consequences of the Council's ambivalence about these matters more graphically than its failure to respond to the massacre of the Israeli athletes at the 1972 Munich Olympics. There was insufficient support for a US draft to even put it to a vote, China and the Soviet Union vetoed a watered down Western European draft, and the US Permanent Representative, future President George H. W. Bush, vetoed a nonaligned draft that neglected to mention either terrorism or the tragedy in Munich. Significantly, this was the first lonely veto cast by the United States, and only its second overall. Such were the disabling politics of the Council in those days.[14]

During the latter half of the Cold War, at least, the politics in the Council concerning nuclear proliferation were more nuanced, and in some ways more promising, than those related to terrorism. Following the conclusion of the Limited Test Ban Treaty in 1963, there was a modest thaw in Soviet-American relations and the beginning of a mutual understanding that Moscow and Washington shared an interest in discouraging the spread of nuclear weapons technology and capacity to additional countries. The bilateral nuclear arms race was dangerous enough; multilateralizing it would impose multiple layers of risk and uncertainty. Following several years of on-and-off negotiations, on both the bilateral and multilateral planes, the Treaty on the Non-Proliferation of Nuclear Weapons (NPT) was endorsed by the General Assembly in June 1968.[15]

As part of the negotiations, the US, the United Kingdom and the Soviet Union agreed to seek a Security Council resolution providing positive assurances that the Council would act if any non-nuclear-weapon state party to the NPT was "a victim of an act or an object of a threat of aggression in which nuclear weapons are used." The subsequent resolution, adopted a week after the Assembly endorsed the NPT,

> recognizes that aggression with nuclear weapons or the threat of such aggression against a non-nuclear-weapon State would create a situation in

which the Security Council, and above all its nuclear-weapon State permanent members, would have to act immediately in accordance with their obligations under the United Nations Charter.[16]

On this issue, East and West largely stood together, with most of the reservations and dissents coming from the South. The resolution, tellingly, passed the Council by a 10-0-5 vote, with the abstentions coming from Algeria, Brazil, France, India, and Pakistan.

Under the NPT regime, moreover, problem cases are eventually to be referred to the Council, possibly for enforcement action.[17] The treaty requires non-nuclear parties to undertake safeguards arrangements with the International Atomic Energy Agency (IAEA), whose Statute requires notification of the Council if "there should arise questions that are within the competence of the Security Council . . . as the organ bearing the main responsibility for the maintenance of international peace and security" or if a state fails to remedy any non-compliance with the safeguards program.[18] Under Article X of the NPT, moreover, a party planning to withdraw from the treaty must first notify the Council and provide it with a statement of the "extraordinary events" leading to its decision. Similar provisions are included in the Chemical Weapons Convention[19] and the Biological Weapons Convention,[20] giving the Council ultimate enforcement responsibilities across the whole WMD spectrum. Even if none of these provisions existed, the Council's generic responsibility for the maintenance of international peace and security would certainly imply an obligation for it to monitor potentially dangerous developments in WMD proliferation. Nevertheless, no such referrals were made to the Council before 1993 and it generally managed to avoid the topic for the life of the Cold War.[21]

The thaw: opportunity knocks

Two years before Mikhail Gorbachev's celebrated articles in *Pravda* and *Izvestia* foreshadowed a radical shift in Soviet foreign and domestic policies, 1985 marked a watershed in the Security Council's handling of terrorism. It was a year of bold and highly publicized terrorist strikes, such as the hijacking of the Italian cruise ship the *Achille Lauro*, bloody assaults on the Rome and Vienna airports, and, critically, even the kidnapping and murder of Soviet diplomats.[22] As a result, in December the Assembly unanimously condemned terrorism in all its forms as criminal and the Council, also unanimously, condemned "unequivocally all acts of hostage-taking and abduction," affirmed the legal and humanitarian obligations of those states on whose territory such acts have occurred, called for the prevention, prosecution and punishment of such acts, and appealed to all states to become parties to the growing array of global counter-terrorism conventions.[23] In mid-1989, two more unanimous Council counter-terrorism resolutions confirmed that the body no longer had any doubts about where it stood *vis-à-vis* terrorism. Resolution 635 condemned all acts of terrorism against civil aviation and called on states to cooperate with the International Civil Aviation Organization (ICAO) in devising a system for marking sheet or plastic explosives.[24] A month later, Resolution 638 condemned unequivocally all acts of hostage-taking and abduction, demanded the immediate release of all hostages, and appealed for wider ratification of the Convention Against the Taking of Hostages.[25]

Though this flurry of resolutions may have removed any remaining ambiguity about the normative stance of the Council, it was not until the 1990s that the Council made its concerns about curbing terrorism operational. As earlier chapters have chronicled, on a number of fronts the 1990s were, for the Security Council, the enforcement decade. Not only did the decade commence with an unprecedented vote to authorize member states "to use all necessary means" to expel the Iraqi invaders from Kuwait,[26] the success of that collaborative effort was capped with an unprecedented gathering of the Security Council at the summit level as "a timely recognition of the fact that there are new favourable international circumstances under which the Security Council has begun to fulfil more effectively its primary responsibility for the maintenance of international peace and security."[27] Among the issues highlighted were curbing terrorism and the proliferation of WMD. Therefore, the years that followed witnessed record numbers of Chapter VII resolutions invoking economic sanctions and/or military interventions to enforce Council decisions.[28] Three times over the course of the 1990s, the Council imposed sanctions on states and groups accused of aiding or abetting terrorism. The Council had not invoked that many sanctions regimes, for any purpose, during the preceding forty-five years.

On 31 March 1992, the Council, in Resolution 748, found that Libya had failed "to demonstrate by concrete actions its renunciation of terrorism" or to respond fully and effectively to an earlier resolution (731) calling for its full cooperation in establishing responsibility for the terrorist bombings of Pan Am flight 103 and UTA flight 772. As a result, 748 imposed a series of measures to limit the movement, use and refurbishing of Libyan aircraft and airfields, and to reduce Libyan diplomatic staffs posted abroad. Similarly, in 1996 the Council acted twice to impose sanctions on Sudan for its refusal to extradite three suspects in the attempted assassination of Egyptian President Hosni Mubarak. Resolution 1054 of 26 April called for the reduction of Sudanese embassy staffs, while Resolution 1070 of 16 August imposed restrictions on Sudanese aircraft similar to those in effect on Libya. Though these measures were targeted so as not to cause unnecessary humanitarian or economic effects, none of these resolutions received the unanimous support of the Council members. The vote on the Libyan sanctions (748), the first taken for counter-terrorism purposes, included abstentions from five developing countries, including the world's two most populous ones: Cape Verde, China, India, Morocco and Zimbabwe. Two permanent members, China and the Russian Federation, abstained on the two resolutions on the Sudan (1054 and 1070).

The third set of counter-terrorism sanctions, on the Taliban regime in Afghanistan, had several novel features. One, the initial resolution (1267 of 15 October 1999), which focused on the provision of sanctuary and training for Osama bin Laden and associated terrorists following the August 1998 bombing of the US embassies in Nairobi and Dar es Salaam, was the first counter-terrorism sanctions resolution to be passed unanimously by the Council. Two, it applied only to the portions of Afghanistan territory occupied by the Taliban regime. Three, its scope, in terms both of targets and measures taken, varied over time through a series of successor resolutions. Initially addressing just the Taliban regime, 1267 not only imposed the by then familiar aircraft restrictions but also froze Taliban financial assets. Resolution 1333 of 19 December 2000, on the other hand, went further, adding an arms embargo, as well as financial sanctions on non-state actors: Osama bin Laden, the Al-Qaida organization, and their associates.[29] And four, this is the only one of the 1990s counter-terrorism sanctions regimes to remain in place today, as the Council's 1267 sanctions committee and a related expert monitoring group, established by Resolution 1363 of 30 July 2001, are still quite active. All of these resolutions and measures, it should be noted, were in place prior to the terrorist attacks on the United States of 11 September 2001.

Unlike these more purposeful efforts to confront states and groups assisting terrorism, the Council inadvertently backed into an operational role in attempting to curb the further proliferation of WMD. Indeed, had Saddam Hussein not decided to invade, occupy, and absorb a much smaller neighbor, Kuwait, the Council might well have continued to keep its distance from proliferation issues for years to come. None of its resolutions prior to or during the Council-authorized war with Iraq in 1991 featured the goal of eliminating Iraqi WMD capabilities, though that regime's previous use of chemical weapons against its own Kurdish population, as well as against Iran, was widely known and reported. With the conclusion of hostilities, Resolution 687 of 3 April 1991 – the so-called "mother of all resolutions" – included a provision calling for "the destruction, removal, or rendering harmless" of Iraq's chemical and biological weapons and ballistic missiles with a range over 150km, for the establishment of a UN Special Commission (later known as UNSCOM) to carry this out, for IAEA inspections and reporting, and for the renunciation and destruction of any Iraqi nuclear capabilities.

Thus began the most ambitious and innovative, initially promising, but ultimately frustrating chapter in the history of Council attempts to enforce its decisions taken under Chapter VII.[30] The UNSCOM inspectors, despite persistent resistance from the Iraqi government,[31] managed both to uncover the latter's extensive but well hidden program to develop biological weapons, and to destroy more of Iraqi WMD and missile stocks than had been accomplished through the coalition's massive bombing raids.[32] Despite these impressive accomplishments, the UNSCOM operation could not entirely overcome two major political-legal hurdles: one, that the Iraqi government was still deemed by the international community to be sovereign over its territory; and two, that the Security Council was deeply divided over how far the sanctions and inspections regimes could be pushed under the circumstances.[33] In December 1998, the UNSCOM contingent was finally withdrawn from Iraq on the eve of a renewed bombing campaign by the US and United Kingdom aimed at destroying remaining Iraqi WMD assets. A year later, the Council voted to replace UNSCOM with UNMOVIC, the United Nations Monitoring, Verification and Inspection Commission (Resolution 1284 of 17 December 1999), with a somewhat weaker mandate. It was not until late November 2002, however, that UNMOVIC was able to exercise any operational responsibilities on the ground in Iraq and the inspectors' brief stay ended with the military intervention by the US-led coalition in March 2003.

In 1993, the Council faced a distant, distinct, but equally difficult case of WMD proliferation: North Korea.[34] In March of that year, Pyongyang informed the Security Council of its intention to withdraw from the NPT.[35] Through its inspections of North Korean facilities in 1992 and 1993, the IAEA had found numerous discrepancies in Pyongyang's reporting of the amount of nuclear material in its possession. These events, plus North Korea's refusal to permit special inspections by the Agency, led the IAEA Board of Governors to find that North Korea was in non-compliance and the IAEA Director-General to make the first such referral to the Security Council. Some members of the Council, however, were less than eager to take up the issue, much less to impose sanctions on the country caught violating the NPT and the IAEA statute.

The Council responded to the crisis with a much more measured and temperate stance than it had in the case of Iraq. Resolution 825 of 11 May 1993 merely (1) called on the North Koreans to "reconsider" their withdrawal announcement, to "reaffirm" their commitment to the Treaty, and to comply with their safeguards agreement with the IAEA; (2) requested the Director-General of the IAEA to continue to consult with Pyongyang; and (3) urged all member states to encourage North Korea to respond positively and to facilitate a solution. China and Pakistan, however, apparently finding even this language too strong, abstained. While Washington was reported to want stronger measures, North Korea's neighbors sought to avoid sanctions or other steps that might escalate an already tense situation. Besides, Pyongyang had long favored bilateral talks with the US and the Council, in essence, found the notion of punting the matter to Washington to be the path of least resistance. The resulting bilaterals produced, in October 1994, something the multilateral channels could not: an Agreed Framework that some saw as rewarding the North for bad behavior but that had the considerable virtue of freezing the North Korean nuclear program.

For the third time in that decade, the Council faced a WMD proliferation crisis when India and then Pakistan conducted a series of nuclear weapon tests in May 1998.[36] This time, the Council spoke with one voice. Following the three Indian underground tests on 11 and 13 May, the President of the Council issued a statement on its behalf strongly deploring the tests and reiterating the assertion from the summit-level meeting of the Council in January 1992 that "the proliferation of all weapons of mass destruction constitutes a threat to international peace and security."[37] A similar presidential statement was issued on 29 May following Pakistan's underground tests.[38] The foreign ministers of the five permanent members, in a rare display of unity, then met in Geneva to issue a strong statement condemning the tests, expressing their deep concern about the danger to peace and security in the region, and pledging collaborative efforts on a number of fronts.[39] This was followed by a unanimous resolution of the Council (1172 of 6 June 1998) that condemned the tests, demanded that the two rivals refrain from any further testing, and urged a series of steps to ease tensions.

Though the vigor and unity of purpose expressed in the flurry of statements was impressive, equally striking was the absence of sanctions or even the threat of such measures in any of them. The US, as national legislation required, invoked sanctions against both states, but then quickly eased them.[40] Unlike Iraq or North Korea, India and Pakistan had not violated the NPT because they were not parties. Moreover, it would be difficult to effectively sanction such large and diverse economies. Besides, both countries were strategically significant (a status that would be further enhanced in the post-9/11 global struggle against terrorism). So the Council, in this case, managed to have its cake and eat it too. It spoke out loudly and unambiguously against further WMD proliferation, yet once again demonstrated that it is a highly political body that addresses even major matters of principle on a case-by-case basis.

Merging agendas in the post-9/11/01 world

As the foregoing discussion suggests, the Security Council's handling of terrorism can be roughly described as having evolved through three stages: Cold War, post-Cold War, and post-9/11/01. The post-Cold War period saw a great leap in terms of the Council's sense of unity and commitment to counter-terrorism as one of its core responsibilities, even to the extent of employing sanctions in several cases. With ambiguity about the Council's mission already largely dispelled, the terrorist assault on the US of 9/11/01 led, as chronicled below, to (1) the institutionalization of the Council's counter-terrorism efforts; (2) the refinement and development of a wide range of techniques for curbing terrorism; (3) the globalization and standardization of efforts to prevent and deter terrorism; and (4) the convergence, to some degree, of the counter-proliferation and counter-terrorism agendas.

For many member states, of course, the most immediate threats came not from terrorists acquiring WMD, but from their use of more conventional means – car bombings, suicide bombers, assassinations, abductions, hijackings, etc. – and from their targeting of governmental, legal, and social-economic institutions. Likewise, concerns about the acquisition of WMD by additional states, particularly those that do not fit easily into the norms, rules, and expectations of the so-called "international community," remain unabated (in part because of worry that rogue states would become conduits for passing WMD assets on to terrorists). But beyond state-to-state proliferation, the scale and ambitions of the 9/11 attacks and the global rhetoric and goals of transnational groups, such as Al-Qaida, have fueled apprehensions of the possible consequences of the terrorist acquisition of usable WMD capabilities. The most powerful members of the Security Council, of course, would seem to be among the most likely targets of such violent groups seeking to overturn the status quo. Hence the permanent members have sought to enlist the UN, and especially the Security Council, in a global prevention strategy.

The Council responded to the 9/11 attacks with unaccustomed vigor, unity, and dispatch. Some of the delegates could see the collapse of the World Trade Center from their offices. They could not have had a more dramatic introduction into the dangers posed by newer, more globalized forms of terrorism. The next day, the Council and the Assembly passed unanimous resolutions condemning the attacks in no uncertain terms.[41] The Council resolution (1368) included far-reaching language of a generic, as well as specific, character. It pronounced terrorism to be a threat to international peace and security and, employing much of the wording of Article 51, affirmed that the right of individual and collective self-defense justified a forceful response by a state victimized by terrorism. Things had come full circle from the Cold War days, when the Council expressed more concern about counter-terrorism than terrorism itself.

Just how far such a response could go and whether preventive or preemptive action would be justified, however, was open to interpretation and debate.[42] But in the months that followed, there was reason to believe that

1368 amounted to the Council's authorization of the use of military force against those who had assisted and/or provided sanctuary for Osama bin Laden and his Al-Qaida associates. It was suggestive, in that regard, that, when the Council subsequently passed a series of resolutions dealing with Afghanistan, it never even mentioned that a US-led military intervention was underway there to overthrow the Taliban regime and, if possible, to capture bin Laden.

On 28 September, little more than two weeks after 1368, the Council again voted unanimously for an ambitious and unprecedented counter-terrorism resolution.[43] Like 1368, 1373 was crafted in sweeping and generic terms. This time, however, the Council supplied a detailed and seemingly exhaustive list of obligations that states should undertake in the collective struggle against terrorism. They were, of course, to "refrain from providing any form of support, active or passive, to entities or persons involved in terrorist acts." Moreover, they were to freeze any assets of such individuals or groups, prohibit them from raising or transferring funds, and bar them sanctuary, safe passage, arms or any other form of material support. In addition, and this spoke to a role for the world body, national governments were to share information on suspected terrorist activities, bolster their national capacities for counter-terrorism, and report to the Council's latest subsidiary body, the Counter-Terrorism Committee (CTC), on their progress in implementing 1373's myriad provisions. Despite these potentially onerous or burdensome undertakings, initially the resolution generated the ungrudging support of the Council's membership, while the relatively transparent, inclusive, and interactive manner in which the CTC conducted its business reassured non-members of the Council.

As broad and inclusive as 1368 and 1373 were, the Council was hardly finished with its enunciation of counter-terrorism resolutions enforceable under Chapter VII. Two more unanimous resolutions followed in 2004. On 28 April, 1540 codified the marriage of the non-proliferation and counter-terrorism agendas, consummated after a long engagement. Spurred by alarming press reports and fresh information produced by Libya's conversion to the anti-proliferation camp, 1540 stressed that the Council was "gravely concerned" by the efforts of terrorists to acquire WMD and "by the threat of illicit trafficking in nuclear, chemical, or biological weapons and their means of delivery, and related materials." Similar in form and content to 1373, 1540 called on all states to "refrain from providing any form of support" to such groups, to adopt and enforce effective counter-trafficking legislation, to take a series of steps to control such weapons and materials, to adopt and implement the relevant international conventions, to enhance their cooperation with international agencies, industry and the public, to assist those states facing implementation problems, and, of course, to report to a new subsidiary committee of the Council on progress in implementing this resolution.[44]

The rationale for the Council's second counter-terrorism resolution in 2004 was less clear and, to some, less compelling. The chief sponsor of Resolution 1566 (8 October 2004) was the Russian Federation, whose long-standing concerns about terrorism had been heightened by the extensive loss of young life when terrorists occupied a school in Beslan. The resolution was wide-ranging, to say the least. It provided a further working definition of terrorism (operational para. 3); called for the completion and adoption of a comprehensive convention and a convention on acts of nuclear terrorism; requested the CTC to develop a set of best practices in implementing 1373's curbs on terrorist financing; and established a working group, rather than a fully fledged committee, to consider practical measures for dealing with terrorist groups other than Al-Qaida/Taliban, and to assess the prospects for developing an international fund to compensate the victims of terrorism and their families.

Again inspired by a disturbing terrorist incident, this time the July 2005 assault on London's public transportation system, the Council adopted yet another unanimous counter-terrorism resolution on 14 September 2005. Resolution 1624, however, was adopted at a summit-level meeting held in conjunction with the global summit. For once not taken under Chapter VII, 1624 calls on states to "prohibit by law incitement to commit a terrorist act or acts," to "prevent such conduct," and to "deny safe haven" for those engaging in such behavior, as well as to strengthen the security of their borders and to continue a dialogue among civilizations. As always, states were to report to the CTC on the steps they were taking to implement the provisions of the resolution.

One of the striking features of these five post-9/11 resolutions is their generic character. Four of the five seek to establish a global system of standards, expectations, reporting, and assessment that apply equally to all states, not just UN member states. Through these interactions between the Council and individual states, weaknesses in state capacity, laws, and practices are to be identified, along with those governments or organizations that can be of assistance in patching these gaps. While the UN may be short on material support, it can provide expertise and practical experience, while acting as a clearing house between those needing help and those willing to provide it. In some sensitive cases, the UN label could conceivably help to open political doors in societies where direct and visible assistance from one of the major powers might not be welcome. Likewise, on several subjects best practices are to be identified and disseminated so that states can learn from each other. The Council, in this scheme, becomes more of a facilitator than an enforcer. Indeed, the one post-9/11 resolution on enforcement – 1368 – leaves that task to the victim, should an international response not be forthcoming. In contrast, a number of the counter-terrorism resolutions before 9/11 addressed how the international community should respond to individual cases of terrorism. During those years, the more generic resolutions lacked reporting requirements or the establishment of a Council subsidiary body to institutionalize the parent body's ongoing involvement with the matter.[45]

Where there is standard setting, capacity-building, and reporting, of course, there is also likely to be a growing bureaucracy nearby. By national standards, not to mention compared to the magnitude of the task, the size of the UN counter-terrorism bureaucracy remains decidedly modest, but, in the context of support staff for the Council, it casts a comparatively large shadow. At the time of the attacks on the United States, UN headquarters in New York had no staff or office assigned to deal with terrorism and the UN's miscast and misnamed Terrorism Prevention Branch (TPB) in Vienna could only boast two mid-level professional posts (at the P-4 and P-5 levels). A year later, nothing had changed. In December 2002, the General Assembly finally assented to adding an increment of three professional and two support posts to the TPB, which was to carry out the new mandate for administrative and legislative capacity-building in member states around the world.[46]

The CTC, charged with the responsibility of soliciting and reacting to the reports of what 192 countries were doing to curb terrorism, also started small. Without an earmarked budgetary allocation and funded temporarily through a fund for special political missions, for its first two years the CTC was supported by a half-dozen technical experts, on short-term contract from outside the UN system. While the UN secretariat provided some general support service, Sir Jeremy Greenstock, the CTC's first chair and the Permanent Representative of the United Kingdom to the UN, complained that "the CTC tends to be allocated the resources that are left over when everything else has been covered."[47] In 2004, his successor, Inocencio F. Arias, Spain's Permanent Representative to the UN, pressed for the reorganization and enlargement of the CTC's professional staff. The resulting plan called for the creation of a Counter-Terrrorism Committee Executive Directorate (CTED) with twenty professional posts.[48] Adopted by the Council in Resolution 1535 of 26 March 2004, the CTED, headed by Javier Rupérez of Spain at the Assistant Secretary-General level, has since grown to an overall staff of about forty posts, including one seconded from the Office of the High Commissioner for Human Rights (OHCHR) to address the sometimes problematic human rights implications of national counter-terrorism programs.[49] In addition, the 1267 monitoring team and the 1540 committee are supported by eight experts each,[50] while the 1566 working group depends on national missions for support. The Council, therefore, now has around sixty professionals to help carry out its counter-terrorism work.

The reporting process has been a labor-intensive exercise, involving successive rounds of cajoling, clarifying, digesting, assessing, correcting, and discussing the national inputs. The initial CTC results were encouraging.[51] During the first round, all 191 member states submitted reports to the Committee, though some, of course, were far more candid and detailed than others. According to the reports, a substantial number of member states were reassessing their domestic laws and administrative structures and, in many cases, strengthening them to better implement the requirements of resolution 1373. Over time, however, member states began to complain more about "reporting fatigue" with each successive round of reporting-assessment-reporting. According to the CTC, 191 member states and six others responded to the first round, 144 member states and two others to the second, 124 plus one to the third, and 88 to the fourth.[52] Following in the CTC's wake, the response to the 1540 committee's reporting request has been slow and uneven. As of 16 December 2005, only 124 states and one organization had submitted reports.[53]

Written reports, of course, have their limitations as an assessment tool. To no one's surprise, the states of greatest concern have had rather little to say of fresh substantive value in their declarations. In contrast, most states have been quite responsible in their reporting, while others appear to have the will but have lacked the bureaucratic capacity to respond regularly. The problem states are those that appear to have the capacity but not the will to do so. Whether to begin a process of naming and shaming such member states has been debated for many months among the Committee members, but a decision to go that route seems unlikely given the group's consensus rule. Instead, the CTC has been giving renewed attention to the more positive instruments in its toolkit.

For example, with the host's consent, the CTC has begun to take fact-finding visits to selected member states to supplement the written submissions and to inform capacity-building efforts. In 2005, visits were undertaken to Albania, Kenya, Morocco and Thailand, with visits planned in 2006 to Algeria, the Philippines and the United Republic of Tanzania. These missions have helped the CTED staff identify where assistance in capacity building is most needed, whether on the legislative, judicial, administrative, or law enforcement side, and which government or organization might be best placed to provide it. The CTC has also sought to accelerate the number of states signing and ratifying the global counter-terrorism conventions. In this, it appears to have been quite successful.[54] By engaging in such a range of interactions with the member states, the Committee should be in a good position to encourage a best-practices-based learning process, a core focus of the next steps of its work.

The 1267 committee, on the other hand, has taken a harder line, as would be expected for a body tasked with overseeing an ongoing sanctions regime. Based in large part on information provided by member states, the 1267 committee has compiled a Consolidated List of individuals, groups, and entities associated with the Taliban and Al-Qaida and hence subject to the 1267 sanctions. Questions of due process, however, have been raised about the list and, particularly, about how an errant name can be removed.[55] As noted above, an eight-person monitoring team was created to assist the implementation of the sanctions regime and to assess the results achieved. The team has undertaken visits to selected member states.[56] The committee reports that more progress has been made on carrying out the assets freeze than on implementing the travel ban or arms embargo.[57] Like the CTC, the 1267 committee has relied to some extent on written reports from member states and has begun to identify capacity gaps where international assistance could be helpful.

All of this activity has raised questions both about coordination within the growing Security Council sub-structure and about the appropriate scope of the Council's work and authority. To assist internal coherence, as called for in Resolution 1566, the chairs of the three operational counter-terrorism committees (1267, 1373 and 1540) provided joint briefings to the Security Council in April, July and October 2005, with the chair of the 1566 working group providing further comments.[58] In considering lessons learned, best practices, and other steps that it might recommend to the Council as a whole, the 1566 working group in the first half of 2005 held a session open to non-members of the Council and another one at which this author was invited to provide an independent perspective.[59]

More broadly, a number of member states – including Germany, which served as a non-permanent member in 2003–4 – have charged that the Council here and in other substantive areas has assumed legislative and even judicial roles best left to more representative bodies, such as the General Assembly or ECOSOC.[60] In this regard, it is worth noting that, while the September 2005 global summit produced a relatively strong statement condemning terrorism, it failed to mention the counter-terrorism efforts of the Security Council and called on the General Assembly, instead, to develop the elements of a UN counter-terrorism strategy outlined by the Secretary-General.[61]

Not only is the Security Council not the sole counter-terrorism actor in the UN system, the UN is hardly the only planet in the large, and expanding, counter-terrorism solar system. Prominent among the other planets are Interpol for cooperation on policing matters, the Financial Action Task Force (FATF) on terrorist financing, the G-8's Counter-Terrorism Action Group (CTAG) on resources for capacity-building, the various regimes and agencies seeking to stem the proliferation of different types of weapons, and any number of initiatives by regional and sub-regional organizations, as well as the Bretton Woods institutions and more specialized functional agencies.[62]

Moreover, the UN is ill suited to perform several of the more visible tasks involved in fighting terrorism. As the Secretary-General's Policy Working Group on the UN and Terrorism readily acknowledged, the world body is not "well placed to play an active operational role in efforts to suppress terrorist groups, to pre-empt specific terrorist strikes, or to develop dedicated intelligence-gathering capacities."[63] With several of its diverse member states having a history of sponsoring terrorism, the UN would neither seek nor be entrusted with sensitive intelligence information.[64] In laying out his counterterrorism strategy in a March 2005 speech in Madrid, the Secretary-General applauded the Bush administration's Proliferation Security Initiative (PSI), designed to interdict the illicit transfer of materials or components of weapons of mass destruction. The PSI, according to the Secretary-General, aims "to fill a gap in our defences" and the UN is not expected to play any direct role in its implementation.[65] After all, it has become standard UN doctrine, as enunciated by the past two secretaries-general, that the world organization no longer conducts military enforcement operations.[66]

Enforcement, of course, need not entail the use of force, and some analysts argue that military force is becoming a less relevant tool for fighting terrorists as their networks become more decentralized and amorphous.[67] As detailed above, the Security Council invoked economic, financial, travel and/or arms sanctions three times in the 1990s against states and groups that were alleged to have aided and abetted terrorists. As the Secretary-General noted in Madrid,

> In the past the United Nations has not shrunk from confronting States that harbour and assist terrorists, and the Security Council has repeatedly applied sanctions. Indeed, it is largely thanks to such sanctions that several States which used to sponsor terrorists no longer do so. This firm line must be maintained and strengthened. All States must know that, if they give any kind of support to terrorists, the Council will not hesitate to use coercive measures against them.

Indeed, state-sponsored terrorism does appear to be ebbing, as suggested by the one hundred percent response to the CTC's first round of queries. But how certain is it that the Security Council will respond either to terrorism or to acquisitions of WMD with tough enforcement measures in the future? If anything, Council members seem less inclined to consider sanctions this decade than last. The 2006 IAEA referral of Iran to the Security Council may provide a telling test case on the proliferation front. By the late 1990s, debates over the effectiveness and humanitarian consequences of sanctions spawned a concerted effort to develop a new generation that would be better targeted, less destructive, and, hopefully, more effective.[68] So far, none of the

Council's counter-terrorism subsidiary bodies – each preferring the carrot to the stick – have called for even the naming and shaming of any state. Deterrence may be working, as the Secretary-General contends, but more likely it is propelled by the unilateral enforcement steps undertaken by powerful countries than by the UN.

The Security Council, in other words, finds itself in a paradoxical position in terms of its efforts to curb terrorism and WMD proliferation. On the one hand, it has managed over time to shed its ambivalence about the value and priority of these efforts. It no longer questions which side it is on, and it has become a significant norm builder in both of these areas. It has developed a range of techniques and tools of persuasion to encourage member states to meet their obligations under the relevant conventions, as well as a modest technical staff and institutional sub-structure to facilitate member state implementation of its non-proliferation and counter-terrorism decisions. And it has recognized the dangerous ways in which these agendas are converging. In short, the Council has come a long way toward becoming an integral and purposeful player in the global struggles against WMD proliferation and global terrorism.

On the other hand, the Council seems to be increasingly inclined to pursue this struggle with but half of its Charter-given arsenal. As Chapters 5 and 6 above related, the bold experiments with enforcement in the 1990s have given way to a much softer and more nuanced form of enforcement in the new millennium. Chapter VII is still invoked with great frequency, as a sort of standard rhetorical form, but now with a more shallow and subtle meaning. Denial and prevention seem to be the successors to deterrence and enforce-ment in the Council's lexicon. In terms of forestalling the acquisition and use of WMD by global terrorists, the emerging strategy based on norms, institu-tions, information, and capacity-building may prove to be sensible and sound as well as politically convenient. It certainly has a better chance of uniting the diverse members of the Council and of facilitating collaboration between the Council and other institutional players. What happens when push comes to shove and an imminent and destructive proliferation and/or terrorist threat needs to be confronted directly, however, is less clear. The Council blinked when North Korea challenged it, and Iran could well be its next big test.

Part of the answer lies in the Council's efforts to develop a range of tools that might be labeled soft or non-coercive enforcement. They involve dissua-sion, persuasion, information, visits, peer pressure, and generally raising the political costs for potential violators of non-proliferation and counter-terrorism norms. Another part of the answer involves capacity-building and a best-practices-based learning process aimed at boosting implementation efforts on the national level to advance both sets of norms. It may be that these are the areas where the Council's – and the UN's – comparative advantages lie at this stage of history. Resolution 1368, after all, implied that it would be up to the member states, not the Council, to defend against and respond to individual acts of terrorism. The Council's role would be more in the realm of facilitator, convenor, and legitimator in the longer-term effort to prevent such things from happening in the first place. According to this line of reasoning, prevention is key, for, as the Secretary-General put it, "even one such attack and the chain of events it might set off could change our world forever."[69] In such a dire scenario, the demise of the Security Council as one of the guardians of international peace and security could well be part of the collateral damage.

10 Reform, adaptation, and evolution

The Security Council, from its very inception, has been controversial. In part, this has stemmed from the prevalent perception that the Council has been the one place in the UN system that really matters. In part, it has derived from the pervasive frustration that the Council has never fulfilled the overly high expectations many people and governments have had for it. And, importantly, it reflects an unresolved tension between the sharply but somewhat narrowly defined concept the convening powers had for how the Council should function and the more inclusive and participatory model favored by the UN's larger membership. These differences were as vigorously contested at the founding conference in San Francisco as they have been in the successive rounds of deliberations on Council reform that have since absorbed so much high-level attention in capitals as well as in the General Assembly Hall.

Round one: San Francisco

Franklin Roosevelt knew what he did and did not want in the way of a Security Council. He and the leaders of the other three convening countries, the United Kingdom, the Soviet Union, and China, were determined not to repeat the high-principled, low-performance experience of the League of Nations. The League's Council did not suffer from a democracy deficit: it boasted equal rights, consensus rules, and a growing membership. The League's Council, however, did not get better as it got bigger: it reached its greatest girth in the mid-1930s, on the eve of the Second World War.

Instead of going this failed route, Roosevelt turned to what had worked: the great-power alliance that had led the resistance to the aggression of the Axis powers. His vision revolved around the "four policemen" – later five when France was added at San Francisco – who would, he hoped, band together to enforce the peace and prevent the outbreak of a third world war in the twentieth century.[1] To be certain that the others could not gang up on any of these core countries, the decision to use collective force would have to be taken by unanimity – hence each would have a veto – a sine qua non provision from Moscow's perspective and presumably from the US Senate's as well. Surely there would be room on the Council for a few lesser members of the alliance, for they too had played their part in defeating the Axis powers, but their place in the peace, as in the war, was deemed to be of secondary importance. Indeed, the draft Charter presented by the four convening powers to the San Francisco conference included no criteria for the election of non-permanent members. The key was to perpetuate the security ties among the four policemen for as long as possible into the postwar era, so they were to have permanent seats in the Council. The first test of their capacity to stick together amidst the competing pressures and disparate voices of multilateral forums came, as Chapter 2 chronicled, in San Francisco. At issue, naturally, were the prerogatives that they had reserved for themselves in the Council.

Clearly, the plans for the Council presented by the four convenors to the San Francisco preparatory conference were anything but representative, democratic or equitable. As a result, many of the invited delegations were not about to accept the draft as a fait accompli without a fight over those missing values. Vigorous challenges were voiced in San Francisco to the size of the Council (many preferred fifteen to the proposed eleven); to the notion of permanent seats set aside for the self-selected few; and, most adamantly, to the veto or unanimity provision.[2] More elaborate criteria for the non-permanent, or elected, seats were suggested by several delegations, as was the concept of reserving these places for countries chosen by their regions to represent them.[3]

Though the Big Five – the four convening powers plus France – rejected the notion of regional seats, they did propose an amendment to the Dumbarton Oaks language to add the criteria for non-permanent members that now appears in Article 23(1) of the Charter. The phrase "equitable geographical distribution" was deliberately chosen to avoid any implication that elected members would carry the weight and the burden of representing their neighbors in Council deliberations. According to the official summary of the deliberations in San Francisco, it was also "pointed out that the members of the Security Council should be regarded as trustees of the whole Organization and not as representatives of different world regions" and that those "who could help to preserve peace and security should be elected to non-permanent seats."[4] The geographical criterion, therefore, was also placed last in 23(1).

Through all the debates, however, the convening powers remained largely unified on these core issues, conceding little and insisting, on many grounds and on many fronts, that their vision was the only acceptable vision for the new Council. The challengers had to make do with the promise under Article 109 for a "General Conference of the Members of the United Nations for the purpose of reviewing the present Charter" to be held by the General

Assembly's tenth session in 1955. By that point, however, with the world body deeply divided by Cold War tensions, the Assembly and Council wisely decided to let that opportunity pass.[5] Nevertheless, the Council reform agenda first framed at San Francisco before the Charter was adopted has been pursued, with varying degrees of energy, ever since.

Round two: 1955–65

During the 1950s and 1960s, the UN's substantive pursuits may have been repeatedly frustrated by the Cold War divide, but the influx of new members proved unstoppable. Spurred by the UN's facilitation of the process of decolonization, the world body's membership more than doubled from 1945 (51) to 1963 (114) (compared to today's 192 members). Only three African and three Asian countries were represented at San Francisco, yet more than half of the membership by the early 1960s was from those two developing regions.[6] Pressures for enlarging the Security Council were inevitable and, following the admission of twenty more members over the two previous years, the calls for expansion became more urgent and vocal in 1956. The "gentleman's agreement" on the geographical distribution of non-permanent seats, that had held for a decade was, by that point, becoming untenable. To the socialist and newly independent countries, Latin America and Europe appeared to be over-represented on the Council to the disadvantage of the new majority. The Soviets called for redistributing the six non-permanent seats, while the constitutionally dubious practice of splitting the two-year terms for some of the seats was employed as a temporary measure. For its part, Washington faced two unattractive options: expanding the Council or watching the seats of its Latin American friends and Western European allies continue to be squeezed.

At the eighteenth General Assembly session in 1963, following eight years of frustration, the issue of amending the Charter to permit Council enlargement finally came to a head.[7] Earlier that year, the very first summit resolution from the Organization of African Unity (OAU) had called for Council expansion. By that point, there was little doubt that a large majority in the General Assembly supported such an enlargement, but the Council's five Permanent Members – whose satisfaction would be required for Charter amendment – were still not on board. Each, in fact, had asked for further consultations before the matter was put to a vote.[8] When the vote was nevertheless taken on 17 December, of the five only China – then represented by the Taipei-based Republic of China – gave its assent.[9] France and the Soviet Union voted no, and the United Kingdom and United States abstained. The developing countries were not deterred, however, and Resolution 1991 (XVIII) to expand the Security Council from 11 to 15 members (and the Economic and Social Council, ECOSOC, from 18 to 27 members), to increase the super-majority required to pass non-procedural matters from seven to nine, and to indicate the geographical distribution of the ten non-permanent members passed easily, by a vote of 97 to 11, with four abstentions. So, for the first time, the Assembly had voted to amend the Charter.

The battle then shifted to member state capitals, where any of the five Permanent Members could have killed the measure by failing to ratify the amendment by 1 September 1965, the deadline specified in the resolution. Yet none chose to do so. First the Soviet Union, then China, France, the United Kingdom, and finally the United States relented. Why the change of heart? No doubt Cold War politics and the East-West competition for influence among the newly independent countries of Africa and Asia had a lot to do with it. There may well have been a temptation to free-ride as well, i.e. to leave the onus of going against the tide to Washington. With disunity among the five, the political costs for any one capital to block the will of the rest of the membership would have been substantial.

Another factor appeared to weigh quite heavily in Washington's recalculations. The world body was facing a potentially fateful constitutional and financial crisis triggered by the refusal of the Soviet Union, France, and a number of developing countries to pay their assessed contributions for the pathbreaking UN peacekeeping missions in the Sinai and the Congo, despite Assembly resolutions and a decision of the International Court of Justice (ICJ) calling on them to do so.[10] Under Article 19 of the Charter, the Soviet Union should have been penalized with the loss of its vote in the Assembly in 1964 for being two years behind in its dues payments to the UN, but it threatened to quit the Organization instead. A shaky compromise was reached instead by which no formal votes were taken during that Assembly session, the Soviet and French arrears were set aside, and the US asserted that it too had the right to withhold payments in the future if its supreme national interests required. Concerned about whether the UN could withstand any additional political shocks, and faced with the retreat of the other convening powers, the Johnson administration reversed course and called on the Senate to consent to the ratification of the Charter amendment to expand the Council. By a 71 to zero vote with little debate, the Senate did so on 3 June 1965.[11] Thus, on 31 August 1965, a day before the deadline, the amendments to Articles 23 and 27 enlarging the Council and changing the numbers required for non-procedural votes duly came into force, closing the second chapter in the continuing reform saga.

Round three: 1993–7

Following the enlargement of the Council in 1965, pressures for further expansion eased for a number of years. Cold War tensions insured that the expanded Council remained largely on the sidelines during some of the most serious crises of the 1960s, 1970s and 1980s, such as the Vietnam War, the Iran-Iraq War, and recurrent tensions in the Middle East and Persian Gulf. Much of the reform energies focused on enhancing the UN's capacities for addressing development, economic and social issues. ECOSOC was enlarged in 1973 for the second time, to three times its original size (18 to 27 to 54), with no net gain for its authority, reputation or effectiveness. The General Assembly, and to some extent the Security Council itself, became a battleground for North-South, as well as East-West, struggles over the shape, norms and agendas of global negotiations.

Perversely but understandably, the clamor for reforming the Council returned not during its relatively unproductive years over the last two decades of the East-West contest but rather after its work pace and output surged in the early 1990s with the end of the Cold War. When the General Assembly's Open-Ended Working Group on the Question of Equitable Representation and Increase in the Membership of the Security Council and Other Matters Related to the Security Council was created in 1993, the Council was busier than ever, whether gauged by resolutions passed, presidential statements made, or number of blue helmets and peacekeeping operations deployed in trouble spots around the world.[12] At that point, moreover, no veto had been cast over the previous three years. Questions of equity, representation, transparency, and accountability were being raised once again precisely because the Council had become so active, so consequential, and potentially so intrusive in the political and security affairs of the member states. The Council's rediscovery of its Chapter VII enforcement tools gave a renewed urgency to questions of how, why, and by whom its decisions were being made. With the collapse of the Soviet Union, some also began to ask, less directly, whether the remaining superpower would not begin to dominate the Council's proceedings.

After a few years with scant results, however, many delegates and pundits began to refer to the Assembly Working Group with the impossibly long title as simply the "never-ending Working Group." They had forgotten that the last Council reform round had taken a decade to produce a result. The Working Group divided its mandate in two: Cluster One was to address the higher-visibility issues of membership, including enlargement, the veto and voting procedures, while Cluster Two was to consider how to enhance accountability and transparency by adjusting the Council's working methods and decision-making procedures. The first cluster has produced more rhetorical flourishes and surface concurrence about the urgency of enlargement than convergence about how to do this and who should occupy any additional seats. To date, the second cluster has proven to be the more productive of the two, though it is widely agreed that reform should eventually encompass both clusters.

The first effort to accomplish a simultaneous breakthrough on both fronts came when Razali Ismail of Malaysia was President of the General Assembly in 1996–7. Teaming with the co-chairs of the Working Group, Razali consulted individually with almost all of the member states in an effort to identify a set of reform steps, including both enlargement and working methods, that could gain the support of most of them. The resulting formula had several elements: (1) the addition of five more permanent and four more non-permanent seats, for a total of 24; (2) a date by which the members of the General Assembly would have to select the five Permanent Members according to a specified geographic and economic distribution; (3) a provision that the new Permanent Members would not have veto power and the current ones would be asked to exercise restraint in their employment of that essentially negative instrument; (4) a rule that new and original Permanent Members would be subject to the same calculations in terms of paying a premium surcharge for peacekeeping assessments; (5) the elimination of the enemies clauses in the Charter; (6) the convening of a review conference after ten years to assess the implementation of these reforms; and (7) a raft of eighteen alterations of the Council's working methods to enhance transparency, accountability and inclusiveness.[13] Having received the assurances of two thirds of the membership that they would support this package, Razali submitted his plan to the Working Group for consideration on 20 March 1997.[14] At that point, however, it turned out that only a handful of delegates were willing to endorse the plan publicly and it soon became apparent that there was insufficient political momentum to move forward. As so often in UN reform efforts, another bold initiative had stumbled over the palpable caution, even intransigence, with which most member states approach questions of institutional change.

Round four: 2003–5

This hot-cold pattern was repeated in the most recent round of deliberations, which peaked in mid-2005 with the airing of several alternative proposals, none of which were put to a vote. Once again, the vast majority of member states endorsed the notion of enlargement in theory, but in practice far fewer favored putting any particular formula to a vote. For a number of years, those large countries with ambitions for attaining a permanent seat have been increasingly restive over the slow pace and indecisive deliberations of the Working Group. Sensing their growing frustration and concerned about the Council's performance in the run-up to the use of force in Iraq in the spring of 2003, Secretary-General Kofi Annan decided to highlight Council enlargement in his call that September for a "radical" overhaul of the UN's inter-governmental machinery.[15] Though his predecessors had resisted the temptation to become personally involved in the unending tug of war among the member states over the size and shape of the Council, Annan declared an "urgent need" to make it "more broadly representative of the international community as a whole, as well as the geopolitical realities of today."[16] With a flair for drama, if not historical accuracy, he cautioned the member states that "we have come to a fork in the road. This may be a moment no less decisive than 1945 itself, when the United Nations was founded."

To chart the implications of a range of emerging security threats for the member states and for the world body, the Secretary-General commissioned a High-level Panel on Threats, Challenges and Change (HLP).[17] Much of its December 2004 final report spoke to the interconnections among threats from pandemics to terrorism, from proliferation to poverty, as the security agendas of the North and the South have begun to merge in important respects.[18] But among its diverse collection of 101 recommendations, those few relating to the reform of the Security Council, not surprisingly, gained by far the most public, press, and governmental attention.[19] The Council, the Panel found, had indeed become more active and effective since the end of the Cold War. In its view, however, the Council's decisions had too often lacked realism, equity, and consistency, resulting in inadequate follow-up and implementation by the UN's membership as a whole.[20] To enhance the Council's credibility and capacity, the Panel offered a series of four principles to guide its enlargement, which it termed "a necessity."[21]

Not unlike the member states, however, the Panel could not agree on a single formula for accomplishing this. Instead, it put forward a Model A and a Model B.[22] In several respects, both models resembled the Razali Plan of seven years earlier: they called for an expansion to twenty-four, a geographical distribution of seats, a more equitable North-South balance, the denial of veto power to new members, an appeal to the current Permanent Members to exercise restraint in employing this tool, and a review conference (in 2020). The new plans, however, omitted Razali's emphasis on working methods, instead praising how much the Council had already accomplished in this area.[23] Model A called for six new permanent seats – two for Africa, two for Asia and the Pacific, one for Europe and one for the Americas – and three more non-permanent, two-year, non-renewable seats. Model B, on the other hand, envisioned no additional permanent seats, but rather the creation of a new category of eight four-year, renewable seats, plus one more two-year, non-renewable seat.

Three and a half months later, on 21 March 2005, Secretary-General Annan issued his own reform report, with scores of recommendations for consideration by heads of state and government, at a September 2005 global summit. In some areas, the findings of this new report, *In Larger Freedom: Towards Development, Security and Human Rights for All*, differed from those of the High-level Panel.[24] In the case of the Security Council, however, he simply endorsed the conclusions of the Panel and urged the member states "to consider the two options, models A and B, proposed in that report . . . or any other viable proposals in terms of size and balance that have emerged on the basis of either model." He called for agreement prior to the September summit, by consensus if possible, "but if they are unable to reach consensus this must not become an excuse for postponing action."[25] He reiterated his conviction that "no reform of the United Nations would be complete without reform of the Security Council."[26]

In some respects, the Secretary-General's rationale for Council reform covered familiar ground: its composition needed to be adjusted "to make it more broadly representative of the international community as a whole, as well as of the geopolitical realities of today, and thereby more legitimate in the eyes of the world."[27] But he also offered some novel perspectives. The founders, he noted, had created three Councils to address security, economic and social matters, and trusteeship, respectively. However,

> the division of responsibilities between them has become less and less balanced: the Security Council has increasingly asserted its authority and, especially since the end of the Cold War, has enjoyed greater unity of purpose among its Permanent Members but has seen that authority questioned on the grounds that its composition is anachronistic or insufficiently representative.[28]

His conclusion: "we need to restore the balance."[29] Presumably his intention was not to suggest that the Security Council should be enlarged until it becomes as ineffective as the other two Councils have been. However, as Chapters 2 and 3 above explain, the founders had no intention of equating the three Councils, whose powers, prerogatives and procedures were to be on very different levels. On the one hand, it may seem curious that the Secretary-General did not celebrate the post-Cold War unity and assertiveness of the Security Council. On the other hand, however, this apparent wariness did reflect the tenor of much of the Council reform debate, as member states not on the Council watched its revival with some hesitation and ambivalence.

Among the member states, Models A and B each had their following, though the latter had a less impressive one. Others looked for an alternative model: either one that would be smaller than twenty-four or one that would put more emphasis on working methods and that would speak more directly to the needs of smaller states. Four large aspirants for permanent seats, Brazil, Germany, India and Japan, known as the G-4, put forward a variant of Model A for consideration by the Assembly.[30] Like Model A, the G-4 proposed adding six more permanent seats: two from Africa, two from Asia, one from Latin America and the Caribbean, and one from the Western European and Others Group.[31] The G-4, however, called for an increment of four more non-permanent members, not three, for a total of twenty-five members in the enlarged Council. The G-4 also hedged a bit in terms of the veto, vowing that "the new permanent members shall not exercise the right of veto until the question of the extension of the right of veto to new permanent members has been decided upon in the framework of the review" called for fifteen years after these amendments enter into force.[32] While the Razali Plan had called for a review conference after ten years and the High-level Panel for one in 2020, neither contemplated any reconsideration of the decision not to extend veto power to the new Permanent Members.

The G-4 countries have not been the only would-be reformers to be vexed about what to say or do about the veto. As noted earlier, this was the single most divisive issue at San Francisco. The five Permanent Members insured, in the hurdles established for amending the Charter, that they would retain a veto over relinquishing the veto. Though the veto has few defenders among the 192 member states, other than the five, of course, the best that its detractors can do is raise the political costs of its use. Indeed, as Figure 1.1 illustrates, the veto has been employed much less frequently since the end of the Cold War, only seventeen times in the fifteen years from 1991 through 2005. There apparently has been some degree of self-restraint. Calling its use "anachronistic and undemocratic," the Razali Plan urged "the original permanent members of the Security Council to limit the exercise of their veto power to actions taken under Chapter VII of the Charter."[33] The High-level Panel asked "the permanent members, in their individual capacities, to pledge themselves to refrain from the use of the veto in cases of genocide and large-scale human rights abuses."[34] The Secretary-General, no doubt wisely, passed on the issue.

In 2004–5, as in 1996–7, the notion of expanding the number of Permanent Members was opposed by a geographically diverse group of countries that had qualms about one of their larger neighbors achieving this status and/or concerns about how Council members for life could ever be held accountable. In Razali's time dubbed the "coffee club," this loose coalition of mostly middle powers, such as Pakistan, Italy, Spain, South Korea, Argentina, Mexico, Canada and Turkey, took on the more attractive mantle of "uniting for consensus" in 2005. Their draft resolution proposed doubling the number of non-permanent members from ten to twenty, thereby expanding the Council to twenty-five members as well.[35] They would also amend Article 23(2) of the Charter to permit non-permanent members to be "eligible for immediate re-election, subject to the decision of their respective geographical groups."[36] Under this plan, decisions of the Council would require the affirmative vote of fifteen of its twenty-five members, compared to fourteen of twenty-five under the G-4 proposal and fifteen of twenty-four under the Razali Plan.

With the encouragement of the Secretary-General and the summit approaching, the long-simmering politics of Council reform and expansion reached a boiling point in the spring and summer of 2005. The general membership, however, remained deeply divided over core structural issues, such as whether to add more Permanent Members or to give them the veto, as well as over choosing which states should move up the status ladder. Neither the G-4 nor uniting for consensus plans, therefore, could gain the requisite two thirds vote in the Assembly. Like Razali, they found the uphill climb simply too steep to be completed. Indeed, in several respects the politics of 2005 were even more difficult than those of 1997.[37] China, which had been remarkably quiet during Razali's quest, vigorously opposed a permanent seat for Japan during the latest round. Beijing, faced with (or encouraging) street demonstrations against a Japanese seat, made frustrating Tokyo's ambition a top foreign policy priority.[38] Arguing that differences among the member states were "further expanding instead of narrowing down" and that they "need more time" for dialogue and consultation, the Chinese Permanent Representative to the UN, Ambassador Wang Guangya, stressed in July 2005 that "China is firmly opposed to setting an artificial timeframe for Security Council reform."[39]

US concerns about expansion had also hardened since 1997. The Clinton administration had supported an expansion to twenty or twenty-one members and had endorsed the bids of its two allies, Japan and Germany, for permanent seats. It also favored permanent seats for unnamed developing countries from Africa, Asia and Latin America, as reflected in the Razali Plan.[40] By the next round, however, the Democrats were no longer in control in Washington and the Bush administration had already experienced some trying times in its relations with the world body. In that regard, it is ironic that the very 2003 debate in the Council over the use of force in Iraq that had triggered the Secretary-General's push for Council expansion, had the opposite effect in Washington DC.

In his September 2003 speech to the Assembly calling for the radical overhaul of the Council, the Secretary-General also bemoaned the "unilateral and lawless use of force" without the Council's authorization.[41] It required no stretch of the imagination for US policy-makers to interpret the call for a much larger Council with a raft of new permanent members as an effort to dilute US influence in the Council and to increase the number of members that might oppose future US plans to employ its dominant military assets in the pursuit of narrow objectives. It had been only months before, in the debate over Iraq, that some members of the Council had suggested that one of the purposes of the body should be to counter-balance the ambitions of the last superpower. Given these developments, it is not surprising that the Bush administration did not share its predecessor's enthusiasm for providing a permanent seat for Germany.[42]

Though not submitting a detailed plan, the US did articulate several elements of one. Secretary of State Condoleezza Rice assured the General Assembly that the US "is open to expanding the Security Council" and believes that it should "reflect the world as it is in 2005 – not as it was in 1945."[43] She and other US officials consistently stressed that the Council's effectiveness should be the prime criterion. To this end, the US proposed a series of criteria "to measure a country's readiness for a permanent seat."[44] It insisted that Japan met these criteria and suggested that it would "support adding two or so new permanent members based on those criteria." It would also "endorse the addition of two or three additional non-permanent seats, based on geographic selection, to expand the Council to 19 or 20."[45]

In extremis, of course, either Beijing or Washington could have killed an amendment to enlarge the Council by refusing to ratify it. But in 2005, the advocates of expansion still could not surmount the first hurdle of gathering a two thirds majority in the Assembly. Africa, much more than in 1997, proved to be the elusive key. Though the largest regional bloc in the world body, with fifty-three members, Africa, like Latin America and the Caribbean, has no permanent members in the Council. Under Model A or the G-4 plan, there would be two permanent members from Afria. But which two? In order to preserve trans-African unity to the extent possible and to encourage any new African permanent member to feel some obligation to try to represent the region as a whole on the Council, Africa was the only region to attempt to select regional candidates to serve permanently on the Council. As of mid-2006, it has not succeeded. The most widely discussed possibilities were South Africa, Nigeria and Egypt, with several smaller states nominating themselves. Rather than join the G-4 campaign to make it a more appealing G-6 effort, in the end the potential African candidates concluded that African unity, at least at that point, was a higher priority.[46]

Forty-three African member states did introduce a draft resolution as a third option.[47] It differed from Model A and the G-4 plan in two important respects. One, it insisted that the new permanent members should be accorded "the same prerogatives and privileges as those of the current permanent members, including the right of veto." Two, it contended that Africa should receive two more non-permanent seats – not one as in the other plans – as well as the two permanent seats. This would enlarge the Council to twenty-six members, not the twenty-four contemplated by Razali or the twenty-five by the High-level Panel, seven of these from Africa alone. At a rump summit of the African Union Assembly at the end of October 2005, these demands, as a matter of equity and justice, were reaffirmed.[48] Given the African, US, and Chinese positions, as well as the continuing stalemate between the G-4 and uniting for consensus, the prospects for Council enlargement appeared as murky and doubtful in mid-2006 as they did at the release of the High-level Panel report a year and a half earlier.

Working methods

While most of the headlines and high-level attention in capitals has been focused on who sits around the Council's horseshoe table in its formal Chamber, many insiders have understood that the reform of its working methods is every bit as essential to improving Council performance. Indeed, for most member states the matter of Council working methods would have a more immediate impact than would enlargement. In an organization of 192 member states, relatively few would have realistic chances of becoming a permanent or even semi-permanent member of the Council even if its current membership was doubled or tripled. Composition concerns formal membership, while working methods address how those members relate to and seek to "represent" the much larger membership outside the Council circle. Even an awkwardly large Council would not be representative unless new working methods to assure greater transparency, accountability and inclusiveness were also introduced.

Over the dozen years that the Assembly's Working Group on Security Council reform has been in business, there has been far greater progress on Cluster Two (working methods) than on Cluster One (composition, veto) issues. This is somewhat paradoxical, because the Assembly has no authority over how a parallel inter-governmental body, the Security Council, conducts its affairs. Where it does have authority, over proposing amendments to the Charter, it has been unable to find a political basis for action. On the one hand, the two reform clusters are related substantively, in part because deficits in working methods would be even more apparent in an expanded Council. Politically, on the other hand, the impetus for working methods reform could well ebb once the Council is expanded, particularly if the number of permanent members is enlarged. Recognizing this political reality, as well as the fact that a change in working methods requires neither Charter amendment nor an Assembly resolution, while enlargement requires both, a number of smaller states, led by Switzerland, have been trying to keep working methods reform high on the change agenda.[49] Their efforts have seen some success, as both the G-4 and uniting for consensus draft resolutions contained a series of suggestions for modifications in working methods.[50]

In explaining why it would have little to say on the subject, the High-level Panel commented that, "in recent years, many informal improvements have been made to the transparency and accountability of the Security Council's deliberations."[51] Like other UN organs, the Council has proven to be much more adept at adaptation to changing circumstances than at formal reform. Necessity becomes the mother of invention. For the Council, it is reasonable to assume that the accelerating pace and changing profile of its activities, more than pressures from the Assembly Working Group, induced it to alter its working methods in a number of respects during the 1990s and, to a less dramatic extent, during the early years of the new millennium. Among the modifications undertaken were the following:

- Under the Arria formula, a member of the Council invites the others to meet, outside of the Council Chamber, with one or more independent experts for a candid exchange of views on a pressing issue before the Council. This practice, which permits more direct input from civil society and encourages Council members to reflect on the complexities of the choices facing them, was once considered to be quite innovative, but has now become standard operating behavior. Now there are frequent informal and formal meetings with agency heads and others with knowledge of developments in the field.

- The Council has also participated in a number of retreats, away from headquarters, with the Secretary-General, other UN officials, and sometimes leading independent experts. For the last three years, for example, the Finnish Mission has sponsored a "Hitting the Ground Running" workshop at which the fifteen current and five incoming members of the Council discuss the Council's work, working methods and plans off site.[52]

- The Council members have undertaken a number of missions to visit areas where developments are of particular interest or concern to the Council. This has allowed much more extensive contact with government officials, non-governmental groups, and UN personnel on the ground in regions of crisis. Some of these have been co-sponsored by ECOSOC.

- The Council has met a number of times since the end of the Cold War at either the foreign minister or summit level, including to discuss counter-terrorism at the time of the September 2005 global summit.

- To assist transparency and accountability, it has become common practice for the President of the Council to brief non-members, and often the press, on the results of informal (private) consultations.

- Tentative monthly forecasts and the provisional agendas for the Council's upcoming work are now provided regularly to non-members, as are provisional draft resolutions.[53]

- Consultations among Security Council members and troop contributors, along with key secretariat officials, are now held on a more regular basis.
- As the Council's agenda and responsibilities have grown, so has its reliance on subsidiary bodies. Mostly chaired by non-permanent members and operating by consensus, several of the currently 25 subsidiary bodies have developed expert staffs, receive reports from member states, and undertake fact-finding, monitoring, and capacity-building missions around the world. (For a list of the subsidiary bodies as of February 2006, see Box 3.1 in Chapter 3 above.)
- Through the work of its subsidiary bodies, as well as in plenary, the Council has begun to include non-members in its work on a more regular and substantive basis.

While acknowledging the progress that has been made on working methods, most member states contend that it has not gone nearly far enough. For example, the ten non-permanent members of the Security Council called for the institutionalization of the steps that had been taken, for taking several of them further, and for more public meetings and fewer informal consultations.[54] It is questionable, however, whether all of the transparency and reporting measures called for would result in a more efficient or effective Security Council. The bulk of the negotiations among the members are bound to be carried out in private, and the public sessions of the Council have become highly formal and ritualistic, largely as opportunities for restating official positions and for public rationalizations. Even non-members of the Council frequently complain of the number and repetitiveness of the speeches given in the formal, public sessions. While it would aid accountability to require states to explain why they cast each veto, and the Council could be more analytical and forthcoming in its reports to the General Assembly, excessively detailed or frequent reporting could make it that much harder for an already overburdened Council to devote sufficient time and attention to its wide-ranging substantive work.

Unanswered (unasked?) questions

In his September 2003 speech to the General Assembly urging "radical" reform of the Security Council, Secretary-General Annan sounded reassuring, almost sanguine, about the prospects. "Virtually all Member States agree," he noted, "that the Council should be enlarged, but there is no agreement on the details."[55] As the "never-ending" Working Group has discovered after a dozen years of earnest deliberation, however, in this case the devil lies indeed in the details. Moreover, as this chapter has related, the so-called "details" involve a host of political and security matters that deeply concern capitals. Reforming the Security Council has not languished for lack of attention from national decision-makers. Quite the opposite: it has proven difficult precisely because member states appreciate the importance of what the Council does or fails to do. Though virtually every member state complains about the way the Council functions or who makes its decisions, they keep giving it more and more work to do.

Even the bitterness of the 2005 debate over expansion testified to the centrality of the issues at stake. "Every potential solution," Thomas G. Weiss and Barbara Crossette observe, "brings as many problems as it solves." This debate, in their view, "presents a microcosm of a perpetual problem: the UN is so consumed with getting the process right that it neglects consequences."[56] While much of the debate understandably has revolved around questions of equity, balance, access and representation – things that matter in assessing the legitimacy of a political decision-making body – ultimately the Council will be judged on how well it performs its core function of maintaining international peace and security. The unanswered questions are myriad. On what basis should the Council's performance be assessed? Is it getting better or worse? Is the prognosis so bleak that the only option is radical surgery? Which reform steps would lead to better performance, not just improved process? Have the flaws in the Council's procedures and composition begun to undermine its performance, for example, by reducing its credibility, authority and legitimacy? Or are such claims merely pretexts for advancing narrow status and power interests of those ambitious states that want to be part of a good thing?

Does size matter? On the one hand, would a Council of twenty-four or twenty-five be so much more unwieldy or so much slower to respond than one of fifteen, nineteen, or twenty? On the other hand, what UN intergovernmental body has become stronger or more effective as it has been enlarged? Is it fair to assert that there is an iron law that UN bodies expand until they can no longer perform effectively? In an organization with 192 members, will there not always be pressure for expansion, whatever the extent of the most recent increment? ECOSOC, for example, has been enlarged twice and now the same is being asked of the Security Council.

In an organization composed of independent, sovereign countries, what do terms like "representative" and "accountable" mean in practice? The founders seemed to be of two minds about such things. According to Article 24(2) of the Charter, the Council "shall act in accordance with the Purposes and Principles of the United Nations." Yet nowhere does the Charter employ terms like "democratic," "representative" or "accountable." The notion of naming the convening powers (plus France) as permanent members of the Council with special privileges and responsibilities, but with no explanation or justification, certainly does not speak of accountability. Today's candidates for permanent status, in the name of equity, would claim the right to be just as unaccountable, just as unrepresentative. While many member states resent the exalted position of the current P-5, what would they gain from increasing the size of a charmed circle from which most of them are permanently excluded? Short of instituting some system of wider consultations, information exchange, and/or review between members and non-members of the Council, how could the representative character of the Council be enhanced? Is the latter a property more of composition or working methods (or both)?

The High-level Panel has contended that an enlargement of members would bring a corresponding expansion both of the resources available to implement Council decisions and of the will of countries – on or off the Council – to do so.[57] Which resources, which member states, and why? Would this only be true to the extent that large, wealthy, and militarily potent states are brought onto the Council? If so, how much room should be left on the Council for their smaller or poorer neighbors? There is no doubt that there have been serious problems of inadequate resources and will to implement Council resolutions. What is less clear is whether this has been the result of the ebbing legitimacy and authority of the Council due to its anachronistic composition, of its increasingly ambitious, intrusive and frequent resolutions, or of shifting strategic conditions well beyond its control. Perhaps mixed responses are endemic to its line of work, as the experience of the League's Council would suggest. What is the evidence, in fact, that implementation rates or enthusiasm for assisting the Council in its work are declining?

Academics have no surer answers to such tough questions than do policy-makers and diplomats. In fact, there is nothing close to a consensus diagnosis of what ails the Council. Without some shared sense of what is wrong with the Council, the prospects of agreeing on the best course of treatment are dim. Two points, however, are clear. One, those advocating radical reform need to do a much better job of explaining why an expanded Council would be a better Council, producing different decisions and enhanced results. Two, those who have repeatedly claimed that the time was not ripe or the proposals for reform were not right need to be much more specific and forthcoming in responding to two queries: one, if not now, when? And two, if not this, what? Reform cannot, and should not, be postponed indefinitely. If reform is good for the rest of the UN, then surely it must be good for the Council as well.

11 Conclusion

Reflection and projection

Few institutions are as well known or as little understood as the UN Security Council. It is, in that regard, one of those classic enigmas hiding in plain sight. It has been perpetually shrouded by layers of divergent and even internally contradictory expectations and fantasies. It habitually disappoints, regroups, and then surprises. One day it is heralded, the next disdained or, worse, dismissed. Each action it takes is celebrated by some and despaired by others. It squanders obvious opportunities, only to manufacture something out of nothing the next time around. As it triumphs in one arena, it turns its back on several more.

The public and most policy-makers tend to see the Council through snapshots of a single place and time. Yet it is an unusually dynamic institution, used by different states for distinct purposes at various points in time. Generally judged by its latest success, or too often failure, the Council has an extraordinary and unparalleled history, full of lessons yet to be learned and mistakes likely to be repeated. Compared to the sweeping rhetoric of its declarations and resolutions, the Council's performance appears erratic, uninspired, and grossly inadequate. Enforcement and implementation have been sometime things. Its penchant for grand declarations, unyielding demands, and overly ambitious plans, on the other hand, is legendary. It has a gift for offering simplistic cures for complex and nuanced ailments. It tends, as well, to make its boldest pronouncements after the worst of the danger and carnage is long past. With greater frequency and increasing sophistication, it has become a specialist at cleaning up the pieces where prevention, mediation, moral suasion, and peacekeeping have failed.

Yet, as the previous chapters have related, from other vantage points the Council's record looks much more respectable and its future even encouraging. No other security organization has taken on more than a fraction of its agenda. NATO was a keystone of deterrence during the Cold War years, but fortunately was never tested on the ground. In its more operational guise since then, its ventures have proven to be more expensive and less flexible than comparable UN-authorized missions. Neither its mandate, authority, nor politics would allow it to have the global reach of the Security Council. Other regional bodies have largely been cast in supporting or short-term roles, as their comparative advantages have been more political than operational for the most part. Their strengths of proximity have also been among their most obvious shortcomings.

The Council is unique in human history. No clones can be detected on the horizon. Whatever the Secretary-General might say, the world is nowhere close to "a new San Francisco moment."[1] It took world wars to create the last two great experiments in international organization and the world cannot afford to go that route a third time. The alternative is not stagnation, because neither the Council nor the global organization in which it is embedded function nearly as well as they should. As Chapter 10 emphasized, adaptation, experimentation and reform need to be a way of – even the key to – life for the Council and the UN system. For such institutions, entering their seventh decade, change is good.

Here, the news is encouraging. The surest standard for assessing how the Council is doing is to judge whether its performance is getting weaker or stronger over time. Given its unique stature, structure and ambition, the Council can best be compared to itself. Based on the evidence compiled in each of the preceding chapters, the performance of the Council has improved with each passing decade. Each of its tools has been sharpened either through internal processes of reassessment or, in the case of military enforcement, by delegating some tasks to those better equipped outside of the organization. New interactive tools, such as reporting, monitoring and capacity building, have been added to its repertoire as it seeks ways of addressing the threats posed by terrorism and weapons of mass destruction. Human rights and humanitarian concerns have been largely integrated into its once state-dominated paradigms. Likewise, a wider spectrum of views and voices are now taken into account in its decision-making. Council deliberations are, on the whole, more open and inclusive. Not only is it listening more to independent expertise and experience, it is frequently going to areas of tension to deliver messages in person, to engage with local actors, and to gain a deeper understanding of the issues at stake. The Council has become a norm-setter, as well as a norm-consumer.

The Council's progress, of course, has been anything but linear. Often it has consisted of two steps forward and one step back, sometimes even the reverse. There have been several detours along the way. But the overall direction – of increasing demands, ambitions and scope on the one hand, and new tools, mechanisms and partners on the other – has been unmistakable. The Council, for all its failings, has proven to be remarkably resilient. It is, after all, basically a piece of machinery to be employed by the member states when, where, and how they need it. Surely its work is to be undertaken within the broad purposes and noble principles of the organization, as Article 24(2) underlines. But that leaves it a lot of room to maneuver and to adapt as circumstances require. The founders' genius lay in their restraint in not binding the Council too tightly to the norms, expectations and needs that prevailed six decades ago. Today's reformers should bear that lesson in mind.[2]

The Council's malleable and adaptable nature makes prognostication about its future shape and priorities a risky, even foolhardy enterprise. Nevertheless, there is every reason to believe not only that the Council will have a future, but that it will be a busy one. It shows no signs of going out of business anytime soon. The demand for its services remains at a historically high level, even on the part of some, like US President George W. Bush, who had warned of its pending irrelevance.[3] The League's Council died of disuse as much as poor performance. So long as national leaders find the Council to be a useful place to do some important business some of the time, its doors will remain open and its relevance will be assured. They judge the Council not on whether it has been consistent and fair, but on whether it continues to be a useful instrument when they need it.

The Council's business is maintaining international peace and security. Its market, therefore, is dynamic, elastic and insatiable. Security and insecurity never go out of style. The demand for the Council's services never ceases, as it can never complete the tasks before it. Because of the nature of its business, member states cannot risk abandoning it or the tools it can mobilize. For small countries, it offers hope. For big ones, it offers the prospect of coupling legitimacy with power, thus adding the essential political glue for international coalition building and force multiplying. The five permanent members, moreover, have a vested interest in maintaining a body that identifies them – whether justly or not – as the world's security oligarchy. They know that they have a privileged position and that some of them deserve it more than others. So the latter work doubly hard to demonstrate that both the Council and the P-5 remain as viable and productive as ever: for them, vetoes are a thing of the past and harmony, inclusiveness, transparency, and reform the themes of the present.

True, a multitude of other actors have moved into the security business, leaving the Council at times as more of a broker or service provider than as the sole operator on the ground. But the Council has learned to welcome partnerships and to prosper in the new service-oriented economy. This shift, however, has raised one of a series of dilemmas about the Council's future direction. Which business model fits it better: that of a strong-willed conglomerate or of a more decentralized franchise system in which various actors find it helpful to don the Council's label even as they pursue their independent strategies? While the Council has yet to privatize its work, it has delegated the employment of its most powerful tool – military enforcement – to coalitions of willing – i.e. self-selected – member states for the most challenging and risky missions. Article 53(1) does provide a Charter basis for such a step, when properly authorized by the Council, but rarely have these coalitions reported to the Council in a timely manner as the enforcement operations have unfolded. Nor can the Council claim, in most cases, to have monitored or steered the way force has been used in its name. Even fast food franchises appreciate that their reputations depend on insuring uniformly high standards in each of their outlets.

A related issue – and one familiar to any number of private and public enterprises – is whether the Council can, or should, attempt to deal with so many issues simultaneously. The standard response is that it has no choice. Like a hospital emergency room, it cannot deny treatment to urgent cases brought to it in extremis. To turn away pressing security situations, where many lives and international stability are at risk, would only spur further complaints about the Council's biases and double standards. The greatest stains on its record have been in places like Rwanda and Srebrenica where it looked the other way in part because it had pressing worries elsewhere. Yet in those sad episodes, the Council not only was "seized" of the case, it had actually deployed paper-thin peacekeeping missions with neither the muscle nor authority to prevent the escalation of violence. These tripwires were tested and the Council's will was found wanting. Misleading the vulnerable with a veneer of Council concern may be worse than telling them earlier and more candidly how robust an international response they could reasonably expect.

Much of the Council's time, moreover, is taken up with renewing old mandates or trying to find new band-aids for long-festering, gaping wounds, in other words, with coping rather than curing. That is consonant, of course, with its core mandate of "maintaining" international peace and security. No doubt relatively few items on the Council's very long agenda are ripe for true resolution at any point in time, so maintenance of the status quo is to be preferred to an escalation of tensions. But does this pattern leave the Council members, individually and collectively, with sufficient time, energy, and flexibility to focus on those handful of situations where concerted effort might pay big dividends in the short run? There have been success stories in this regard, where the Council, in tandem with the Secretary-General and regional actors, has been able to concentrate on a single urgent case that hung in the balance. Mazambique, Angola, El Salvador, Cambodia, and Namibia come to mind. But these have been the exceptions, not the rule.

A third dilemma, again relating to the scope and content of the Council's agenda, is its proclivity for taking up thematic issues. Many of these questions have flowed from the need to address in greater depth the kinds of humanitarian, proliferation, and terrorist challenges discussed in Chapters 8 and 9 above. For the sake of its own work, the Council needed to develop standards and define the scope for its engagement with these issues, since they posed relatively fresh doctrinal and operational concerns. The Council's thematic resolutions and, more often, presidential statements on these matters have, in essence, provided it, as well as the UN's larger membership, with sort of a normative compass to guide their exploration of new substantive territory. At the same time, however, the Council's excursion into what could reasonably be characterized as norm building or codification of legal standards has raised legitimate questions about trespassing on territory reserved for the General Assembly or other larger, more representative bodies. Was this a passing exigency or the beginning of a long-term trend? Given how thinly the Council is already stretched, one might hope it is the former and that the Assembly will begin to get its act together to fill these normative gaps in a responsible and timely manner.

The debates over the use of force in Iraq and over Security Council expansion have raised two more fundamental dilemmas of an almost existential character. The first, raised most directly and candidly, relates to the use of force. The second, and related, question concerns the implications for the Council's role, decision-making, and composition of the enormous disparities in national military and economic capacity. Whatever the merits of the case, the rhetorical struggle in the Council over whether to authorize the US-led intervention in Iraq brought to the surface two quite distinct interpretations of the Council's primary function. One view, centered on Article 2(4)'s restraint on the unilateral use of force other than in self-defense, pictured the Council as judge and jury, determining when member states should or should not be authorized to use force.[4] The opposing perspective stressed the need for the Council to be resolute in enforcing its resolutions and defending international security in order to create conditions under which individual states could exercise such restraint without endangering national security. These are not mutually exclusive propositions, of course. If the Council fails to play an active role in boosting international security on the ground, then any pieties its advocates will mouth about the virtues of multilateralism will have little credibility or effect. Likewise, for a powerful state to insist that the Council should simply endorse its pre-packaged plan of action would also serve to undermine the Council's purpose and authority. As the quick review of the development of the Charter presented in the opening chapters of the book suggests, the founders certainly envisioned a Council that would be agile, resolute and forceful in dealing with threats to the peace. They did not foresee the Council as a passive judge commenting on and assessing the action from the sidelines. But they were equally convinced that security could only be sustained in a framework of international law and order, with a Council prepared to take collective action at the center. Finding both sides of the debate to have distorted their founding intent, they probably would have counseled them to go back to the spirit and strategies that animated Dumbarton Oaks and San Francisco.

As sensible as this might sound, it does not take into account the distorting pressures of the currently highly skewed distribution of military and economic capabilities. True, the US was the dominant force behind the creation of the UN and its share of global GDP was higher in 1945 than today.[5] But the gap in force projection capacities is arguably larger today and the US no longer has a global ideological and strategic competitor, as during the Cold War days. No other state, for the foreseeable future, will be in a position to try to counterbalance the US in any of the traditional measures of hard power.[6] The subtext of the pre-Iraq intervention debate in the Council, however, suggests that some states may be tempted to use it and other multilateral bodies to frustrate or counterbalance the US through soft power means.[7] Both Washington and other capitals will need to be careful not to undermine the viability of the Council as such verbal and political tugs-of-war are played out in the years ahead.[8] The Council is a place for political struggle in the effort to find common ground, of course, but it will have trouble serving any of the members' needs if some are convinced they need to demonstrate that they live in a unipolar world and others want to pretend that it is a multipolar one. In conditions of unipolarity, at least in the military realm, it will be a challenge to make multilateral decision-making work, especially if the Council is expanded.[9]

Despite these worries, the likelihood is that the member states will find a way to insure that the Council continues to serve their interests in the face of an evolving strategic environment. The Council, after all, survived the Cold War, the North-South split, and hundreds of vetoes by Moscow and Washington. It can survive even pronounced strategic asymmetries as well. It must do more than simply preserve itself, of course, it must make a positive contribution to international peace and security. As Chapter 8 above and the *2005 Human Security Report* chronicle, there is ample reason to believe that the condition of global security, in the aggregate, is improving. Inter-state war, in particular, is on the decline. And that was to be the Council's core purpose, though surely it has been only one of many contributors to the encouraging trend. Now it is tackling other, more elusive targets, as Chapters 8 and 9 address.

There is no justification for complacency or for inertia, as the Council will need to change to meet new threats, demands and opportunities. But neither is there room for defeatism or for such radical reforms that the baby will be thrown out with the bathwater. Instead, the Council should approach the future with the quiet confidence that its remarkable history of growth and adaptation has earned and should inspire.

Notes

Foreword

1 Edward C. Luck, *Mixed Messages: American Politics and International Organization* (Washington DC: Brookings Institution Press, 1999).

2 High-level Panel on Threats, Challenges and Change, *A More Secure World: Our Shared Responsibility* (New York: UN, 2004); and Kofi Annan, *In Larger Freedom: Towards Development, Security and Human Rights for All* (New York: UN, 2005).

3 See also Thomas G. Weiss, *Overcoming the Security Council Impasse: Envisioning Reform* (Berlin: Friedrich Ebert Stiftung, 2005), occasional paper 14.

1 Grading the great experiment

1 John J. Mearsheimer, "The False Promise of International Institutions," *International Security*, 19, no. 3 (winter 1994–5): 5–49.

2 See, for example, "Views of a Changing World 2003" and "A Year After the Iraq War," two multinational polls conducted by the Pew Research Center for the People and the Press, http://people-press.org/reports/display.php3?ReportID = 185 and http://people-press.org/reports/display.php3?PageID = 796, respectively.

2 The founding vision

1 V. M. Molotov, Speeches and Statement of the People's Commissar of Foreign Affairs of the USSR and Chairman of the Soviet Delegation at the United Nations Conference on International Organization in San Francisco, Embassy of the USSR, 24 May 1945, 6.

2 F. P. Walters, *A History of the League of Nations* (London: Oxford University Press, 1952), vol. II, 812–13.

3 Leland M. Goodrich, "From League of Nations to United Nations," *International Organization*, 1, no. 1 (February 1947): 3.

4 Grayson Kirk, "The Enforcement of Security," *Yale Law Journal*, 55, no. 5 (August 1946): 1082.

5 League of Nations, *The League Hands Over* (Geneva: 1946), 32–3, 46, 51, 59.

6 While Germany and Japan gave notice of their withdrawal from the League in 1933, the two countries did not cease to be League members until 1935. For a

useful summary of the experience of the League's Council without analysis or editorial comment, see League of Nations, *The Council of the League of Nations: Composition, Competence, Procedure* (Geneva, 1938); for a list of the non-permanent members of the League of Nations from 1920 to 1940, see *Essential Facts About the League of Nations*, 9th edn rev. (Geneva: League of Nations, 1938).

7   Declaration by the United Nations, 1 January 1942.

8   *The New York Times*, 25 December 1943.

9   Forrest Davis, "Roosevelt's World Blueprint," *Saturday Evening Post*, 10 April 1943. For a fuller accounting of the President's role in developing the plans for the United Nations, see Townsend Hoopes and Douglas Brinkley, *FDR and the Creation of the U.N.* (New Haven CT: Yale University Press, 1997). Though Roosevelt has properly been credited with being the guiding spirit behind the creation of the UN, he sadly died just two weeks before the opening of the San Francisco founding conference.

10   At least one prominent scholar at the time flagged this distinction between the assumptions behind the League and its successor. See Hans Kelsen, "The Old and the New League: The Covenant and the Dumbarton Oaks Proposals," *American Journal of International Law*, 39, no. 1 (January 1945): 46–7.

11   In addition to Hoopes and Brinkley, *FDR and the Creation of the U.N.*, see Ruth B. Russell, *A History of the United Nations Charter: The Role of the United States 1940–1945* (Washington DC: Brookings Institution Press, 1958).

12   UN Document A/60/L.1, 15 September 2005, 40, para. 177.

13   Russell, *A History of the United Nations Charter*, Appendix I, 1019–28.

14   Some points that stirred little commentary, much less dissent, at Dumbarton Oaks and San Francisco have since proved highly controversial. For example, for a detailed discussion of the US role in introducing the language in Article 2(4) on the non-use of force that it now finds awkward, see Edward C. Luck, "Article 2(4) on the Non-Use of Force: What Were We Thinking?," in David P. Forsythe, Patrice C. McMahon and Andrew Wedeman (eds) *American Foreign Policy in a Globalized World* (New York: Routledge, 2006).

15   For a careful chronicling of the deliberations on these issues at Dumbarton Oaks, see Robert C. Hilderbrand, *Dumbarton Oaks: The Origins of the United Nations and the Search for Postwar Security* (Chapel Hill NC: University of North Carolina Press, 1990), 183–208; and Hoopes and Brinkley, *FDR and the Creation of the U.N.*, 133–58.

16   Chapter V. Section C. Voting, Russell, *A History of the United Nations Charter*, 1022.

17   Stephen C. Schlesinger, *Act of Creation: The Founding of the United Nations* (Boulder CO: Westview Press, 2003), 53–72; Hoopes and Brinkley, *FDR and the Creation of the U.N.*, 172–9; and Russell, *A History of the United Nations Charter*, 515–44.

18   For an explanation of the Yalta agreement by the four sponsoring governments, dated 8 June 1945, see Appendix III, 455–8 of Sydney D. Bailey and Sam Daws, *The Procedure of the UN Security Council*, 3rd edn (Oxford: Clarendon Press, 1998).

19   For Section VI-C of the Dumbarton Oaks Proposals, as agreed at Yalta, see Russell, *A History of the United Nations Charter*, 713.

20   *Ibid.*, 713–49; Hoopes and Brinkley, *FDR and the Creation of the U.N.*, 198–203; and Schlesinger, *Act of Creation*, 193–225.

21   Parliament of the Commonwealth of Australia, *United Nations Conference on International Organization, Report by the Australian Delegation* (Canberra: Government of the Commonwealth of Australia, 1945).

22 Hoopes and Brinkley, *FDR and the Creation of the U.N.*, 199.
23 Russell, *A History of the United Nations Charter*, 737.
24 Senator Tom Connally, *My Name is Tom Connally* (New York: Thomas Y. Crowell, 1954), 283. Emphasis in the original. As he later recalled,

> I felt that the United States should have the veto power. Otherwise, the majority of UN members – who were little countries – could vote us into a war we didn't want. . . . And I was also aware that the Senate would never agree to a document that let other nations decide when the United States should go to war.

> (*Ibid.*, 282)

3 Defining the Council through charter and practice

1 For comments on the evolution of Council procedures, see Sydney D. Bailey and Sam Daws, *The Procedure of the UN Security Council*, 3rd edn (Oxford: Clarendon Press, 1998), 9–18.
2 Table on Number of Security Council Meetings and Consultations, 1988–2002, Global Policy Forum, http://www.globalpolicy.org/security/data/secmgtab.htm (accessed 07/27/04).
3 For reliable and current information on the Council's work and the issues before it, see the Security Council Report, http://www.securitycouncilreport.org.
4 Edward C. Luck, *Reforming the United Nations: Lessons from a History in Progress*, Occasional Paper no. 1 (New Haven CT: The Academic Council on the United Nations System, 2003), 7–10.
5 Ruth B. Russell, *A History of the United Nations Charter: The Role of the United States 1940–1945* (Washington DC: Brookings Institution Press, 1958), 672.
6 *Ibid.*, 657.
7 The Charter arguably puts less emphasis on judicial settlement than had the Covenant, which (Article 12, as amended in 1924) had made this one of the compulsory means that members should employ to resolve a dispute. Clyde Eagleton, "The United Nations: Aims and Structure," *Yale Law Journal*, 55, no. 5 (August 1946): 981–2. Yet the International Court of Justice (ICJ) is much more fully integrated into the UN system, while the Covenant (Article 14) simply calls on the Council to develop proposals for the creation of a Permanent Court of International Justice. US leaders were concerned that the Senate might not consent, once again, to the ratification of the ICJ statute if it was not included as part of the San Francisco package.
8 While the Truman Administration preached a decidedly optimistic line about how well these new mechanisms would perform, not all informed Americans were convinced that the new arrangements would be so superior to those of the League. For some measured scholarly analysis suggesting that the way the League did and the UN would work in practice would not be so different, see Leland M. Goodrich, "From League of Nations to United Nations," *International Organization*, 1, no. 1 (February 1947): 16–18. There were a number of confirmed skeptics in the State Department, including Acting Assistant Secretary of State Joseph Grew and Dean Acheson, an Assistant Secretary of State at the time who managed the presentation of the Charter to the US Senate and who became Truman's Secretary of State in 1949. See, for Grew, Robert C. Hilderbrand, *Dumbarton Oaks: The*

Origins of the United Nations and the Search for Postwar Security (Chapel Hill NC: University of North Carolina Press, 1990), 254; Dean Acheson, *Present at the Creation: My Years in the State Department* (New York: W. W. Norton, 1969), 6–7, 11–12, 111–12; James Chace, *The Secretary of State Who Created the American World* (New York: Simon and Schuster, 1998), 107–8; and Edward C. Luck, *Mixed Messages: American Politics and International Organization, 1919–1999* (Washington DC: Brookings Institution Press, 1999), 18, 30, 260.

 9 See Bailey and Daws, *The Procedure of the UN Security Council* (1946–95); data for 1996–2004 compiled by Marilyn Messer of the Center on International Organization, Columbia University.

10 *The United Nations Conference on International Organization, Selected Documents, 25 April to 26 June 1945, San Francisco* (Washington DC: US Government Printing Office, 1946), 781.

11 Russell, *A History of the United Nations Charter*, 676.

12 These points are elaborated in Edwards C. Luck "A Council for All Seasons: The Creation of the Security Council and Its Relevance Today," in Vaughan Lowe, Adam Roberts, Jennifer Welsh, and Dominik Zaum, eds., *The UN Security Council and War* (Oxford University Press, forthcoming 2006).

13 *Documents of the United Nations Conference on International Organization*, vol. XVII, part 1, Summary Report of the Thirteenth Meeting of the Coordination Committee, WD256, CO/107, 10 June 1945 (New York: United Nations, 1954), 74. This understanding was confirmed in Secretary of State Edward R. Stettinius Jr's report to the President, as follows:

> It should be pointed out that the sequence of Articles 41 and 42 does not mean that the Council must in all cases resort to non-military measures in the first instance. While ordinarily this would be the case, since crises generally take a long time to develop, in a case of sudden aggression the Security Council may resort at once to military action without proceeding through any intermediate step, and the language of Article 42 has been refined to make this clear.
>
> *Report to the President on the Results of the San Francisco Conference by the Chairman of the United States Delegation, The Secretary of State*, Publication 2349, Conference Series 71 (Washington DC: Department of State, 26 June 1945), 93)

> Also see the Report of the Rapporteur of Commission III to Plenary Session, *The United Nations Conference on International Organization*, Selected Documents, 833, and commentary by Grayson Kirk, who served as Executive Officer of Commission III, in "The Enforcement of Security," *Yale Law Journal*, 55, no. 5 (August 1946): 1088–9.

14 Secretary-General Boutros Boutros-Ghali's *An Agenda for Peace* report, prepared in 1992 on the call of the first summit meeting of the Council, remains one of the clearest statements of UN doctrine on the use of force and how it relates to the other tools in its Chapter VI and VII toolkit (UN Document A/47/277, 17 June 1992). For a discussion of preventive deployment, see paras 28–32. Though arguing that military action under Article 42 "should only be taken when all peaceful means have failed," he underlined that "the option of taking it is essential to the credibility of the United Nations as guarantor of international security." (para. 43).

15 Luck, *Mixed Messages*, 168, 187. From the outset of the wartime discussion of the form of the United Nations, moreover, the Roosevelt administration firmly opposed the idea of a truly international force. Russell, *A History of the United Nations Charter*, 467–72.

16 Secretary-General Boutros Boutros-Ghali, Introduction, *The Blue Helmets: A Review of United Nations Peace-keeping*, 3rd edn (United Nations: Department of Public Information, 1996), 7–8.

17 As Secretary-General Boutros Boutros-Ghali noted, moreover, "the role of the Military Staff Committee should be seen in the context of Chapter VII, and not that of the planning or conduct of peacekeeping operations." *An Agenda for Peace*, 25, para. 43. The MSC, in other words, should stay out of the sort of security tasks the Organization regularly conducted and reserve its expertise for the kinds of contingencies rarely undertaken by the world body.

18 For an interesting summary of the Military Staff Committee's frustrating initial efforts, see John Gerard Ruggie, *The United Nations and the Collective Use of Force: Whither – or Whether?* (New York: United Nations Association of the USA, 1996), 3. The Security Council's first resolution, on 25 July 1946, called for the establishment of the Military Staff Committee. The Committee still meets, sometimes as a luncheon club, sometimes as a breakfast club, but has been given nothing of substantive importance to do since those early failings. Secretary-General Kofi Annan and his High-level Panel on Threats, Challenges and Change have recommended that this Committee be disbanded through Charter amendment. See, respectively, Report of the Secretary-General, *In Larger Freedom: Towards Development, Security and Human Rights for All* (New York: United Nations, 2005), 72, para. 219; and *A More Secure World: Our Shared Responsibility* (New York: United Nations, 2004), 114, para. 100.

19 For telling accounts of the negotiations in San Francisco that produced Article 51, see Russell, *A History of the United Nations Charter*, 693–704; and Stephen C. Schlesinger, *Act of Creation: The Founding of the United Nations* (Boulder CO: Westview Press, 2003), 175–92.

20 Russell, *A History of the United Nations Charter*, 696; and Schlesinger, *Act of Creation*, 177.

4 Peace operations

1 Leland M. Goodrich, "From League of Nations to United Nations," *International Organization*, 1, no. 1 (February 1947): 15.

2 Resolution 54 of 15 July 1948 invoked Articles 39 and 40 – the Council's first references to Chapter VII – concerning the first war in Palestine, but it did not impose enforcement measures. The first enforcement action – a very big one – came in response to the North Korean invasion of South Korea in June 1950. That vote was possible only because the Soviet representatives happened to be boycotting the Council at the time in protest of Taipei's continued occupancy of the Chinese seat on the Council.

3 For a detailed inside look at these complex negotiations, see Brian Urquhart, *Ralph Bunche: An American Life* (New York: W. W. Norton, 1993), 139–200.

4 For example, Peter Wallensteen of Sweden's Uppsala University reviewed conflict prevention efforts in thirty inter-state and intra-state disputes from 1992 to 1999. In only five of these cases did he conclude that the UN was a leading outside actor, compared to eleven times for the US and ten for the European Union. "Reassessing Recent Conflicts: Direct vs. Structural Prevention," in Fen Osler Hampson and David M. Malone (eds) *From Reaction to Conflict: Opportunities for the UN System* (Boulder CO: Lynne Rienner, 2002), 205–21, esp. Table 9.1.

5 For a sophisticated quantitative and qualitative analysis of the UN's record since 1945, see Michael W. Doyle and Nicholas Sambanis, *Making War and Building Peace: United Nations Peace Operations* (Princeton NJ: Princeton University Press, 2006).

6 Report of the Panel on United Nations Peace Operations, UN Document S/2000/809, 21 August 2000, 3, para. 15.

7 *Ibid.*, 2–3, paras. 11–13.

8 Kofi Annan, "Reflections on Intervention," Ditchley Park, United Kingdom, 26 June 1998.

9 Boutros Boutros-Ghali, *An Agenda for Peace*, UN Document A/47/277, 17 June 1992, 13, para. 23.

10 For a portrayal of the UN as being engulfed by a sea of local conflicts, see William Shawcross, *Deliver Us from Evil: Peacekeepers, Warlords and a World of Endless Conflict* (New York: Simon and Schuster, 2000).

11 Carnegie Commission on Preventing Deadly Conflict, *Preventing Deadly Conflict: Final Report* (New York: Carnegie Corporation of New York, 1997).

12 Address by the Secretary-General, Forum on the Final Report of the Carnegie Commission on Preventing Deadly Conflict, "The Centrality of the United Nations to Prevention and the Centrality of Prevention to the United Nations," UN Document SG/SM/6454, 5 February 1998. For similar statements by the Secretary-General, see the text of a message by the Secretary-General for the opening of an Inter-Parliamentary Union Conference, "The Importance of Conflict Prevention," UN Document SG/SM/6514, 3 April 1998, and the address by the Secretary-General at Rice University, "The Challenge of Conflict Prevention," UN Document SG/SM/6535, 23 April 1998.

13 Address by the Secretary-General, "Development Is the Best Form of Prevention," First United Nations Lecture (Washington DC: World Bank, 19 October 1999); "The Question of Intervention: Statements by the Secretary-General" (United Nations: Department of Public Information, 1999), 47–55.

14 Address by the Secretary-General to the Security Council, "The Role of the Security Council in the Prevention of Armed Conflict," UN Document SG/SM/7238, 29 November 1999.

15 Statement by the President of the Security Council, UN Document S/PRST/1999/34, 30 November 1999; and Statement by the President of the Security Council, UN Document S/PRST/2000/25, 20 July 2000.

16 For a critique of the notion of structural prevention, see Edward C. Luck, "Prevention in Theory and Practice," in Hampson and Malone, *From Reaction to Conflict Prevention*, 251–71. Also see Elizabeth M. Cousens, "Conflict Prevention," in David M. Malone (ed.) *The UN Security Council: From the Cold War to the 21st Century* (Boulder CO: Lynne Rienner, 2004), 101–15.

17 David Mitrany commented in 1932, for example, that, because of "technical inquiries" and arbitration, "frontier disputes, which in the past had given rise to many a conflict, have almost passed out of the political field." Had the League's Assembly met in the Far East, he contended, it would have been possible to judge and resolve "the issues involved in the Sino-Japanese conflict." *The Progress of International Government* (London: George Allen & Unwin, 1933), 111. Also see F. P. Walters, *A History of the League of Nations*, vol. II (London: Oxford University Press, 1952) 699–703 on the varied views of member states on the opening of the League's new headquarters in the Palais des Nations in 1936, as well as its growing attention to Near Eastern questions from 1936 to 1939 (739–48) and the renaissance of its economic and social work from 1935 to 1939 (749–62).

18 Among the critics, see Saadia Touval, "Why the UN Fails," *Foreign Affairs*, 73, no. 5 (September/October 1994): 44–57; Richard K. Betts, "The Delusion of Impartial Intervention," *Foreign Affairs*, 73, no. 6 (November/December 1994): 20–33; Stephen John Stedman, "UN Intervention in Civil Wars: Imperatives of Choice and Strategy," in Donald C. F. Daniel and Bradd C. Hayes (eds) *Beyond Traditional Peacekeeping* (New York: St Martin's Press, 1998), 40–63; and Ted Galen Carpenter, "The Mirage of Global Collective Security," in Carpenter (ed.) *Delusions of Grandeur: The United Nations and Global Intervention* (Washington DC: Cato Institute, 1997), 13–28.

19 Chester A. Crocker, Fen Osler Hampson and Pamela Aall (eds) *Herding Cats: Multiparty Mediation in a Complex World* (Washington DC: United States Institute of Peace Press, 1999).

20 Report of the High-level Panel on Threats, Challenges and Change, *A More Secure World: Our Shared Responsibility* (New York: United Nations, 2004), 33–4, para. 85.

21 *Ibid.*, 34, para. 86.

22 Fen Osler Hampson, "Can the UN Still Mediate?," in Richard M. Price and Mark W. Zacher (eds) *The United Nations and Global Security* (New York: Palgrave MacMillan, 2004), 75–92.

23 Quoted in Urquhart, *Ralph Bunche*, 265. See 264–90 for an insider's account of the planning for this first peacekeeping force.

24 Though the vote to establish what was to become the first United Nations Emergency Force (UNEF I) was 57 to 0, there were nineteen abstentions, including Egypt, France, Israel, the Soviet Union, and the United Kingdom, i.e. all of the parties to the conflict. Clearly seeking approval in the Security Council would have proven time-consuming and problematic. *The Blue Helmets: A Review of United Nations Peace-keeping*, 3rd edn (New York: UN Department of Public Information, 1996), 37.

25 First deployed in 1964, UNFICYP has kept the peace by preserving the geographical segregation of the two communities since the hostilities and Turkish intervention in 1974. For a detailed history of the operation, see *The Blue Helmets*, 149–70. The Secretary-General has made a number of mediation efforts there through the years. In 2004, it looked as if he might finally succeed, only to fall short again because of the intractability of one of the parties. See "Secretary-General Presents Final Settlement Plan for Cyprus," UN Document SG/SM/9239, 31 March 2004; and " 'Unique and Historic' Chance to Resolve Cyprus Problem Missed, Says Secretary-General After Settlement Plan Rejected," UN Document SG/SM/9269, 26 April 2004; Warren Hoge, "Cyprus Greeks and Turks Agree on Plan to End 40-Year Conflict," *New York Times*, 14 February 2004; and Alan Cowell, "After Negotiations on Unity Fall, Cypriots to Decide on Plan," *New York Times*, 1 April 2004.

26 The very reference to Chapter VI1/2 suggests some awkwardness in trying to fit peacekeeping doctrine and practices within the definitional walls set out in the Charter. There was a substantial literature in the mid-1990s on the doctrinal muddle surrounding UN peacekeeping. For a concise statement of many of these concerns, see John Gerard Ruggie, "Wandering in the Void: Charting the UN's New Strategic Role," *Foreign Affairs*, 72, no. 5 (November/December 1993): 26–31.

27 UN Department of Peacekeeping Operations, http://www.un.org/Depts/dpko/fatalities/ (accessed January 2006).

28 See UN resolutions 143 (1960) and 161 (1961) for ONUC (United Nations Operation in the Congo) and Resolution 751 (1992) for UNISOM I (United Nations Operation in Somalia) and 814 (1993) for UNISOM II. For useful accounts of ONUC and UNISOM, see Indar Jit Rikhye, "The United Nations Operations in the Congo: Peacekeeping, Peacemaking and Peacebuilding," in Daniel and Hayes, *Beyond Traditional Peacekeeping*, 207–27; and Gary Anderson, "UNOSOM II: Not Failure, Not Success," in *ibid.*, 267–81.

29 The initial UNPROFOR mandate derived from Resolution 743 (1992). For an assessment of the failure to protect the safe haven at Srebrenica, see the *Report of the Secretary-General pursuant to General Assembly Resolution 53/35: The Fall of Srebrenica*, UN Document A/54/549, 15 November 1999. On the larger frustrations produced by UNPROFOR, see Marrack Goulding, *Peacemonger* (Baltimore MD: Johns Hopkins University Press, 2003), 291–329; and Mats Berdal, "Bosnia," in Malone, *The UN Security Council*, 451–66.

30 See peacekeeping statistics compiled by the Global Policy Forum, http://www.globalpolicy.org/security/peacekpg/data/index.htm (accessed August 2004).

31 Evidently the practice of developing countries providing most of the forces for operations in the developing world, especially in Africa, is not without precedent. Indar Rikhye points out that, "of the 93,000 men from 35 states who served with UNOC during the four-year operation, 82.4 percent came from 19 Afro-Asian states, with most of the technical units and specialists being provided by Western countries." "The United Nations Operations in the Congo," in Daniel and Hayes, *Beyond Traditional Peacekeeping*, 218.

32 Michael W. Doyle, Ian Johnstone and Robert C. Orr (eds) *Keeping the Peace: Multidimensional UN Operations in Cambodia and El Salvador* (Cambridge: Cambridge University Press, 1997), 1.

33 Report of the Panel on United Nations Peace Operations, 9, para. 48.

34 *Ibid.*, 9, para. 50.

35 As Indar Rikhye has noted, "had its length, manpower commitment and financial cost been foreseen, there is little doubt that it would never have taken place – the cost alone would have deterred the member states." "The United Nations Operations in the Congo," 216. Indeed, the Soviet Union, France, and a number of developing countries refused to pay their assessments for the cost of the Congo operation, plunging the world body into a serious financial crisis and, with the subsequent Article 19 controversy, into a severe political crisis as well. See Chapter 10 below.

36 For the initial Council mandate for these missions, see, respectively, resolutions 632 (1989), 693 (1991), 745 (1992) and 797 (1992).

37 See James Dobbins, Keith Crane, Seth G. Jones, Andrew Rathmell, Brett Steele and Richard Teltschik, *The UN's Role in Nation-Building: From Congo to Iraq* (Santa Monica CA: Rand Corporation, 2005); and Stephen John Stedman, Donald Rothchild and Elizabeth M. Cousens, *Ending Civil Wars: The Implementation of Peace Agreements* (Boulder CO: Lynne Rienner, 2002).

38 Boutros-Ghali, *An Agenda for Peace*, 34, para. 59, and 33, para. 57.

39 Report of the Panel on United Nations Peace Operations, 5, para. 28.

40 Stephen John Stedman, "Policy Implications," in Stedman *et al.*, *Ending Civil Wars*, 668.

41 James Dobbins *et al.*, *The UN's Role in Nation-Building*, xxxvii. For the US study, see James Dobbins, John G. McGinn, Keith Crane, Seth G. Jones, Rollie Lal,

Andrew Rathmell, Rachel Swanger and Anga Timilsina, *America's Role in Nation-Building: From Germany to Iraq* (Santa Monica CA: Rand Corporation, 2003).

42 *Ibid.*, xxx.

43 Kofi Annan, *In Larger Freedom: Towards Development, Security and Human Rights for All* (New York: United Nations, 2005), 41–2, paras 114–19. While the High-level Panel had envisioned the Commission dealing with countries sliding into conflict as well as those emerging from conflict, the preventive dimension proved controversial with a number of member states and was not included in the Secretary-General's proposal. See *A More Secure World*, 83–5, paras 261–9.

44 UN Document A/60/L.1, 25–26, 15 September 2005, paras 97–105.

45 A/RES/60/180 of 30 December 2005 and S/RES/1645 of 20 December 2005, op. para. 2. Also see S/RES/1646 of 20 December 2005.

46 See, for example, the Uppsala Conflict Data Program (UCDP), http://www.pcr.uu.se/research/UCDP/ (accessed August 2004); Peter Wallensteen, *Understanding Conflict Resolution: War, Peace, and the Global System* (London: Sage, 2002); Monty G. Marshall and Ted Robert Gurr, *Peace and Conflict 2003* (College Park MD: University of Maryland, Center for International Development and Conflict Management (CIDCM), 2003); and Ted Robert Gurr, "Ethnic Warfare on the Wane," *Foreign Affairs*, 79, no. 3 (May/June 2003): 52–64. Also see the discussion and endnotes in Chapter 8 below.

47 Marshall and Gurr, *Peace and Conflict 2003*, 12.

48 *2003 Global Refugee Trends* (Geneva: United Nations High Commissioner for Refugees, 15 June 2004), 2 and 6.

49 Institute for Strategic Studies, *Military Balance* (New York: Routledge), vol. 103 (2003), Table 33, 240. The same table shows a marked reduction in global military expenditures for those years as well, though the Stockholm International Peace Research Institute (SIPRI) suggests that global outlays rose from 1994 to 2003 by 18 percent, http://web.sipri.org/contents/milap/milex/mex_wnr_table.html (accessed August 2004). Both sets of calculations are based on constant 2000 US dollars.

50 *Ibid.*, 47. Peter Wallensteen and Patrick Johansson similarly characterize the post-Cold War period as "one of unusual peacemaking" with "an unprecedented record of peace agreements." "Security Council Decisions in Perspective," in Malone, *The UN Security Council*, 28.

5 Military enforcement

1 For a chronology of MSC activities, see Sydney D. Bailey and Sam Daws, *The Procedure of the UN Security Council*, 3rd edn (Oxford: Clarendon Press, 1998), 278–9, Table 14. Following the Iraqi invasion of Kuwait in August 1990, the US sought to revive the MSC, apparently in part as a way of demonstrating to Saddam Hussein the collective will to repel his aggression. In Resolution 665 (1990), the Committee was cited in connection with helping to coordinate member state maritime forces seeking to monitor the UN sanctions regime imposed on Iraq in Resolution 661 (1990).

2 Moscow cast 107 vetoes in the Council before Washington cast its first in 1970. The first "lonely" US veto came in 1972, twenty-seven years after San Francisco. Since then, the US has employed the veto more often than the other four permanent members combined. From 1970 through 2005, the US cast 80, the United

Kingdom 25, France 14, USSR/Russia 13, and China 4. For the overall trend lines in the use of the veto, see Figure 1.1.

3 During the years of McCarthyism, far-right critics of the UN in the US came to see the world body as a "Trojan horse" to get communists and their sympathizers into the country. See Edward C. Luck, *Mixed Messages: American Politics and International Organization, 1919–1999* (Washington DC: Brookings Institution Press, 1999), 83–9.

4 Resolution 377 (V) of 3 November 1950.

5 Bailey and Daws, *The Procedure of the Security Council*, 229–30.

6 For example, the Council called on the Assembly to undertake emergency special sessions in regard to the Suez (1956), Hungary (1956), Lebanon and Jordan (1958), the Congo (1960), Afghanistan (1980), and the Occupied Arab Territories (1982), http://www.un.org/ga/documents/liemsps.htm (accessed August 2004).

7 Resolution 479 (1980). The Council's handling of the situation in 1980 added to Iranian ire about perceived bias in the Council's deliberations.

8 Resolution 461 (1979).

9 Resolutions 674 and 677 (1990).

10 Resolution 678 (1990) passed by a 12 to 2 to 1 vote, with China casting the lone abstention and Cuba and Yemen the negative votes.

11 See Luck, *Mixed Messages*, 134–5 and the results of 1989 and 1992 Roper polls conducted for the United Nations Association of the USA (UNA-USA), as discussed in Jeffrey Laurenti, *Directions and Dilemmas in Collective Security: Reflections from a Global Roundtable* (New York: UNA-USA, 1992), 18–19.

12 Boutros Boutros-Ghali, *An Agenda for Peace*, UN Document A/47/277, 17 June 1992, 25, para. 43.

13 *Ibid.*, 26, para. 44.

14 Luck, *Mixed Messages*, 189–91.

15 Boutros Boutros-Ghali, *Supplement to An Agenda for Peace: Position Paper of the Secretary-General on the Occasion of the Fiftieth Anniversary of the United Nations*, UN Document A/50/60-S/1995/1, 3 January 1995, 14, para. 77.

16 *Ibid.*, 14, para. 80. This caveat was softened with an acknowledgment that "Member States so authorized have in recent operations reported more fully and more regularly to the Security Council about their activities." *Ibid.*

17 Secretary-General Kofi Annan, *Renewing the United Nations: A Programme for Reform*, UN Document A/51/950, 14 July 1997, 36, para. 109.

18 *Ibid.*, 36, para. 107.

19 George Bush and Brent Scowcroft, *A World Transformed* (New York: Alfred A. Knopf, 1998), 415.

20 Secretary-General Kofi Annan, "Two Concepts of Sovereignty," Address to the 54th Session of the United Nations General Assembly, UN Document SG/SM/7136, 20 September 1999.

21 Many in the UN community felt that the American action was justified under Resolution 1368 (2001), passed the day after the 9/11 attacks, because it reaffirms a state's right of self-defense against terrorist attacks. The generic resolution makes no mention, however, of the right to attack presumed sponsors of terrorism. For more discussion of this episode and of the larger question of the Council's handling of terrorism and counter-terrorism, see Chapter 9 below.

22 Two caveats should be taken into account in attempting to assess the Council's role in determining the levels of investment in post-conflict peace-building missions. One, the Council does not have authority under the Charter to decide

matters of appropriations or assessments for the Organization. It is one of the few cases in which the Assembly has the ultimate say. Two, the funding of peace-building projects is generally done on a voluntary, not assessed, basis and is often decided outside of a UN context. A major study by the Rand Corporation has uncovered an enormous disparity between the postwar per capita assistance devoted to Bosnia and Kosovo, on the one hand, and Afghanistan and Haiti, on the other. James Dobbins, John G. McGinn, Keith Crane, Seth G. Jones, Rollie Lal, Andrew Rathmell, Rachel Swanger and Anga Timilsina, *America's Role in Nation-Building: From Germany to Iraq* (Santa Monica CA: Rand Corporation, 2003), 157–8, Figure 9.8.

23 Figures documenting this trend are given in Chapter 4 above.

24 Grayson Kirk, who had served as the Executive Officer of the Third Commission (Security Council) at the San Francisco founding conference, made much the same point in 1946 in explaining why the founders eschewed the option of assembling a UN army: "it was realized that the character of modern warfare is such that military effort demands the closest coordination of a bewildering array of industrial and technical facilities." Grayson Kirk, "The Enforcement of Security," *Yale Law Journal*, 55, no. 5 (August 1946): 1083. Moreover, he went on to point out,

> it is obvious that in any given military action it would be impracticable to assemble small units from a large number of countries. The problems of command and control would become enormously complicated. Combat efficiency would give way to a nightmare of confusion.
>
> (*Ibid.*, 1085)

25 International Institute for Strategic Studies, *Military Balance* (New York: Routledge) vol. 103 (2003), 335–40, Table 33.

26 This is one of the four characteristics of American exceptionalism identified by this author. See Edward C. Luck, "American Exceptionalism and International Organization: Lessons from the 1990s," in Rosemary Foot, S. Neil MacFarlane and Michael Mastanduno (eds) *US Hegemony and International Organizations: The United States and Multilateral Institutions* (Oxford: Oxford University Press, 2003), 27.

6 Economic sanctions, arms embargoes, and diplomatic instruments

1 *World Peace: A Written Debate Between William Howard Taft and William Jennings Bryan* (New York: George H. Doran Company, 1970), 33.

2 For a useful summary of sanctions under the League, see Margaret P. Doxey, *International Sanctions in Contemporary Perspective*, 1st edn (New York: St Martin's Press, 1987), 24–31.

3 Such appeals were made by the Security Council in two cases, relating to the sanctions imposed on Iraq after its invasion of Kuwait in 1990 and on the former Yugoslavia in the early 1990s. In the case of the sanctions on Haiti, the Dominican Republic made such a request after the sanctions had been terminated, so this was handled by the secretariat and the General Assembly. See an informal background paper prepared by the UN Sanctions Secretariat, Department of Political Affairs, "A Brief Overview of Security Council Applied Sanctions," for the Second Expert Seminar on Smart Sanctions, The Next Step: Arms Embargoes and Travel Sanctions, Berlin, 3–5 December 2000, 27–9.

4 Further efforts to bolster economic and financial sanctions on Southern Rhodesia produced resolutions 388 (1976) and 409 (1977).

5 The fact that the Council rarely agreed on imposing economic sanctions during the Cold War does not mean that they were not employed by one side or the other at times. For an extensive list of economic sanctions imposed for foreign policy reasons between 1914 and 1990, see Table 1.1, 16–27 of Gary C. Hufbauer, Jeffrey J. Schott and Kimberly Ann Elliott, *Economic Sanctions Reconsidered: History and Current Policy*, 2nd edn (Washington DC: Institute for International Economics, 1990).

6 See, for instance, W. Andy Knight, "Improving the Effectiveness of UN Arms Embargoes," in Richard M. Price and Mark W. Zacher (eds) *The United Nations and Global Security* (New York: Palgrave MacMillan, 2004), 39–55; Michael Brzoska (ed.) *Smart Sanctions: The Next Steps, The Debate on Arms Embargoes and Travel Sanctions Within the 'Bonn-Berlin Process'* (Baden-Baden: Nomos Verlagsgesellschaft, 2001); and David Cortright and George A. Lopez, *Sanctions and the Search for Security: Challenges to UN Action* (Boulder CO: Lynne Rienner, 2002), 153–79.

7 Two additional resolutions, 558 (1984) and 591 (1986), reminded member states of their obligations under the existing arms embargo on South Africa.

8 Though some observers have credited efforts to isolate apartheid South Africa, such as through banning sports contacts, as being among the more powerful measures to persuade it to change, the Security Council has never called for the total isolation of any member state. The General Assembly went a good deal farther in this direction, though its decisions were not binding. See, for example, Margaret Doxey, *International Sanctions in Contemporary Perspective*, 127 and 163–4, note 5.

9 As Margaret Doxey has pointed out, the drafters failed to specify the need to freeze Iraqi assets, which was only accomplished through Resolution 670 seven weeks later. Two years later, the same mistake was repeated in Council sanctions on Serbia-Montenegro. *United Nations Sanctions: Current Policy Issues*, rev. edn (Halifax, Canada: Center for Foreign Policy Studies, Dalhousie University, 1999), 33.

10 For a lucid account of the UN's experience with sanctions over these years, see David Cortright and George A. Lopez, *The Sanctions Decade: Assessing UN Strategies in the 1990s* (Boulder CO: Lynne Rienner, 2000).

11 See, for instance, Cortright and Lopez, *Sanctions and the Search for Security*, 93–114.

12 *Ibid.*, 181–200.

13 See, for example, Hufbauer *et al.*, *Economic Sanctions Reconsidered*, 102; and Cortright and Lopez, *The Sanctions Decade*, 208.

14 Cortright and Lopez, *ibid.*, Table 11.1, 205–7.

15 Boutros Boutros-Ghali, *Agenda for Peace*, UN Document A/47/277, 17 June 1992, 24, para. 41.

16 Boutros Boutros-Ghali, *Supplement to An Agenda for Peace: Position Paper of the Secretary-General on the Occasion of the Fiftieth Anniversary of the United Nations*, UN Document A/50/60-S/1995/1, 3 January 1995, 12, para. 67.

17 *Ibid.*, 13, para. 70.

18 Kofi Annan, *Renewing the United Nations: A Programme for Reform*, UN Document A/51/950, 14 July 1997, 36, para. 108.

19 UN Document S/1995/300, 13 April 1995, Annex.

20 Thomas G. Weiss, David Cortright, George A. Lopez and Larry Minear (eds) *Political Gain and Civilian Pain: Humanitarian Impacts of Economic Sanctions* (Lanham MD: Rowman and Littlefield, 1997).

21 See, for example, Strategic Planning Unit, Executive Office of the UN Secretary-General, "UN Sanctions: How Effective? How Necessary?," paper prepared for the 2nd Interlaken Seminar on Targeting UN Financial Sanctions, 29–31 March, 1999, Switzerland, http://www.smartsanctions.ch/Papers/I2/2unintro.pdf, 104–5.

22 UN Document S/1999/92, 29 January 1999. Sanctions committees, like most other subsidiary bodies of the Security Council, include all fifteen members of the Council and make decisions by consensus. They are usually chaired by non-permanent members of the Council.

23 Knight, "Improving the Effectiveness of UN Arms Embargoes," 48–9; and David Cortright and George A. Lopez, "Reforming Sanctions," in David M. Malone (ed.) *The UN Security Council: From the Cold War to the 21st Century* (Boulder, CO: Lynne Rienner, 2004), 172–3.

24 On the internet, see http://www.smartsanctions.ch. In print, see Swiss Confederation, United Nations Secretariat, and the Watson Institute for International Studies, *Targeted Financial Sanctions: A Manual for Design and Implementation* (Providence RI: Watson Institute for International Studies, Brown University, 2001).

25 Michael Brzoska (ed.) *Design and Implementation of Arms Embargoes and Travel and Aviation Related Sanctions: Results of the 'Bonn-Berlin Process'* (Bonn: Bonn International Center for Conversion, 2001).

26 Peter Wallensteen, Carina Staibano and Mikael Eriksson (eds) *Making Targeted Sanctions Effective: Guidelines for the Implementation of UN Policy Options* (Uppsala: Department of Peace and Conflict Research, Uppsala University, 2003).

27 For a review of sanctions reform efforts, see Michael Brzoska, "From Dumb to Smart? Recent Reforms of UN Sanctions," *Global Governance*, 9, no. 4 (October–December 2003): 519–35.

28 For an insider's account of the politics and inner workings of the Council's sanctions committee on Iraq, named the 661 Committee for the resolution establishing the sanctions, see Peter van Walsum, "The Iraq Sanctions Committee," in Malone, *The UN Security Council*, 181–93.

29 The story of the turnaround of the Angolan sanctions is told in David J. R. Angell, "The Angolan Sanctions Committee," in Malone, *ibid.*, 195–204.

30 For a detailed history and political analysis of the Council's dealings with Iraq, see David M. Malone, *The International Struggle Over Iraq: Politics in the UN Security Council, 1980–2005* (Oxford: Oxford University Press, 2006).

31 The effort to curb Iraqi programs to acquire weapons of mass destruction is addressed in Chapter 9 below.

32 Cortright and Lopez, *The Sanctions Decade*, 45–51; Cortright and Lopez, *Sanctions and the Search for Security*, 21–46; and van Walsum, "The Iraq Sanctions Committee."

33 The revenues were also to be used for payments to the UN Compensation Panel for victims of the war, to meeting half the costs of the Iraq-Kuwait Boundary Demarcation Commission, and to cover the costs of administering the program. Resolution 706 of 15 August 1991.

34 For the voluminous results of the Volcker inquiry, see http://www.iic-offp.org/documents.htm

35 For contributions to this debate, see Andrew Mack and Asif Khan, "UN Sanctions: A Glass Half Full?," in Price and Zacher, *The United Nations and Global Security*, 109–21; Simon Chesterman and Beatrice Pouligny, "Are Sanctions Meant to Work? The Politics of Creating and Implementing Sanctions Through the

United Nations," *Global Governance*, 9, no. 4 (October–December 2003): 503–18,
Robert A. Pape, "Why Sanctions Do Not Work," *International Security*, 22, no. 2
(fall 1997): 90–136; David A. Baldwin, "The Sanctions Debate and the Logic of
Choice," *International Security*, 24, no. 3 (winter 1999/2000): 80–107; Hufbauer *et
al.*, *Economic Sanctions Reconsidered*, 91–115; and Cortright and Lopez, *The Sanctions
Decade*, 203–20.

7   Enlisting and empowering partners

1 The Council was to advise on possible responses to aggression and to address
matters of disarmament, arbitration, and setting up a Permanent Court of
International Justice, but members were "to bring to the attention of the
Assembly or of the Council" possible threats to the peace (Article 11(2)).

2 For more on the relationship between the Secretary-General and the Security
Council, see Leon Gordenker, *The UN Secretary-General and Secretariat* (New York:
Routledge, 2005).

3 For an exception to this general rule, see Sydney D. Bailey and Sam Daws, 3rd
edn, *The Procedure of the UN Security Council* (Oxford: Clarendon Press, 1998), 292.

4 M. J. Peterson, *The UN General Assembly* (New York: Routledge, 2006).

5 Ruth B. Russell, *A History of the United Nations Charter: The Role of the United
States, 1940–1945* (Washington DC: Brookings Institution Press, 1958), 751.

6 Moscow has, at times, argued that the Council should determine how such
missions should be financed. Bailey and Daws, *The Procedure of the UN Security
Council*, 299–300.

7 In the case of the deployment of the United Nations Transition Assistance Group
(UNTAG) to Namibia in 1989, however, concerns in the Assembly about the size
and shape of the budget for the operation presented by the Secretary-General
resulted in a delay in the deployment of the blue helmets that could have had
serious consequences. See *The Blue Helmets: A Review of United Nations Peace-keeping*,
3rd edn (New York: United Nations Department of Public Information, 1996),
208–9.

8 The Article 19 crisis of the early 1960s resulted from the refusal of the Soviet
Union, France, and a number of developing countries to pay their peacekeeping
assessments on the grounds that the Sinai and Congo missions had been authorized only by the General Assembly and that the use of peacekeepers is not
mentioned in the Charter and thus should be funded through voluntary payments.
It not only led to a financial crippling of the Organization, but also to no votes
being taken in the General Assembly in 1964, when Moscow was due to lose its
vote for being two years in arrears, under the provisions of Article 19. For the
latter half of the 1990s, the US paid less than its full assessment for peacekeeping
based on a Congressionally-imposed cap. For accounts of these episodes, see
Edward C. Luck, *Mixed Messages: American Politics and International Organization,
1919–1999* (Washington DC: Brookings Institution Press, 1999), 233–8, and
214 and 244 respectively.

9 Thomas M. Franck, *Nation Against Nation: What Happened to the U.N. Dream and
What the U.S. Can Do About It* (New York: Oxford University Press, 1985), 39–41.

10 General Assembly Resolution 377(V), 3 November 1950.

11 A. LeRoy Bennett, *International Organizations: Principles and Issues*, 5th edn
(Englewood Cliffs NJ: Prentice Hall, 1991), 138.

12 This distancing of ECOSOC from the Security Council may reflect the Soviet preferences at the end of World War II. At Dumbarton Oaks, the American and British delegates had to convince a reluctant Soviet delegation to include ECOSOC in a broad-based conception of the new world body, which Moscow felt should be devoted simply to security, narrowly conceived. Robert C. Hilderbrand, *Dumbarton Oaks: The Origins of the United Nations and the Search for Postwar Security* (Chapel Hill NC: University of North Carolina Press, 1990), 86–93.

13 Bailey and Daws, *The Procedure of the UN Security Council*, 301–3.

14 Kofi Annan, *In Larger Freedom: Towards Development, Security and Human Rights for All* (New York: United Nations, 2005), 59–60, paras. 165–6.

15 *Ibid.*, 63, para. 178. For further discussion of structural prevention, see Chapter 4 above and the Carnegie Commission on Preventing Deadly Conflict, *Preventing Deadly Conflict: Final Report* (New York: Carnegie Corporation of New York, 1997); Address by the Secretary-General to the Security Council, "The Role of the Security Council in the Prevention of Armed Conflict," UN Document SG/SM/7238, 29 November 1999; Statements by the President of the Security Council, UN Document S/PRST/1999/34, 30 November 1999; and UN Document S/PRST/2000/25, 20 July 2000, Fen Osler Hampson, "Preventive Diplomacy at the United Nations and Beyond"; and Edward C. Luck, "Prevention: Theory and Practice," both in Fen Osler Hampson and David M. Malone (eds) *From Reaction to Conflict Prevention: Opportunities for the UN System* (Boulder CO: Lynne Rienner, 2002), 139–57 and 251–71, respectively.

16 High-level Panel on Threats, Challenges and Change, *A More Secure World: Our Shared Responsibility* (New York: United Nations, 2004), 87, para. 276.

17 Kofi Annan, *In Larger Freedom*, 42, para. 116. The High-level Panel initially had a somewhat broader conception of the Commission's mandate, to include countries sliding into chaos and conflict, as well as those emerging from such conditions. *A More Secure World*, 83–5, paras 261–9.

18 A/RES/60/180 of 30 December 2005 and S/RES/1645 of 20 December 2005, op. para. 2. Also see S/RES/1646 of 20 December 2005.

19 The permanent members do not have a veto in such elections (Article 10(2) of the Statute).

20 For a more extensive discussion of these cases, see Bailey and Daws, *The Procedure of the UN Security Council*, 307–20; and Bennett, *International Organizations*, 172–85. On a number of occasions, affected states have asked the Court to pronounce on Council decisions, but it has understandably been reluctant to do so.

21 There is a substantial literature of personal accounts and case studies that shed light on the range of UN-regional experiences in peace operations. For the former, see, for instance, Marrack Goulding, *Peacemonger* (Baltimore MD: Johns Hopkins University Press, 2003); and William Shawcross, *Deliver Us From Evil: Peacekeepers, Warlords and a World of Endless Conflict* (New York: Simon and Schuster, 2000). For case studies, see *Blue Helmets*; Donald C. F. Daniel and Bradd C. Hayes (eds) *Beyond Traditional Peacekeeping* (New York: St Martin's Press, 1995); Herbert Howe, "Lessons of Liberia: ECOMOG and Regional Peacekeeping," *International Security*, 21, no. 3 (winter 1996/7): 145–76; Michael W. Doyle, Ian Johnstone and Robert C. Orr (eds) *Keeping the Peace: Multidimensional UN Operations in Cambodia and El Salvador* (Cambridge: Cambridge University Press, 1997); Stephen John Stedman, Donald Rothchild and Elizabeth M. Cousens (eds) *Ending Civil Wars: The Implementation of Peace Agreements* (Boulder CO: Lynne Rienner, 2002); Michael Pugh and Waheguru Pal Singh Siddhu (eds) *The United Nations and Regional*

Security: Europe and Beyond (Boulder CO: Lynne Rienner, 2003); and Adekeye Adebajo and Ismail Rashid (eds) *West Africa's Security Challenges: Building Peace in a Troubled Region* (Boulder CO: Lynne Rienner, 2004).

22 UN Document A/47/277 – S/24111, 17 June 1992, 35–7, paras 60, 63 and 64.

23 UN Document A/50/60-S/1995/1, 3 January 1995, 7 and 21, paras 24, 87 and 88.

24 Brian L. Job, "The UN, Regional Organizations, and Regional Conflict: Is there a Viable Role for the UN?," in Richard M. Price and Mark W. Zacher (eds) *The United Nations and Global Security* (New York: Palgrave MacMillan, 2004), 233, Table 14.2.

25 Alex J. Bellamy and Paul D. Williams, "Who's Keeping the Peace? Regionalization and Contemporary Peace Operations," *International Security*, 29, no. 4 (spring 2005), 166, Table 2.

26 James O. C. Jonah, "The United Nations," in Adebajo and Rashid, *West Africa's Security Challenges*, 342.

27 Goulding, *Peacemonger*, 217–18.

28 Job, "The UN, Regional Organizations, and Regional Conflict," 239.

29 *SIPRI Yearbook: World Armament and Disarmament, 1993* (Stockholm: Almquist and Wiksell, 1993).

30 United Nations website, "Contributions to UN Peacekeeping Operations," http://www.un.org/depts/dpko

31 See White House, Press Secretary, President Speaks to the United Nations General Assembly, 21 September 2004; White House, Press Secretary, Background Briefing on Peace Support Operations, 8 June 2004; and, on initial problems, Sonni Efron, "Demise of a Peacekeeping Initiative," *Los Angeles Times*, 23 October 2004.

32 Kofi Annan, *In Larger Freedom*, 71, paras 213–15. For the more modest recommendations of his High-level Panel, see *A More Secure World*, 85–6, para. 272.

33 Non-governmental associations have historically played important roles both in national and transnational political dynamics. See, for example, Steve Charnovitz, "Two Centuries of Participation: NGOs and International Governance," *Michigan Journal of International Law*, 18, no. 2 (winter 1997): 183–286 and Ann M. Florini (ed.) *The Third Force: The Rise of Transnational Civil Society* (Washington DC: Carnegie Endowment for International Peace, 2000), 8–13.

34 Thomas G. Weiss (ed.) *Beyond UN Subcontracting: Task-Sharing with Regional Security Arrangements and Service-Providing NGOs* (London: Macmillan, 1998).

35 Andrew S. Natsios, "NGOs and the UN System in Complex Humanitarian Emergencies: Conflict or Cooperation?," in Thomas G. Weiss and Leon Gordenker (eds) *NGOs, the UN, and Global Governance* (Boulder CO: Lynne Rienner, 1996), 80.

36 See, for example, James A. Paul, "Working with Nongovernmental Organizations," in David M. Malone, *The UN Security Council: From the Cold War to the 21st Century* (Boulder CO: Lynne Rienner, 2004), 373–87.

37 See, for instance, the Council's 2004 sessions on the role of civil society in postconflict peace building. UN Document S/PV.4993 (and Resumption 1), 22 June 2004.

38 UN Document A/58/817, 11 June 2004, 45, para. 95.

39 *Ibid.*, 45, para. 98, plus Proposal 12 on 46. For the Secretary-General's comments on these proposals, see UN Document A/59/354, 13 September 2004, 4, paras 13–14.

40 Stephen John Stedman, "Spoiler Problems in Peace Processes," *International Security*, 22, no. 2 (fall 1997): 5–53.

41 For a range of perspectives on what motivates armed groups, see Mats Berdal and David Malone (eds) *Greed and Grievance: Economic Agendas in Civil Wars* (Boulder CO: Lynne Rienner, 2001); and Eboe Hutchful and Kwesi Aning, "The Political Economy of Conflict," in Adebajo and Rashid (eds) *West Africa's Security Challenges*, 192–222.

42 Andrés Franco, "Armed Nonstate Actors," in Malone, *The UN Security* Council, 117–30. Also see P. J. Simmons and Chantal de Jonge Oudraat (eds) *Managing Global Issues: Lessons Learned* (Washington DC: Carnegie Endowment for International Peace, 2001).

43 Jeffrey Herbst, "International Laws of War and the African Child: Norms, Compliance, and Sovereignty," in Edward C. Luck and Michael W. Doyle (eds) *International Law and Organization: Closing the Compliance Gap* (Lanham MD: Rowman and Littlefield, 2004), 185–203.

8   The humanitarian imperative

1 "Unifying the Security Council in Defence of Human Rights," Address to the Centennial of the First International Peace Conference, The Hague, 18 May 1999, in *The Question of Intervention: Statements by the Secretary-General* (New York: United Nations, 1999), 33.

2 For a searching discussion of these challenges, see Thomas G. Weiss and David A. Korn, *Internal Displacement: Conceptualization and its Consequences* (London: Routledge, 2006).

3 "Reflections on Intervention," Ditchley Park, United Kingdom, 26 June 1998 in *The Question of Intervention*, 6. For an early discussion of state responsibility, see Francis M. Deng, Sadikiel Kimaro, Terence Lyons, Donald Rothchild and I. William Zartman, *Sovereignty As Responsibility: Conflict Management in Africa* (Washington DC: Brookings Institution Press, 1996).

4 As Thomas G. Weiss commented in the early 1990s, "too many pleas for consistency or against inevitable selectivity amount to arguing that the United Nations should not intervene anywhere unless it can intervene everywhere. These objections justify inaction." "On the Brink of a New Era?: Humanitarian Interventions, 1991–94," in Donald C. F. Daniel and Bradd C. Hayes (eds) *Beyond Traditional Peacekeeping* (London: Macmillan Press, 1995), 8.

5 Michael Ignatieff, "The Stories We Tell: Television and Humanitarian Aid," in Jonathan Moore (ed.) *Hard Choices: Moral Dilemmas in Humanitarian Intervention* (Lanham MD: Rowman and Littlefield, 1998), 287–302.

6 Boutros Boutros-Ghali, *Supplement to An Agenda for Peace*, UN Document A/ 50/60 – S/1995/1, 3 January 1995, 6, para. 18.

7 Kofi Annan, *In Larger Freedom: Towards Development, Security and Human Rights for All* (New York: United Nations, 2005), 48, para. 134.

8 Thomas G. Weiss, "The Humanitarian Impulse," in David M. Malone (ed.) *The UN Security Council: From the Cold War to the 21st Century* (Boulder CO: Lynne Rienner, 2004), 38.

9 UN Document S/23500, 31 January 1992.

10 Boutros Boutros-Ghali, *An Agenda for Peace: Preventive Diplomacy, Peacemaking, and Peace-keeping*, UN Document A/47/277, 17 June 1992, 8, para. 29.

11 *Ibid.*, 8, para. 30.

12 Boutros-Ghali, *Supplement to An Agenda for Peace*, 6, para. 18.

13 *Ibid.*, 6, para. 19.

14 Boutros-Ghali, *An Agenda for Peace*, 4, para. 17.

15 Five of these addresses can be found in *The Question of Intervention*.

16 *Ibid.*, 42.

17 In the face of so much resistance, the Secretary-General found a tactical retreat to be the most practical course. The next year, his Millennium Report, *"We the Peoples": The Role of the United Nations in the 21st Century*, only included a brief discussion of "the dilemma of intervention." UN Document A/54/2000 (2000), 47–8.

18 Report of the International Commission on Intervention and State Sovereignty, *The Responsibility to Protect* (Ottawa: International Development Research Centre, 2001), xi. Also see the Supplementary Volume, edited by Thomas G. Weiss and Don Hubert, of research, bibliography, and background materials.

19 *Ibid.*, xiii.

20 Kofi Annan, *In Larger Freedom*, 49, para. 135.

21 UN Document SG/A/880, 14 July 2004.

22 For a thoughtful analysis of the UN's role in developing and promoting the notion of human security, see S. Neil MacFarlane and Yuen Foong Khong, *Human Security and the UN: A Critical History* (Bloomington, IN: Indiana University Press, 2006).

23 UN Document, A/60/L.1, para. 138.

24 *Ibid.*, para. 139.

25 As Joanna Weschler notes, the Security Council's record on human rights has had its ups and downs, but its "attitude has been evolving toward a general acceptance of the responsibility to take steps, whenever possible, to prevent massive human rights violations and to protect the most vulnerable." "Human Rights," in Malone, *The UN Security Council*, 66.

26 The Security Council, however, never embraced the amorphous concept of "human security" to the extent that Secretary-General Kofi Annan and others in the UN community seemed to. According to the Secretary-General, "freedom from want, freedom from fear, and the freedom of future generations to inherit a healthy environment – these are the interrelated building blocks of human – and therefore national – security." UN Document SG/SM/7382 of 8 May 2000. In his view, "the prevention of conflict begins and ends with the protection of human life and the protection of human development. Ensuring human security is, in the broadest sense, the United Nations' cardinal mission." UN Document SG/SM/6534 of 22 April 1998. Also see the report of the Commission on Human Security, *Human Security Now: Protecting and Empowering People* (New York: Commission on Human Security, 2003). For a balanced critique, see Roland Paris, "Human Security: Paradigm Shift or Hot Air?," *International Security*, 26, no. 2 (fall 2001): 87–102.

27 Human Security Centre, University of British Columbia, Canada, *Human Security Report: War and Peace in the 21st Century* (Oxford: Oxford University Press, 2005), 31; Bethany Lacina and Nils Petter Gleditsch, *Monitoring Trends in Global Combat: A New Dataset of Battle Deaths 2005* (Oslo: Centre for the Study of Civil War, 2004). Also see Monty G. Marshall, "Measuring the Societal Impact of War," in Fen Osler Hampson and David M. Malone (eds) *From Reaction to Conflict Prevention: Opportunities for the UN System* (Boulder CO: Lynne Rienner, 2002), 63–104.

28 *Human Security Report, ibid.*, 31, Figure 1.8; Meredith Reid Sarkees, Frank Whelon Wayman and J. David Singer, "Inter-State, Intra-State and Extra-State Wars: A

Comprehensive look at Their Distribution Over Time, 1816–1997," *International Studies Quarterly*, 47 (March 2003): 49–70.

29 Lotta Harborn and Peter Wallensteen, "Armed Conflict and its International Dimensions, 1946–2004," *Journal of Peace Research*, 42, no. 5 (September 2005), Table II, 624 (as revised, http://www.prio.no/page/CSCW_research_detail/Programme_detail_CSCW/9649/47173.html). Also see *A More Secure World: Our Shared Responsibility*, Report of the High-level Panel on Threats, Challenges and Change (New York: United Nations, 2004), 11, para. 5 and figure.

30 Harborn and Wallensteen, "Armed Conflict and its International Dimensions," *ibid.*, 623 and Table 1, 624, as revised, *ibid.*

31 *A More Secure World*, 33, para. 85.

32 *Human Security Report 2005*, 31 and 24 respectively.

33 For a summary of Security Council actions relevant to this conflict, see the Security Council Report, Update Report No. 1, Ethiopia/Eritrea, 9 November 2005, http://www.securitycouncilreport.org.

34 Boutros-Ghali, *Supplement to An Agenda for Peace*, 5, para. 12.

35 Stefan Elbe, "HIV/AIDs and the Changing Landscape of War in Africa," *International Security*, 27, no. 2 (fall 2002): 159–77.

36 Security Council Resolution 1308 of 17 July 2000.

37 See Jeffrey Herbst, "International Law of War and the African Child: Norms, Compliance, and Sovereignty," and James R. Katalikawe, Henry M. Onoria, and Baker G. Wairama, "Crisis and Conflicts in the African Great Lakes Region: The Problem of Noncompliance with Humanitarian Law," in Edward C. Luck and Michael W. Doyle (eds) *International Law and Organization: Closing the Compliance Gap* (Lanham MD: Rowman and Littlefield), 2004, 185–203 and 121–52, respectively.

38 UN Document A/51/306, 26 August 1996, 90, para. 318. The study was mandated by General Assembly resolution 48/157 of 20 December 1993.

39 S/RES/1612 of 26 July 2005, S/RES/1539 of 22 April 2004, S/RES/1460 of 20 January 2003, S/RES/1379 of 20 November 2001, S/RES/1314 of 11 August 2000, and S/RES/1261 of 30 August 1999. For the latest report of the Secretary-General, see UN Document A/59/695-S/2005/72 of 9 February 2005.

40 S/RES/1325 of 31 October 2000, op. paras 10 and 11.

41 S/RES/955 of 8 November 1994. Also see Navanethem Pillay, "Sexual Violence in Times of Conflict: The Jurisprudence of the International Criminal Tribunal for Rwanda," in Simon Chesterman (ed.) *Civilians in War* (Boulder CO: Lynne Rienner, 2001), 165–76.

42 See, for example, UN Documents S/PRST/2001/31 of 31 October 2001, S/PRST/2002/6 and Annex of 15 March 2002, S/PRST/2003/27 of 15 December 2003, S/PRST/2004/40 of 28 October 2004, and S/PRST/2004/46 of 14 December 2004.

43 Report of the Secretary-General on Women and Peace and Security, UN Document S/2004/814 of 13 October 2004, 2, para. 6.

44 *Ibid.*, 7–9, paras 31–40.

45 A/RES/57/306 of 22 May 2003, UN Document A/57/465 of 11 October 2002, S/RES/1400 of 28 March 2002, and UN Document S/PRST/2002/41 of 20 December 2002. For the Secretary-General's bulletin on these issues, see UN Document ST/SGB/2003/13 of 9 October 2003.

46 UN Document S/PRST/2002/41 of 20 December 2002. The Secretary-General similarly appealed to member states to insure "that military personnel serving with United Nations peacekeeping operations are held accountable for any acts of sexual exploitation and abuse." UN Document A/58/777 of 23 April 2004, 4, para. 14.

47 UN Document A/59/710 of 24 March 2005.

48 UN Document A/59/19/Add. 1 of 11 April 2005.

49 UN Documents S/PRST/2005/21 of 31 May 2005 and S/PRST/2005/52 of 27 October 2005.

50 Arthur C. Helton, *The Price of Indifference: Refugees and Humanitarian Action in the New Century* (Oxford: Oxford University Press, 2002), 18.

51 Former US Permanent Representative to the United Nations Richard C. Holbrooke insisted that the legal and policy distinction between "internally displaced" and "refugees" – those whose forced dislocations moved them across state borders – was dysfunctional, especially in light of the growing numbers of internal refugees who did not qualify under traditional rules for assistance by the UN High Commissioner for Refugees (UNHCR). See USUN Press Release #6 (00) of 13 January 2000 and Richard Holbrooke, "A Borderline Difference: We Ignore Millions Who Are Refugees in Their Own Countries," *Washington Post*, 8 May 2000. For views on the role of economic motivations in conflict, see Eboe Hutchful and Kwesi Animy, "The Political Economy of Conflict," in Adekeye Adebajo and Ismail Rashid (eds) *West Africa's Security Challenges: Building Peace in a Troubled Region* (Boulder CO: Lynne Rienner, 2004), 195–222; and Mats Berdal and David Malone (eds) *Greed and Grievance: Economic Agendas in Civil Wars* (Boulder CO: Lynne Rienner, 2000).

52 Boutros-Ghali, *Supplement to An Agenda for Peace*, 5, para. 12.

53 According to the UN High Commissioner for Refugees (UNHCR), the total "population of concern" was 19.8 million in 1997 and 19.2 million in 2004. Over this period, the number of those who qualified as refugees fell from 12 million to 9.2 million. *Refugees by Numbers, 2005 Edition* (Geneva: UNHCR, 2005), 10.

54 *Human Security Report*, 103, Figure 3.1.

55 Luc Côté, "Compliance with the Laws of War: The Role of the International Criminal Tribunal for Rwanda," in Luck and Doyle (eds) *International Law and Organization*, 155.

56 For a brief history, see Steven R. Ratner and Jason S. Abrams, *Accountability for Human Rights Atrocities in International Law: Beyond the Nuremburg Legacy*, 2nd edn (Oxford: Oxford University Press, 2001), 3–25.

57 Resolution 771 was passed unanimously, while China, India, and Zimbabwe abstained on 770.

58 Resolution 827 of 25 May 1993. Earlier, the Council had expressed its intent to establish such a body and requested the Secretary-General to report on options for implementing that resolution. Resolution 808 of 22 February 1993.

59 For assessments of the ICTY's work, see Ratner and Abrams, *Accountability*, 190–201; Philippe Kirsch, John T. Holmes and Mora Johnson, "International Tribunals and Courts," in Malone, *UN Security Council*, 281–94, and Côté, "Compliance."

60 Resolution 872 of 5 October 1993.

61 Resolution 912 of 21 April 1994. For the cogent reflections of the President and a member of the Security Council in April 1994, see Colin Keating, "An Insider's Account," and Ibrahim A. Gambari, "An African Perspective," in Malone, *UN Security Council*, 500–11 and 512–20, respectively.

62 Resolutions 935 of 1 July 1994 and 955 of 8 November 1994, respectively.

63 Katalikawe *et al.*, "Crisis and Conflicts in the African Great Lakes Region," 140, Tables 5.1 and 5.2. Also see Ratner and Abrams, *Accountability*, 201–6, and Côté, "Compliance."

64 For a thoughtful critique of the employment of international tribunals as a deterrent to further violence and human rights abuses, see Jack Snyder and Leslie Vinjamuri, "Trials and Error: Principle and Pragmatism in Strategies of International Justice," *International Security*, 28, no. 3 (winter 2003/04): 5–44; and Gary Jonathan Bass, *Staying the Hand of Vengeance: The Politics of War Crimes Tribunals* (Princeton NJ: Princeton University Press, 2000).

65 Statement to the General Assembly, UN Document SG/SM/7136 – GA/9596, 20 September 1999.

66 This line of thought is further developed in Edward C. Luck, "The Enforcement of Humanitarian Norms and the Politics of Ambivalence," in Simon Chesterman, *Civilians in War*, 197–218.

9 Terrorism and weapons of mass destruction

1 League of Nations, *Convention for the Prevention and Punishment of Terrorism*, L.546(1).M.383(1).1937V, Geneva, 16 November 1937; and, for the draft convention on the ICC, see League of Nations, *Committee for the International Repression of Terrorism*, C222.M.162.1937.V, Geneva, 26 April 1937, Appendix II. For a fuller discussion of these conventions, see Edward C. Luck, "Another Reluctant Belligerent: The United Nations and the War on Terrorism," in Richard Price and Mark Zacher (eds) *The United Nations and Global Security* (New York: Palgrave Macmillan, 2004), 96–7.

2 League of Nations, *Proceedings of the International Conferences on the Repression of Terrorism*, C.94.M.47.1938V, Geneva, 1–16 November 1937, 50; League of Nations, *International Repression of Terrorism, Draft Conventions, Observations by Governments, Series III*, A.24(b).1936V, Geneva, 21 February 1938, 2.

3 The widespread use of poison gas in the First World War had led to the 1925 Geneva Protocol for the Prohibition of the Use in War of Asphyxiating, Poisonous or Other Gases, and of Bacteriological Methods of Warfare. The US signed but never ratified the Protocol. From 1932 to 1937, the League's Disarmament Conference tried unsuccessfully to negotiate an agreement to prohibit the production and stockpiling of biological and chemical weapons. US Arms Control and Disarmament Agency, *Arms Control and Disarmament Agreements: Text and Histories of Negotiations*, 1980 edn (Washington DC: US Government Printing Office, 1980), 120.

4 Resolution 1(1), "Establishment of a Commission to Deal with the Problem Raised by the Discovery of Atomic Energy," 24 January 1946.

5 US Arms Control and Disarmament Agency, *Agreements*, 82.

6 The Charter's wording in that regard is a bit inconsistent, as Article 47(1) calls on the Military Staff Committee to advise and assist on "the regulation of armaments, and possible disarmament."

7 Quoted in Grayson Kirk, "The Enforcement of Security," *Yale Law Journal*, 55, no. 5 (August 1946): 1091–2. Also see Dean Acheson, *Present at the Creation: My Years in the State Department* (New York: W. W. Norton, 1969), 155.

8 Debates also ensued about the extent to which the UN's arms control and disarmament efforts should focus on nuclear arms or conventional forces, given that the Soviet bloc was widely credited with having an advantage in the latter. In February 1947, the Security Council, despite a Soviet abstention, voted to establish a Commission on Conventional Armaments. The next month, in a unanimous

vote, the Council urged the Atomic Energy Commission to submit a draft treaty on the international control of atomic energy. Resolutions 18 (1947) of 13 February 1947 and 20 (1947) of 10 March 1947. In 1952, the two commissions were merged to form the UN Disarmament Commission. For the Council resolution to dissolve the Commission for Conventional Armaments, see Resolution 97 (1952) of 30 January 1952. Also see General Assembly Resolution 502 (VI) of 11 January 1952.

9 The State Department identified more than 150 international terrorist incidents in 1968 and almost 200 in 1969. These annual totals rose to more than 600 for the period 1985–8 and ebbed somewhat since. US Department of State, Office of the Coordinator for Counterterrorism, *Patterns of Global Terrorism, 1992, 1995, and 2001* (Washington DC: US Department of State series).

10 Resolution 286 (1970), 9 September 1970.

11 For broader accounts of the roles of the Security Council and the General Assembly in addressing terrorism, see Chantal de Jonge Oudraat, "The Role of the Security Council," and M. J. Peterson, "Using the General Assembly," in Jane Boulden and Thomas G. Weiss (eds) *Terrorism After September 11th* (Bloomington IN: Indiana University Press, 2004), 151–72 and 173–97, respectively.

12 This point is further developed in Edward C. Luck, "The Uninvited Challenge: Terrorism Targets the United Nations," in Edward Newman and Ramesh Thakur (eds) *Multilateralism Under Challenge: Power, International Order and Structural Change* (Tokyo: United Nations University and the Social Science Research Council, 2006).

13 For a fuller discussion of how the politics of the Middle East have shaped the Security Council's response to terrorism, see Edward C. Luck, "Tackling Terrorism," in David M. Malone (ed.) *The United Nations Security Council: From the Cold War to the 21st Century* (Boulder CO: Lynne Rienner, 2004), 88–93 and 97–8.

14 The Assembly's will to fight terrorism, of course, was no more promising. Hoping to save the day, Secretary-General Kurt Waldheim then urged the Assembly to address the growing threat from terrorism. It produced, instead, a resolution condemning not terrorism but the "continuation of repressive and terrorist acts by colonial, racist and alien regimes in denying peoples their legitimate right to self-determination and independence and other human rights and fundamental freedoms." Resolution 3034 (XXVII) of 18 December 1972, para. 4. Also see Robert Alden, "Strong Legal Action to Combat Terrorism is Rebuffed at U.N.," *New York Times*, 12 December 1972.

15 General Assembly Resolution 2373 (XXII), annex. For a brief history of the negotiating process, see US Arms Control and Disarmament Agency, *Agreements*, 82-9.

16 Resolution 255 (1968), 19 June 1968, para. 1. The previous quote is from para 2. In 1995, in conjunction with the NPT Review Conference, the Security Council adopted a refinement of these assurances, in this case with all five permanent members and nuclear weapons states firmly on board. S/RES/984 (1995), 11 April 1995.

17 For a forward-looking discussion of the Council's potential role in stemming WMD proliferation, see McGeorge Bundy *et al.*, *Confronting the Proliferation Danger: The Role of the U.N. Security Council* (New York: United Nations Association of the USA, 1995).

18 Article III, para. B4 and Article XII, para. C.

19 Article VII.C.36 and Article XVI.

20 Articles VI and XIII.

21 In 1981, however, the Council did unanimously condemn the unilateral actions of one member state, Israel, when it undertook air strikes to destroy Iraqi nuclear facilities that it perceived to be a threat to its national security. Resolution 487 (1981) of 19 January 1981. A decade later, of course, the Council found that Iraqi efforts to develop WMD, including nuclear weapons, constituted a threat to international peace and security.

22 Robert C. McFadden, "Terror in 1985: Brutal Attacks, Tough Responses," *New York Times*, 30 December 1985.

23 A/RES/40/61 of 9 December 1985 and Council Resolution 579 (1985) of 18 December 1985.

24 Resolution 635 (1989) of 14 June 1989.

25 Resolution 638 (1989) of 31 July 1989.

26 Resolution 678 of 29 November 1990. On that vote, China abstained, while Cuba and Yemen voted against the resolution, making it 12–2–1. The closest analogy would have been Resolution 83 of 27 June 1950 recommending that member states assist the Republic of Korea in repelling the armed attack from North Korea. At that point, however, the Soviet Union was boycotting the Council and did not participate in the voting.

27 UN Document S/23500 of 31 January 1992.

28 David Cortright and George A. Lopez, *The Sanctions Decade: Assessing UN Strategies in the 1990s* (Boulder CO: Lynne Rienner, 2000), 107–33.

29 See paras 5(a) and 8(c), respectively. While the other Taliban-related resolutions were adopted unanimously, China and Malaysia abstained on this one.

30 For accounts by UNSCOM's two Executive Chairmen, see Rolf E. Ekeus, "Compliance or Non-Compliance with Arms Control and Disarmament," in Ian Anthony and Adam Daniel Rotfeld (eds) *A Future Arms Control Agenda: Proceedings of Nobel Symposium 118, 1999* (Oxford: Oxford University Press, 2001), 190–8; and Richard Butler, *The Greatest Threat: Iraq, Weapons of Mass Destruction, and the Crisis of Global Security* (New York: Public Affairs, 2000).

31 For Council resolutions condemning Iraq's lack of cooperation, see 1060 of 12 June 1996, 1115 of 21 June 1997, 1134 of 23 October 1997, 1137 of 12 November 1997, 1194 of 9 September 1998, and 1205 of 5 November 1998.

32 Jean Pascale Zanders, "The Elimination of Chemical and Biological Weapons," in Anthony and Rotfeld, *A Future Arms Control Agenda*, 310–17; and Pascal Teixeira da Silva, "Weapons of Mass Destruction: The Iraqi Case," in Malone, *The United Nations Security Council*, 208.

33 These same divisions, with the US and United Kingdom on one side and China, France, and Russia on the other, persisted into the 2002–3 Council debate over the use of force in Iraq.

34 For an account of the international community's contrasting approaches to handling the Iraqi and North Korean cases, see Harold A. Feiveson and Jacqueline W. Shire, "Dilemmas of Compliance with Arms Control and Disarmament Agreements," in Edward C. Luck and Michael W. Doyle, *International Law and Organization: Closing the Compliance Gap* (Lanham MD: Rowman and Littlefield, 2004), 217–225.

35 It would have been the first state party to do so. It had joined the NPT in 1985, but had only signed a safeguards agreement with the IAEA in 1992.

36 India had exploded a small device in 1974, but had declared it to be a "peaceful" nuclear explosion and had refrained from following up for more than two decades.

37 UN Document S/PRST/1998/12 of 14 May 1998.

38 UN Document S/PRST/1998/17 of 29 May 1998.
39 UN Document S/1998/473 of 5 June 1998 and Annex.
40 Zia Mian, "The American Problem: The United States and Noncompliance in the World of Arms Control and Nonproliferation," in Luck and Doyle, *International Law and Organization*, 282.
41 A/RES/56/1 and 1368, respectively.
42 See, for example, José E. Alavarez, "Hegemonic and International Law Revisited," *The American Journal of International Law*, 97, no. 4 (October 2003): 879–82; de Jonge Oudraat, "Role of the Security Council," in *Terrorism After September 11th*, 158–61; and Nico Schrijver, "September 11 and Challenges to International Law," in Boulden and Weiss, *Terrorism and the UN*, 55–73.
43 Given subsequent differences over the use of force in Iraq, it is worth recalling that both 1368 and 1373 were adopted during a French presidency of the Council.
44 The adoption of 1540 did not proceed as quickly or smoothly as 1368 and 1373 had. First worked out among the five permanent members, the text of 1540 was then considered in debates among a much wider group of countries, including many non-members of the Council, before something close to a consensus could be obtained. While the US was supportive of 1540, it initially favored giving the committee only a six-month tenure and then went along with the two-year term eventually adopted.
45 As is normal practice, each resolution setting up a sanctions regime included a provision for setting up a corresponding Council sanctions committee, such as the one for 1267, which is still functioning.
46 Luck, "Another Reluctant Belligerent," 102.
47 UN Document S/PV.4512, 15 April 2002, 2. Regarding the trust fund, see UN Document S/PV.4453, 18 January 2002, 4.
48 United Nations Security Council, *Proposal for the Revitalization of the Counter-Terrorism Committee*, UN Document S/2004/124, 19 February 2004.
49 The High Commissioner had pressed, unsuccessfully, for the CTC to include human rights criteria in its assessment of member state reports. See OHCHR, Note to the Chair of the Counter-Terrorism Committee: A Human Rights Perspective on Counter-Terrorist Measures, 23 September 2002. Alternatively, the Secretary-General has proposed a special rapporteur to report to the Commission on Human Rights "on the compatibility of counter-terrorism measures with international human rights laws." Kofi Annan, *In Larger Freedom: Towards Development, Security and Human Rights for All* (New York: United Nations, 2005), 36, para. 94. In the same report, however, he lauded "the increasing frequency of the Security Council's invitations to the High Commissioner" (51, para. 144).
50 UN Documents S/2004/1039, 6 and S/2005/799, 3, respectively.
51 Eric Rosand, "Security Council Resolution 1373, the Counter-Terrorism Committee, and the Fight Against Terrorism," *The American Journal of International Law*, 97, no. 2 (April 2003): 333–41; and David Cortright, George A. Lopez, Alistair Miller and Linda Gerber, *An Action Agenda for Enhancing the United Nations Program on Counter-Terrorism* (Goshen IN: Fourth Freedom Forum, 2004).
52 *Work Programme of the Counter-Terrorism Committee, 1 April – 30 June 2005*, UN Document S/2005/266, 22 April 2005, para. 3.
53 UN Document S/2005/799, 19 December 2005, Annex, 4, para. 15. Given differences among its members, the 1540 Committee got off to a slow start. Originally, the national reports had been due by 28 October 2004.

54 For a breakdown of signatories and parties by convention and by country, as of 1 November 2004, see Annex VI and VII of UN Document S/2005/83, Second Report of the Analytical Support and Sanctions Monitoring Team appointed pursuant to Resolution 1526 (2004) concerning Al-Qaida and the Taliban and associated individuals and entities. For the post-9/11/01 acceleration of adherence to the conventions, see Cortright *et al.*, *Action Agenda*, 6–7.

55 For example, see the December 2004 report of the Secretary-General's High-level Panel on Threats, Challenges and Change, *A More Secure World: Our Shared Responsibility* (New York: United Nations, 2004), 50, paras 152–3. For comments by the 1267 committee on this and other matters, see UN Document S/2005/760, 6 December 2005.

56 For the third report of the Analytical Support and Sanctions Monitoring Team, see UN Document S/2005/572, 2 September 2005.

57 UN Document S/2004/1037, 31 December 2004, 4.

58 UN Documents S/PV.5168, S/PV.5229, and S/PV.5293.

59 25 May 2005, talking points for the latter session are available at http://www.sipa.columbia.edu/cio.

60 Eric Rosand cites similar statements from a range of developing countries as well; see "The Security Council as 'Global Legislator': *Ultra Vires* or Ultra Innovative," *Fordham International Law Journal*, 28 (May 2005): 542–90.

61 UN Document, A/60/L.1, 15 September 2005, 22, paras 81–3.

62 For a discussion of the CTC's outreach and coordination efforts, see Cortright *et al.*, *Action Agenda*, 17–23.

63 UN Document A/57/273, S/2002/875, Annex, 4, para. 9.

64 As noted earlier, UNSCOM, the UN's first substantial effort to identify, locate, and destroy Iraqi programs to develop and deploy weapons of mass destruction and their delivery systems, was something of an exception. In the end, this mix proved to be a factor in the demise of what had been a largely productive mission. See David Kay, *Information Resources for Assessing Emerging Threats to International Peace and Security* (New York: United Nations Association of the USA, 1997); Daniel Byman, "A Farewell to Arms Inspections," *Foreign Affairs*, 79, no. 1 (January/February 2000); and Richard Butler, *The Greatest Threat*.

65 UN Document SG/SM/9757, 10 March 2005.

66 Secretary-General Kofi Annan, *Renewing the United Nations: A Programme for Reform*, UN Document A/51/950, 14 July 1997, 36, para. 107; and Secretary-General Boutros Boutros-Ghali, *Supplement to An Agenda for Peace*, UN Document A/50/60, 3 January 1995, 18–19, paras 77–80.

67 According to Rik Coolsaet of Brussels' Royal Institute for International Relations, "within the EU, there is a widely shared belief that the war in Afghanistan was and will remain the only part of the post-9/11 counterterrorism effort where military means played a significant role." In his view,

> the international mechanisms of sanctions and suppression have been very effective immediately after 9/11, but are gradually becoming less and less relevant, because – as a result of the decentralisation and atomization of jihadism – they address a set of circumstances which no longer apply.
> (Rik Coolsaet, "Between al-Andalus and a Failing Integration: Europe's Pursuit of a Long-term Counterterrorism Strategy in the Post-Al-Qaeda Era," Egmont Paper 5, Brussels: Royal Institute for International Relations (IRRI-KIIB), May 2005, 6–7)

68 For the debate on arms embargoes and travel sanctions within the "Bonn-Berlin Process," see Michael Brzoska (ed.) *Smart Sanctions: The Next Steps* (Baden-Baden: Nomos Verlagsgesellschaft, 2001); and for the "Stockholm Process on the Implementation of Targeted Sanctions," see Peter Wallensteen, Carina Staibano and Mikael Eriksson (eds) *Making Targeted Sanctions More Effective: Guidelines for the Implementation of UN Policy Options* (Uppsala: Uppsala University, 2003).

69 Kofi Annan, *In Larger Freedom*, 35, para. 87.

10 Reform, adaptation, and evolution

1 For a good sense of FDR's views on postwar organization, see Forrest Davis, "Roosevelt's World Blueprint," *Saturday Evening Post*, 10 April 1943, 20–1, 109–10. In terms of criteria for permanent membership, it is worth recalling that the so-called "policemen" were not necessarily the five strongest powers at that time, as France and China had been occupied during the war, but they were the five principal allies. Clauses concerning the "enemies" were included in the Charter, and they were only to be considered for admission once they were judged to have become "peace-loving."

2 See Chapter 2 above, as well as Ruth B. Russell, *A History of the United Nations Charter: The Role of the United States 1940–1945* (Washington DC: Brookings Institution Press, 1958), 646–55 and 713–49; Stephen C. Schlesinger, *Act of Creation: The Founding of the United Nations* (Boulder, CO: Westview Press, 2003), 159–74 and 193–207; and Townsend Hoopes and Douglas Brinkley, *FDR and the Creation of the U.N.* (New Haven CT: Yale University Press, 1997), 184–204.

3 Among those advocating regional seats were Brazil, Colombia, Cuba, Egypt, Philippines and Uruguay. Speaking on 20 June 1945, the Egyptian delegate, Badawi Pasha, sounded the same themes as many of those calling for enlargement today:

> The Security Council, in our view, would be more democratic if this amendment [to expand the Council from 11 to 14] were adopted and would represent all of the great regions of the world. In our opinion, this would not have in any way diminished its capacity for acting very quickly. ... In connection with the method of election of non-permanent members, we think that the method should be based on geographical distribution by region.
>
> (Verbatim minutes of the Fourth Meeting of Commission III, 20 June 1945, *United Nations Conference on International Organization (UNCIO), Selected Documents*, Washington DC: US Government Printing Office, 1946, 798)

4 *Documents of the United Nations Conference on International Organization 1945*, Commission III: Security Council, Volume XI (New York: UN Information Organizations, 1945), 291.

5 See General Assembly Resolution 992(X) of 21 November 1955 and Security Council Resolution 110 (1955) of 16 December 1955. Article 109(1) was subsequently amended in 1968.

6 This count excludes Australia, New Zealand, and several Middle Eastern states.

7 For key points in the Assembly debate, see UN Document A/PV.1285, 17 December 1963, 6–17. For the report of the Committee on Arrangements for a Conference for the Purpose of Reviewing the Charter, see UN Document A/5487,

4 September 1963, 1–7. A summary of Security Council resolutions from the preceding years on these issues can be found in Report of the Security Council, 16 July 1962–15 July 1963, UN Document A/5502, 95–6. For a somewhat fuller summary of the events of this period, see Edward C. Luck, *Reforming the United Nations: Lessons from a History in Progress*, Occasional Paper no. 1 (New Haven CT: The Academic Council on the United Nations System, 2003), 8–10.

8 The United States stated on 14 December, for instance, that it could go along with "modest" expansion of the Council from 11 to 13 members (and of ECOSOC, the Economic and Social Council, from 18 to 24 members), as had been suggested by the Latin American and Caribbean countries.

9 None of the five voted for enlarging ECOSOC in the two-part resolution.

10 Edward C. Luck, *Mixed Messages: American Politics and International Organization, 1919–1999* (Washington DC: Brookings Institution Press, 1999), 233–8.

11 United States Senate, *Congressional Record*, 89th Cong., 1st Sess., 1965, vol. III, pt. 9 (Washington DC: US Government Printing Office, 1965), 12547–59. Had they been present for the vote, three Senators – Richard Russell (D-Georgia), Alan Simpson (R-Wyoming) and Strom Thurmond (R-South Carolina) – indicated that they would have opposed the measure.

12 The Working Group was mandated in resolution A/RES/48/26 of 3 December 1993. While its meetings have been closed, there have been annual reports of its proceedings, see UN Documents A/49-59/47 (1994–2005).

13 This author served as an advisor to President Razali in the development of his plan.

14 Though the Razali Plan is in the form of a draft Assembly resolution, it was presented as a conference room paper to the Working Group. Since the sessions of the group were closed, there is no UN number assigned to the paper and it cannot be found among the UN's public papers. It can be found, however, through the website of the Global Policy Forum, http://www.globalpolicy.org/security/reform/raz-497.htm

15 Press conference, UN Document SG/SM/8855, 8 September 2003 and Address to the General Assembly, UN Document SG/SM/8891-GA/10157, 23 September 2003.

16 UN Document SG/SM/8891.

17 For the group's mandate and membership, see http://www.un.org/secureworld/panelmembers.html

18 High-level Panel on Threats, Challenges and Change, *A More Secure World: Our Shared Responsibility*, UN Document A/59/565, 2 December 2004. For thoughtful critiques, see Ernesto Zedillo (ed.) *Reforming the United Nations for Peace and Security* (New Haven CT: Yale Center for the Study of Globalization, 2005); Michael J. Glennon, "Idealism at the U.N.," *Policy Review*, 129 (February-March 2005): 3–13; and Mats Berdal, "The United Nations at 60: A New San Francisco Moment?," *Survival*, 47, no. 3 (autumn 2005), 7–31. Also see, by this author, "How Not to Reform the United Nations," *Global Governance*, 11, no. 4 (October-December 2005): 407–14.

19 *A More Secure World*, 79–83, paras 244–60.

20 *Ibid.*, 79, paras 245–6.

21 *Ibid.*, 80, paras 249–50.

22 *Ibid.*, 80–2, paras 250–6.

23 *Ibid.*, 82–3, para. 258. The Panel also failed to address, as Razali had, how many of the twenty-four votes would be needed to pass a resolution. Razali placed that hurdle at 15 of the 24, compared to the current 9 of 15.

24　For example, while the Panel had called for the universalization of the Commission on Human Rights, the Secretary-General urged its elimination and replacement by a smaller and more dedicated Human Rights Council. UN Document A/59/2005, 21 March 2005, 63–4, paras 181–3. There was an obvious inconsistency, of course, between the conclusion that smaller was better for human rights but that larger numbers were needed to lend legitimacy to the Security Council.

25　*Ibid.*, 61, para. 170.

26　*Ibid.*, 60, para. 169.

27　*Ibid.*, 60, para. 168.

28　*Ibid.*, 59, para. 165.

29　*Ibid.*, 59, para. 166.

30　Draft resolution UN Document A/59/L.64, 6 July 2005.

31　The geographical groupings in the G-4 proposal followed the standard five divisions used in the General Assembly, while the High-level Panel endorsed a simpler, four-part division. For the latter, *A More Secure World*, 81, para. 251.

32　UN Document A/59/L.64, paras 5(b) and 7. According to para. 6(b), the subsequent resolution to amend the Charter should "reflect the fact that the extension of the right of veto to the new permanent members has not been decided."

33　UN Document A/AC.247/1997/CRP. 1, 20 March 1997, para. 4. Similar recommendations had been made by the Independent Working Group on the Future of the United Nations, *The United Nations in Its Second Half Century* (New York: The Ford Foundation and Yale University, 1995) and by Bruce Russett, Barry O'Neill and James Sutterlin, "Breaking the Security Council Logjam," *Global Governance*, 2, no. 1 (January-April 1996): 77.

34　*A More Secure World*, 82, para. 256.

35　UN Document A/59/L.68, 21 July 2005.

36　*Ibid.*, para. 3(2).

37　For an incisive analysis of the political obstacles to Council expansion in 2005, see Thomas G. Weiss, *Overcoming the Security Council Impasse: The Implausible Versus the Plausible*, Occasional Paper no. 14 (Berlin: Friedrich-Ebert-Stiftung, 2005).

38　Robert Marquand, "Anti-Japan Protests Jar an Uneasy Asia," *Christian Science Monitor*, 11 April 2005; Norimitsu Onishi, "Tokyo Protests Anti-Japan Rallies in China," *New York Times*, 11 April 2005; and Chris Buckley, "Anti-Japan Protests Sweep Across China; Japan Won't Get Apology, Beijing Says," *International Herald Tribune*, 18 April 2005. On Japan's campaign, see Edward C. Luck, "Tokyo's Quixotic Quest for Acceptance," *Far Eastern Economic Review*, 168, no. 5 (May 2005): 5–10.

39　Press release, People's Republic of China Mission to the United Nations, 11 July 2005.

40　Barbara Crossette, "U.S., Bending a Bit, Will Offer Wider Role for 3d World at U.N.," *New York Times*, 17 July 1997; Ambassador Bill Richardson, US Permanent Representative to the UN, Statement to the Open-Ended Working Group of the General Assembly on Security Council Reform, USUN Press Release no. 128(97), 17 July 1997; and Ambassador Richard C. Holbrooke, US Permanent Representative to the UN, Statement to the Open-Ended Working Group of the General Assembly on Security Council Reform, USUN Press Release no. 46(00), 3 April 2000.

41　UN Document SG/SM/8891.

42　Steven R. Weisman, "U.S. Rebuffs Germans Anew on Bid for Security Council," *New York Times*, 9 June 2005; and Nicholas Kralev, "U.S. Declines to Back German Bid," *Washington Post*, 9 June 2005.

43 US Department of State, Remarks by the Secretary of State Condoleezza Rice in the United Nations General Assembly, 17 September 2005.

44 US Department of State, Testimony of R. Nicholas Burns, Under Secretary for Political Affairs, to the Senate Foreign Relations Committee, 21 July 2005.

45 *Ibid.*

46 Anthony Mitchell, "African Leaders Press for Permanent Seats, Veto Powers in U.N. Security Council Reform," Associated Press report, 31 October 2005.

47 UN Document A/59/L.67, 14 July 2005.

48 Ext/ASSEMBLY/AU/Dec.1 (V), Decision on the Reform of the UN System and the Security Council, and Mitchell, "African Leaders Press for Permanent Seats."

49 In the spring of 2005, the Swiss Mission to the United Nations convened a series of informal roundtable meetings of member states to discuss further steps toward working methods reform based on a background paper prepared by this author, "Reforming the Security Council – Step One: Improving Working Methods," 25 April 2005. Some of the discussion in this sub-section draws on that paper. More recently, the so-called S-5 (Switzerland, Costa Rica, Jordan, Lichtenstein and Singapore) have prepared a draft resolution on working methods. This took the form of an annex to a letter of 3 November 2005 signed by the five permanent representatives, http://www.reformtheun.org/index.php/government_statements/c466?theme = alt2.

50 See UN Documents A/59/L.64, para. 8 and A/59/L.68, paras 7, 8 and 9, respectively.

51 *A More Secure World*, 82, para. 258. For the latest wrinkles in working methods, see UN Documents S/2006/507 of 19 July 2006 and S/2006/78 of 7 February 2006.

52 For summaries of the first two workshops, see UN Documents S/2004/135 of 20 February 2004 and S/2005/228 of 6 April 2005. These are organized by the Center on International Organization of Columbia University in cooperation with the Security Council Affairs Division of the UN secretariat.

53 For an independent monthly account of the Council's deliberations and activities, see the Security Council Report at http://www.securitycouncilreport.org. An initiative of the governments of Canada and Norway and the MacArthur, Rockefeller, and Hewlett Foundations, and undertaken in affiliation with Columbia University, the Report published its first *Monthly Forecast* in November 2005. The founders saw this as one way of adding to the transparency of the Council's work.

54 Letter to the President of the Security Council Signed by All Ten Non-Permanent Members of the Council, Annex: Position Paper on Working Methods of the Security Council, reprinted in the Report of the General Assembly Working Group on Security Council Reform, UN Document A/53/47, 5 August 1999.

55 UN Document SG/SM/8891.

56 Thomas G. Weiss and Barbara Crossette, "The United Nations: The Post-Summit Outlook," *Great Decisions 2006* (New York: Foreign Policy Association, 2006).

57 *A More Secure World*, 79, paras 245–6.

11 Conclusion

1 Kofi Annan, " 'In Larger Freedom': Decision Time at the UN," *Foreign Affairs*, 84, no. 3 (May/June 2005): 65. In September 2003, the Secretary-General cautioned the member states that, "Excellencies, we have come to a fork in the road. This

may be a moment no less decisive than 1945 itself, when the United Nations was founded." Address to the General Assembly, UN Document SG/SM/8891–GA/ 10157, 23 September 2003.

2 These points are elaborated in Edward C. Luck "A Council for All Seasons: The Creation of the Security Council and Its Relevance Today," in Vaughan Lowe, Adam Roberts, Jennifer Welsh, and Dominik Zaum, eds., *The UN Security Council and War* (Oxford University Press, forthcoming 2006).

3 In his statement to the UN General Assembly on 12 September 2002, President Bush warned that, because of a decade of Iraqi defiance,

> all the world now faces a test, and the United Nations a difficult and defining moment. Are Security Council resolutions to be honored and enforced, or cast aside without consequence? Will the United Nations serve the purpose of its founding, or will it be irrelevant?
>
> (USUN Press Release no. 131(02))

4 For some historical speculations by the author about the origins of Article 2(4) and why the United States initially proposed that language, see "Article 2(4) on the Non-Use of Force: What Were We Thinking?," in David P. Forsythe, Patrice C. McMahon and Andrew Wedeman (eds) *American Foreign Policy in a Globalized World* (New York: Routledge, 2006): 51–80.

5 G. John Ikenberry largely attributes the difference in US attitudes toward international organization from 1945 to the present to distinctive strategic views and political orientations in Washington DC. See *After Victory: Institutions, Strategic Restraint, and the Rebuilding of Order After Major Wars* (Princeton NJ: Princeton University Press, 2001); and "Getting Hegemony Right," *The National Interest*, 64 (spring 2001): 17–24.

6 Stephen G. Brooks and William C. Wohlforth, "American Primacy in Perspective," *Foreign Affairs*, 81, no. 4 (July/August 2002): 20–33.

7 Joseph S. Nye Jr, *The Paradox of American Power: Why the World's Only Superpower Can't Go It Alone* (New York: Oxford University Press, 2002).

8 See Chapter 5 above on the implications for military enforcement missions.

9 In the World Trade Organization (WTO), where the US and the European Union confront each other as equals, bipolarity works reasonably well.

Appendix 1
Provisional rules of procedure of the Security Council

(Adopted by the Security Council at its 1st meeting and amended at its 31st, 41st, 42nd, 44th and 48th meetings, on 9 April, 16 and 17 May, 6 and 24 June 1946; 138th and 222nd meetings, on 4 June and 9 December 1947; 468th meeting, on 28 February 1950; 1463rd meeting, on 24 January 1969; 1761st meeting, on 17 January 1974; and 2410th meeting, on 21 December 1982. Previous versions of the provisional rules of procedure were issued under the symbols S/96 and Rev. 1–6)

Chapter I. Meetings

Rule 1

Meetings of the Security Council shall, with the exception of the periodic meetings referred to in rule 4, be held at the call of the President at any time he deems necessary, but the interval between meetings shall not exceed fourteen days.

Rule 2

The President shall call a meeting of the Security Council at the request of any member of the Security Council.

Rule 3

The President shall call a meeting of the Security Council if a dispute or situation is brought to the attention of the Security Council under Article 35 or under Article 11(3) of the Charter, or if the General Assembly makes recommendations or refers any question to the Security Council under Article 11(2), or if the Secretary-General brings to the attention of the Security Council any matter under Article 99.

Rule 4

Periodic meetings of the Security Council called for in Article 28(2) of the Charter shall be held twice a year, at such times as the Security Council may decide.

Rule 5

Meetings of the Security Council shall normally be held at the seat of the United Nations.

Any member of the Security Council or the Secretary-General may propose that the Security Council should meet at another place. Should the Security Council accept any such proposal, it shall decide upon the place and the period during which the Council shall meet at such place.

Chapter II. Agenda

Rule 6

The Secretary-General shall immediately bring to the attention of all representatives on the Security Council all communications from States, organs of the United Nations, or the Secretary-General concerning any matter for the consideration of the Security Council in accordance with the provisions of the Charter.

Rule 7

The provisional agenda for each meeting of the Security Council shall be drawn up by the Secretary-General and approved by the President of the Security Council.

Only items which have been brought to the attention of the representatives on the Security Council in accordance with rule 6, items covered by rule 10, or matters which the Security Council had previously decided to defer, may be included in the provisional agenda.

Rule 8

The provisional agenda for a meeting shall be communicated by the Secretary-General to the representatives on the Security Council at least three days before the meeting, but in urgent circumstances it may be communicated simultaneously with the notice of the meeting.

Rule 9

The first item of the provisional agenda for each meeting of the Security Council shall be the adoption of the agenda.

Rule 10

Any item of the agenda of a meeting of the Security Council, consideration of which has not been completed at that meeting, shall, unless the Security Council otherwise decides, automatically be included in the agenda of the next meeting.

Rule 11

The Secretary-General shall communicate each week to the representatives on the Security Council a summary statement of matters of which the Security Council is seized and of the stage reached in their consideration.

Rule 12

The provisional agenda for each periodic meeting shall be circulated to the members of the Security Council at least twenty-one days before the opening of the meeting. Any subsequent change in or addition to the provisional agenda shall be brought to the notice of the members at least five days before the meeting. The Security Council may, however, in urgent circumstances, make additions to the agenda at any time during a periodic meeting.

The provisions of rule 7, paragraph 1, and of rule 9, shall apply also to periodic meetings.

Chapter III. Representation and credentials

Rule 13

Each member of the Security Council shall be represented at the meetings of the Security Council by an accredited representative. The credentials of a representative on the Security Council shall be communicated to the Secretary-General not less than twenty-four hours before he takes his seat on the Security Council. The credentials shall be issued either by the Head of the State or of the Government concerned or by its Minister of Foreign Affairs. The Head of Government or Minister of Foreign Affairs of each member of the Security Council shall be entitled to sit on the Security Council without submitting credentials.

Rule 14

Any Member of the United Nations not a member of the Security Council and any State not a Member of the United Nations, if invited to participate in a meeting or meetings of the Security Council, shall submit credentials for the representative appointed by it for this purpose. The credentials of such a representative shall be communicated to the Secretary-General not less than twenty-four hours before the first meeting which he is invited to attend.

Rule 15

The credentials of representatives on the Security Council and of any representative appointed in accordance with rule 14 shall he examined by the Secretary-General who shall submit a report to the Security Council for approval.

Rule 16

Pending the approval of the credentials of a representative on the Security Council in accordance with rule 15, such representative shall be seated provisionally with the same rights as other representatives.

Rule 17

Any representative on the Security Council, to whose credentials objection has been made within the Security Council, shall continue to sit with the same rights as other representatives until the Security Council has decided the matter.

Chapter IV. Presidency

Rule 18

The presidency of the Security Council shall be held in turn by the members of the Security Council in the English alphabetical order of their names. Each President shall hold office for one calendar month.

Rule 19

The President shall preside over the meetings of the Security Council and, under the authority of the Security Council, shall represent it in its capacity as an organ of the United Nations.

Rule 20

Whenever the President of the Security Council deems that for the proper fulfilment of the responsibilities of the presidency he should not preside over the Council during the consideration of a particular question with which the member he represents is directly connected, he shall indicate his decision to the Council. The presidential chair shall then devolve, for the purpose of the consideration of that question, on the representative of the member next in English alphabetical order, it being understood that the provisions of this rule shall apply to the representatives on the Security Council called upon successively to preside. This rule shall not affect the representative capacity of the President as stated in rule 19, or his duties under rule 7.

Chapter V. Secretariat

Rule 21

The Secretary-General shall act in that capacity in all meetings of the Security Council. The Secretary-General may authorize a deputy to act in his place at meetings of the Security Council.

Rule 22

The Secretary-General, or his deputy acting on his behalf, may make either oral or written statements to the Security Council concerning any question under consideration by it.

Rule 23

The Secretary-General may be appointed by the Security Council, in accordance with rule 28, as rapporteur for a specified question.

Rule 24

The Secretary-General shall provide the staff required by the Security Council. This staff shall form a part of the Secretariat.

Rule 25

The Secretary-General shall give to representatives on the Security Council notice of meetings of the Security Council and of its commissions and committees.

Rule 26

The Secretary-General shall be responsible for the preparation of documents required by the Security Council and shall, except in urgent circumstances, distribute them at least forty-eight hours in advance of the meeting at which they are to be considered.

Chapter VI. Conduct of business

Rule 27

The President shall call upon representatives in the order in which they signify their desire to speak.

Rule 28

The Security Council may appoint a commission or committee or a rapporteur for a specified question.

Rule 29

The President may accord precedence to any rapporteur appointed by the Security Council.

The Chairman of a commission or committee, or the rapporteur appointed by the commission or committee to present its report, may be accorded precedence for the purpose of explaining the report.

Rule 30

If a representative raises a point of order, the President shall immediately state his ruling. If it is challenged, the President shall submit his ruling to the Security Council for immediate decision and it shall stand unless overruled.

Rule 31

Proposed resolutions, amendments and substantive motions shall normally be placed before the representatives in writing.

Rule 32

Principal motions and draft resolutions shall have precedence in the order of their submission.

Parts of a motion or of a draft resolution shall be voted on separately at the request of any representative, unless the original mover objects.

Rule 33

The following motions shall have precedence in the order named over all principal motions and draft resolutions relative to the subject before the meeting:

1   To suspend the meeting;
2   To adjourn the meeting;
3   To adjourn the meeting to a certain day or hour;
4   To refer any matter to a committee, to the Secretary-General or to a rapporteur;
5   To postpone discussion of the question to a certain day or indefinitely; or
6   To introduce an amendment.

Any motion for the suspension or for the simple adjournment of the meeting shall be decided without debate.

Rule 34

It shall not be necessary for any motion or draft resolution proposed by a representative on the Security Council to be seconded before being put to a vote.

Rule 35

A motion or draft resolution can at any time be withdrawn so long as no vote has been taken with respect to it.

If the motion or draft resolution has been seconded, the representative on the Security Council who has seconded it may require that it be put to the vote as his motion or draft resolution with the same right of precedence as if the original mover had not withdrawn it.

Rule 36

If two or more amendments to a motion or draft resolution are proposed, the President shall rule on the order in which they are to be voted upon. Ordinarily, the Security Council shall first vote on the amendment furthest removed in substance from the original proposal and then on the amendment next furthest removed until all amendments have been put to the vote, but when an amendment adds to or deletes from the text of a motion or draft resolution, that amendment shall be voted on first.

Rule 37

Any Member of the United Nations which is not a member of the Security Council may be invited, as the result of a decision of the Security Council, to participate, without vote, in the discussion of any question brought before the Security Council when the Security Council considers that the interests of that Member are specially affected, or when a Member brings a matter to the attention of the Security Council in accordance with Article 35(1) of the Charter.

Rule 38

Any Member of the United Nations invited in accordance with the preceding rule, or in application of Article 32 of the Charter, to participate in the discussions of the Security Council may submit proposals and draft resolutions. These proposals and draft resolutions may be put to a vote only at the request of a representative on the Security Council.

Rule 39

The Security Council may invite members of the Secretariat or other persons, whom it considers competent for the purpose, to supply it with information or to give other assistance in examining matters within its competence.

Chapter VII. Voting

Rule 40

Voting in the Security Council shall be in accordance with the relevant Articles of the Charter and of the Statute of the International Court of Justice.

Chapter VIII. Languages

Rule 41

Arabic, Chinese, English, French, Russian and Spanish shall be both the official and the working languages of the Security Council.

Rule 42

Speeches made in any of the six languages of the Security Council shall be interpreted into the other five languages.

Rule 43

[Deleted]

Rule 44

Any representative may make a speech in a language other than the languages of the Security Council. In this case, he shall himself provide for interpretation into one of those languages. Interpretation into the other languages of the Security Council by the interpreters of the Secretariat may be based on the interpretation given in the first such language.

Rule 45

Verbatim records of meetings of the Security Council shall be drawn up in the languages of the Council.

Rule 46

All resolutions and other documents shall be published in the languages of the Security Council.

Rule 47

Documents of the Security Council shall, if the Security Council so decides, be published in any language other than the languages of the Council.

Chapter IX. Publicity of meetings, records

Rule 48

Unless it decides otherwise, the Security Council shall meet in public. Any recommendation to the General Assembly regarding the appointment of the Secretary-General shall be discussed and decided at a private meeting.

Rule 49

Subject to the provisions of rule 51, the verbatim record of each meeting of the Security Council shall be made available to the representatives on the Security Council and to the representatives of any other States which have participated in the meeting not later than 10 a.m. of the first working day following the meeting.

Rule 50

The representatives of the States which have participated in the meeting shall, within two working days after the time indicated in rule 49, inform the Secretary-General of any corrections they wish to have made in the verbatim record.

Rule 51

The Security Council may decide that for a private meeting the record shall be made in a single copy alone. This record shall be kept by the Secretary-General. The representatives of the States which have participated in the meeting shall, within a period of ten days, inform the Secretary-General of any corrections they wish to have made in this record.

Rule 52

Corrections that have been requested shall be considered approved unless the President is of the opinion that they are sufficiently important to be submitted to the representatives on the Security Council. In the latter case, the representatives on the Security Council shall submit within two working days any comments they may wish to make. In the absence of objections in this period of time, the record shall be corrected as requested.

Rule 53

The verbatim record referred to in rule 49 or the record referred to in rule 51, in which no corrections have been requested in the period of time required by rules 50 and 51, respectively, or which has been corrected in accordance with the provisions of rule 52, shall be considered as approved. It shall be signed by the President and shall become the official record of the Security Council.

Rule 54

The official record of public meetings of the Security Council, as well as the documents annexed thereto, shall be published in the official languages as soon as possible.

Rule 55

At the close of each private meeting the Security Council shall issue a *communiqué* through the Secretary-General.

Rule 56

The representatives of the Members of the United Nations which have taken part in a private meeting shall at all times have the right to consult the record of that meeting in the office of the Secretary-General. The Security Council may at any time grant access to this record to authorized representatives of other Members of the United Nations.

Rule 57

The Secretary-General shall, once each year, submit to the Security Council a list of the records and documents which up to that time have been considered confidential. The Security Council shall decide which of these shall be made available to other Members of the United Nations, which shall be made public, and which shall continue to remain confidential.

Chapter X. Admission of new members

Rule 58

Any State which desires to become a Member of the United Nations shall submit an application to the Secretary-General. This application shall contain a declaration made in a formal instrument that it accepts the obligations contained in the Charter.

Rule 59

The Secretary-General shall immediately place the application for membership before the representatives on the Security Council. Unless the Security Council decides otherwise, the application shall be referred by the President to a committee of the Security Council upon which each member of the Security Council shall be represented. The committee shall examine any application referred to it and report its conclusions thereon to the Council not less than thirty-five days in advance of a regular session of the General Assembly or, if a special session of the General Assembly is called, not less than fourteen days in advance of such session.

Rule 60

The Security Council shall decide whether in its judgement the applicant is a peace-loving State and is able and willing to carry out the obligations contained in the Charter and, accordingly, whether to recommend the applicant State for membership.

If the Security Council recommends the applicant State for membership, it shall forward to the General Assembly the recommendation with a complete record of the discussion.

If the Security Council does not recommend the applicant State for membership or postpones the consideration of the application, it shall submit a special report to the General Assembly with a complete record of the discussion.

In order to ensure the consideration of its recommendation at the next session of the General Assembly following the receipt of the application, the Security Council shall make its recommendation not less than twenty-five days in advance of a regular session of the General Assembly, nor less than four days in advance of a special session.

In special circumstances, the Security Council may decide to make a recommendation to the General Assembly concerning an application for membership subsequent to the expiration of the time limits set forth in the preceding paragraph.

Chapter XI. Relations with other United Nations organs

Rule 61

Any meeting of the Security Council held in pursuance of the Statute of the International Court of Justice for the purpose of the election of members of the Court shall continue until as many candidates as are required for all the seats to be filled have obtained in one or more ballots an absolute majority of votes.

Appendix

Provisional procedure for dealing with communications from private individuals and non-governmental bodies

A   A list of all communications from private individuals and non-govern-mental bodies relating to matters of which the Security Council is seized shall be circulated to all representatives on the Security Council.

B   A copy of any communication on the list shall be given by the Secretariat to any representative on the Security Council at his request.

(*source*: http://www.un.org/Docs/sc/scrules.htm)

Appendix 2

Size of UN peacekeeping forces, 1947–2005

Highest month for each year, rounded to the nearest hundred. Figures include troops, military observers, and police.

Year	Total
2005	70,100
2004	64,720
2003	45,800
2002	46,800
2001	47,800
2000	38,500
1999	18,400
1998	14,600
1997	25,000
1996	29,100
1995	68,900
1994	76,500
1993	78,500
1992	52,200
1991	15,300
1990	13,700
1989	17,900
1988	13,000
1987	12,500
1986	12,500
1985	12,500
1984	12,500
1983	12,500
1982	12,500
1981	12,500
1980	13,000

1979	13,300
1978	16,700
1977	11,500
1976	11,500
1975	11,300
1974	11,100
1973	9,800
1972	7,200
1971	7,200
1970	7,200
1969	7,200
1968	6,900
1967	13,000
1966	13,000
1965	13,000
1964	13,000
1963	12,600
1962	26,500
1961	22,500
1960	26,200
1959	6,800
1958	7,200
1957	6,800
1956	700
1955	700
1954	700
1953	700
1952	700
1951	700
1950	700
1949	700
1948	600
1947	30

(*source*: http://www.globalpolicy.org/security/peacekpg/data/pcekprs1.htm. Data through 1994 by William Durch, Stimson Center; data from 1995 forward, http://www.un.org/Depts/dpko/dpko/contributors/)

Bibliographical essay

In terms of understanding the purposes and unique qualities of the Security Council, the place to start is with its often dismissed predecessor, the Council of the League of Nations. See the League Covenant, of course, plus the following:

Goodrich, Leland M., "From League of Nations to United Nations," *International Organization*, 1, 1 (February 1947): 3–21. Argues insightfully, if not convincingly, that there was a lot more continuity between the League and the UN than the boosters of the latter cared to admit.

League of Nations, *The Council of the League of Nations: Composition, Competence, Procedure* (Geneva: League of Nations, 1938a).
——*Essential Facts About the League of Nations*, 9th edn rev. (Geneva: League of Nations, 1938b).
——*The League Hands Over* (Geneva: League of Nations, 1946).
Walters, F. P., *A History of the League of Nations*, 2 vols (London: Oxford University Press, 1952). The classic account from a League insider.

For a revealing look at how US President Franklin Delano Roosevelt saw the postwar order, see Forest Davis, "Roosevelt's World Blueprint," *The Saturday Evening Post*, 10 April 1943. A particularly able and readable narrative on American, as well as British and Soviet, planning for the new organization is contained in Townsend Hoopes and Douglas Brinkley, *FDR and the Creation of the U.N.* (New Haven: Yale University Press, 1997).

A remarkably full account of the State Department planning process can be found in the annual volumes of the series *Foreign Relations of the United States* (Washington DC: US Government Printing Office). The single most thorough yet accessible source on both the planning and negotiating processes is Ruth B. Russell, *A History of the United Nations Charter: The Role of the United States, 1940–1945* (Washington DC: Brookings Institution Press, 1958). Robert C. Hilderbrand provides a lively and detailed account of the Big Four negotiations prior to the founding conference in *Dumbarton Oaks:*

The Origins of the United Nations and the Search for Postwar Security (Chapel Hill NC: University of North Carolina Press, 1990).

While Russell's thick volume provides the most authoritative unofficial account of the founding conference in San Francisco, Stephen C. Schlesinger tells the story with a much lighter touch and an eye for the importance of personalities in *Act of Creation: The Founding of the United Nations* (Boulder CO: Westview Press, 2003). For those who want to dig deeper, it is worth looking both at the autobiographical accounts provided by a number of the key representatives at San Francisco and at the reports and dispatches various delegations sent to their capitals at the time. The official records of the conference are very extensive and occasionally revealing: *Documents of the United Nations Conference on International Organization 1945*, 22 vols (New York: UN Information Organizations, 1954); and the US Department of State, *The United Nations Conference on International Organization: Selected Documents, April 25 to June 26, 1945, San Francisco* (Washington DC: US Government Printing Office, 1946).

For a feel for how the framework established at San Francisco has been carried out in practice, see Sydney D. Bailey and Sam Daws, *The Procedure of the UN Security Council*, 3rd edn (Oxford: Clarendon Press, 1998). This is the standard reference work on the topic, though for recent developments this should be supplemented by official sources. In that regard, though it lacks analytical content, the Security Council's annual report to the General Assembly (A/60/2 for the most current report) provides a useful and authoritative overview of what it has been up to. Though always kept in a state of limbo by the Permanent Members to permit flexible interpretation as needed, the Council's Provisional Rules of Procedure (see Appendix 1) are worth a quick read. Also see the UN's website and those provided by two independent entities, the Security Council Report and the Global Policy Forum (http://www.un.org/Docs/sc/; http://www.securitycouncilreport.org; and http://www.globalpolicy.org).

As noted in the Preface, there is a much larger literature on the things the Council mandates – such as peace operations, sanctions, and humanitarian measures – and on specific crises it has addressed, than on its development as an institution. Though less focused on the latter than the former, David Malone's edited collection of essays, *The United Nations Security Council: From the Cold War to the 21st Century* (Boulder CO: Lynne Rienner, 2004) has a wealth of valuable material. No doubt his forthcoming book, *The International Struggle Over Iraq: Politics in the UN Security Council, 1980–2005* (Oxford: Oxford University Press, 2006), will be a useful addition as well.

The statements and reports of the last two Secretaries-General, Boutros Boutros-Ghali and Kofi Annan, reflect the remarkable evolution of UN security doctrine during the turbulent post-Cold War years. In particular, see

Agenda for Peace, A/47/277, 17 June 1992.

Supplement to An Agenda for Peace: Position Paper of the Secretary-General on the Occasion of the Fiftieth Anniversary of the United Nations, UN Document A/50/60-S/1995/1, 3 January 1995.

"Reflections on Intervention," 35th Annual Ditchley Foundation Lecture, 26 June 1998, reprinted in *Questions of Intervention*, New York: United Nations, 1999.

Report of the Panel on UN Peace Operations, UN Document S/2000/809, 21 August 2000.

A More Secure World: Our Shared Responsibility, Report of the High-level Panel on Threats, Challenges and Change, New York: United Nations, 2004.

In Larger Freedom: Towards Development, Security and Human Rights for All, New York: United Nations, 2005.

The reports on the failings – of the Council and others – in Rwanda and Srebrenica make for particularly sober and important reading:

Report of the Secretary-General pursuant to General Assembly Resolution 53/35: The Fall of Srebrenica, UN Document A/54/549, 15 November 1999.

Report of the Independent Inquiry into the Actions of the United Nations During the 1994 Genocide in Rwanda, UN Document S/1999/1257, 16 December 1999.

Index